Stratification and Inequality Series
The Center for the Study of Social Stratification and Inequality,
Tohoku University, Japan
Volume 4

Deciphering Stratification and Inequality

Stratification and Inequality Series
The Center for the Study of Social Stratification and Inequality,
Tohoku University, Japan

Inequality amid Affluence: Social Stratification in Japan
Junsuke Hara and Kazuo Seiyama

Intentional Social Change: A Rational Choice Theory
Yoshimichi Sato

Constructing Civil Society in Japan: Voices of Environmental Movements
Koichi Hasegawa

Deciphering Stratification and Inequality: Japan and Beyond
Yoshimichi Sato

Social Justice in Japan: Concepts, Theories and Paradigms
Ken-ichi Ohbuchi

Stratification and Inequality Series

The Center for the Study of Social Stratification and Inequality,
Tohoku University, Japan
Volume 4

Deciphering Stratification and Inequality

Japan and Beyond

Edited by

Yoshimichi Sato

This English edition first published in 2007 by
Trans Pacific Press, PO Box 120, Rosanna, Melbourne, Victoria 3084, Australia
Telephone: +61 3 9459 3021 Fax: +61 3 9457 5923
Email: info@transpacificpress.com
Web: http://www.transpacificpress.com

Copyright © Trans Pacific Press 2007

Designed and set by digital environs, Melbourne. http://www.digitalenvirons.com

Printed by BPA Print Group, Burwood, Victoria, Australia

Distributors

Australia and New Zealand
UNIREPS
University of New South Wales
Sydney, NSW 2052
Australia
Telephone: +61(0)2-9664-0999
Fax: +61(0)2-9664-5420
Email: info.press@unsw.edu.au
Web: http://www.unireps.com.au

USA and Canada
International Specialized Book
Services (ISBS)
920 NE 58th Avenue, Suite 300
Portland, Oregon 97213-3786
USA
Telephone: (800) 944-6190
Fax: (503) 280-8832
Email: orders@isbs.com
Web: http://www.isbs.com

Asia and the Pacific
Kinokuniya Company Ltd.

Head office:
Shin-Mizonokuchi Bldg. 2F
5-7 Hisamoto 3-chome
Takatsu-ku, Kawasaki 213-8506
Japan
Telephone: +81(0)44-874-9642
Fax: +81(0)44-829-1025
Email: bkimp@kinokuniya.co.jp
Web: www.kinokuniya.co.jp

Asia-Pacific office:
Kinokuniya Book Stores of Singapore Pte., Ltd.
391B Orchard Road #13-06/07/08
Ngee Ann City Tower B
Singapore 238874
Telephone: +65 6276 5558
Fax: +65 6276 5570
Email: SSO@kinokuniya.co.jp

All rights reserved. No production of any part of this book may take place without the written permission of Trans Pacific Press.

ISBN 978-1-876843-90-8 (Hardback)
ISBN 978-1-876843-96-0 (Paperback)

Contents

Figures	vi
Tables	viii
Preface	xi
List of Contributors	xv

Part I: Advancing Theoretical Frontiers

1. Contemporary Japanese Society and the New Inequalities: A Frontier of Social Stratification and Inequality Research *Junsuke Hara* — 3
2. Parsons' Discourses on Social Stratification: Some Reflections on Equality and Inequality *Kazuyoshi Takagi* — 18
3. Market, Trust and Inequality: An Agent-based Model of Effect of Market Attractiveness on Trusting Behavior and Inequality *Yoshimichi Sato* — 31

Part II: Exploring Realities in Japan

4. Local Leaders' Network Structure in the Edo Period: The Case of 'Busyu-gi Bo' of the Suzukis in Ushu Area *Daisuke Sato* — 47
5. Migration and Status Attainment during the High Growth Period *Yutaka Ginya* — 88
6. The Effects of Spatial Characteristics on the Determinants of Class Identification *Daisuke Kobayashi* — 112
7. Deterioration in Employment Practice and Career Images *Yoshimichi Sato* — 127
8. Long-term Trends in Status Homogamy *Satoshi Miwa* — 140

Part III: Inquiring beyond Japan

9. Educational Reform and Inequality in Japan and Korea *Ki Hun Kim and Satoshi Miwa* — 163
10. Market Transition of Laid-off Workers in Urban China *Guihua Xie* — 183
11. Generational Differences in Mexican-American's Earnings: Comparing the Second, 2.5th and Third Generations *Yukio Kawano, Katharine M. Donato and Charles M. Tolbert II* — 216

Notes	237
References	246
Index	262

Figures

1.1	Household income disparity and GNP per capita	5
1.2	University advancement rates by social strata	6
1.3	Intra-age-group and inter-age-group personal income disparity	9
1.4	Personal annual income distribution by social strata and gender	13
1.5	Employment and wage rates for part-time female workers	15
2.1	Population composition in Yankee City by social stratification	19
2.2	Foci of integrative balances in the societal community	30
3.1	Trusting game	33
3.2	Steps of the agent-based model	34
3.3	Prisoner's dilemma game	36
3.4	Correlation between endowments and accumulated payoff	38
3.5	Difference in accumulated payoff between members of group A and members of group B	39
3.6	Percentage of agents in the market	39
3.7	Percentage of trusting behavior in the market	40
3.8	Percentage of cooperating behavior in the market	40
4.1	Location of Obanazawa village and seven other villages and areas	48
5.1	Changes in worker ratios by industry	91
5.2	Occupational mobility from first job to second job by migration pattern	106
5.3	Occupational mobility from first job to current job by migration pattern	107
5.4	Occupational mobility from first job to current job by mobility pattern after first job	109
6.1	Intra-prefectural migrants and inter-prefectural migrants (1954–2002)	124
7.1	Percentage of part-time workers	128
7.2	Unemployment rates in Japan	129
8.1	Multivariate model of status homogamy	147
8.2	Absolute in-marriage rates in Japan	149
8.3	In-marriage trend by father's occupation	150
8.4	In-marriage trend by educational level	150

8.5	Bivariate trends in UNIDIFF parameter for homogamy of social origin	155
8.6	Bivariate trends in UNIDIFF parameter for educational homogamy	155
8.A	Design matrices for homogamy	160
9.1	Change in the enrollment rates between the old and new systems in Japan	167
9.2	Change in the enrollment (advancement) rates between the old and new systems in Korea	168
9.3	Change in the rate of advancing to higher education, 1965–1990	169
9.4	Percentage of female students enrolled in universities, 1970–2003	170
9.5	Percentage of female students enrolled in junior colleges, 1970–2003	170
9.A	Methodological notes for the system effect model	182
10.1	Six surveyed cities in China	189
11.1	Image of cross-generational adaptation	222

Tables

3.1	Design of the simulation	37
3.2	Summary of the findings	41
4.0	Total gifts by category and locality	53
4.1.A	Number of gift bearers and return rates/Continuity of gifts by category – ① Obanazawa village	56
4.1.B	Single/multiple gift categories and changes in subsequent occasions – ① Obanazawa village	58
4.2.A	Number of gift bearers and return rates/Continuity of gifts by category – ② Ōishida village and environs	60
4.2.B	Single/multiple gift categories and changes in subsequent occasions – ② Ōishida village and environs	62
4.3.A	Number of gift bearers and return rates/Continuity of gifts by category – ③ Other villages in Murayama	65
4.3.B	Single/multiple gift categories and changes in subsequent occasions – ③ Other villages in Murayama	66
4.4.A	Number of gift bearers and return rates/Continuity of gifts by category – ④ Shinjō, Sakata and Yuri-gun	69
4.4.B	Single/multiple gift categories and changes in subsequent occasions – ④ Shinjō, Sakata and Yuri-gun	70
4.5.A	Number of gift bearers and return rates/Continuity of gifts by category – ⑤ Obanazawa Kamigō	73
4.5.B	Single/multiple gift categories and changes in subsequent occasions – ⑤ Obanazawa Kamigō	74
4.6.A	Number of gift bearers and return rates/Continuity of gifts by category – ⑥ Shōgon, Niu and Akudo villages	77
4.6.B	Single/multiple gift categories and changes in subsequent occasions – ⑥ Shōgon, Niu and Akudo villages	78
4.7.A	Number of gift bearers and return rates/Continuity of gifts by category – ⑦ Tōgō, Yokosawa and Nobesawa areas	81
4.7.B	Single/multiple gift categories and changes in subsequent occasions – ⑦ Tōgō, Yokosawa and Nobesawa areas	82
4.8.A	Number of gift bearers and return rates/Continuity of gifts by category – ⑧ Obanazawa Shimogō	85

4.8.B	Single/multiple gift categories and changes in subsequent occasions – ⑧ Obanazawa Shimogō	86
5.1	Outflow and inflow numbers of new graduates by prefecture	94
5.2	Logistic regression analysis with migration as the dependent variable	98
5.3	Distribution of first jobs by migration pattern	100
5.4	Distribution of first jobs amongst employees only	102
5.5	Multiple regression analysis with the size of the company where first employed as the dependent variable	103
5.6	Event history analysis with leaving the first job as the dependent variable	105
6.1	Hierarchical linear regression model with class identification as the dependent variable for the 1995 data	118
6.2	Hierarchical linear regression model with class identification as the dependent variable for the 1975 data	122
6.3	Descriptive statistics of region-level variables at two time points	125
7.1	Basic statistics	134
7.2	Results of simple multinomial logit regression analysis	135
7.3	Results of multinomial logit regression analysis	138
8.1	Sample size by cohort	146
8.2	Categories of father's occupation and educational level	146
8.3	Fitting statistics for the homogamy pattern	152
8.4	Parameter estimates in bivariate and multivariate models	153
8.5	Fitting statistics for the homogamy trends	154
8.6	Fitting and slopes for multivariate trend models	156
9.1	Binary logit models of high school attendance conditional on junior high school male graduates born from 1928 to 1937 in Japan in Point A (N = 3,017)	174
9.2.	Binary logit models of junior high school attendance conditional on elementary school male graduates born from 1930 to 1939 in Korea in Point A (N = 740)	176
9.3.	Multinomial logit models of attending university or junior college conditional on high school graduates born from 1953 to 1962 in Japan in Point B (N = 2,418)	177
9.4.	Multinomial logit models of attending university or junior college conditional on high school graduates born from 1958 to 1967 in Korea in Point B (N = 1,998)	179

10.1	Characteristics of surveyed enterprises by city	190
10.2	Descriptive statistics on workers in survey sample	191
10.3	Logit estimates on layoff status	198
10.4	Descriptive statistics of laid-off workers' reemployment and earnings	204
10.5	Probit estimates for reemployment	206
10.6	OLS regressions for rewards from post-layoff jobs (with sample selection for reemployment)	209
10.7	OLS regressions for rewards from laid-off workers' pre-layoff job	210
11.1	Definition of the three generations	225
11.2	Mean characteristics of Mexican generation groups, black and white natives, 1994–2003	227
11.3	Industry composition of Mexicans, native blacks and whites, 1994–2003	228
11.4	Tests of cross generational difference in industry and occupation	230
11.5a	Multivariate analysis of logged hourly earnings (Male Mexican workers), 1994–2003	232
11.5b	Multivariate analysis of logged hourly earnings (Female Mexican workers), 1994–2003	233
11.A	Mean characteristics of the first and second generations who did not identify themselves Mexican but have certain family connections to Mexico	236

Preface

This volume is a collection of the fruits of research activities at the Division of the Study of Structure and Change of Social Stratification and Inequality (hereafter: the Division), the Center for the Study of Social Stratification and Inequality (hereafter: the CSSI). The CSSI was established in the summer of 2003 to break through limitations concerning the study of social stratification and inequality in Japan. The Division has particularly focused on two limitations. The first is that the study of social stratification and inequality in Japan has been weak in theoretical development; it has rather emphasized empirical analysis of survey data. Although empirical studies of social stratification and inequality are important, theories that lead such studies are indispensable. Theories of industrialization and modernization gave directions for empirical studies, but have lost their explanatory power as Japanese society becomes a post-industrialized society. The second limitation is that Japanese specialists on social stratification and inequality have tended to confine themselves temporally and spatially. That is, they have mainly focused on the *modern Japanese* society. In other words, they have paid less attention to social stratification and inequality in pre-modern Japan and other societies.

The Division held several workshops to discuss these limitations. Its members presented working papers at the workshops to explore the possibility of breaking through them. As for the first limitation, rational choice theory was used to study the emergence of inequality, while Talcott Parsons' theory of social stratification was revisited to find cues for new developments of theories on social stratification and inequality. As for the second limitation, a historian who studies inequality in the Edo era, specialists on social stratification and inequality in Korea and China, and a specialist on Mexican immigrants in the U.S.A. contributed to this volume. Their papers have made the spectrum of this volume wider than expected. Some readers might think that this volume is so eclectic that it has no coherent organization. However, the 'core' of this volume is very clear. It is a reflection on conventional studies of social stratification and inequality in modern Japanese society.

This volume consists of three parts. Part I houses three papers that attempt to provide new perspectives on theories of social stratification and inequality. In Chapter 1 Junsuke Hara discusses the impact of 'new inequality' on the study of social stratification and inequality. The study has focused on such social problems as poverty and starvation. However, the social problems are no longer primary political issues in affluent advanced societies. Has the study of social stratification and inequality, then, lost its target? Hara's answer is no. Rather, he argues that the study should properly analyze 'new inequality.' 'New inequality' means new aspects of inequality amid affluence; it includes inequality between the old and the young, inequality of superior goods, and inequality within minorities. Hara points out new directions of the study of social stratification and inequality to explore these types of 'new inequality.' In Chapter 2 Kazuyoshi Takagi revisits Talcott Parsons' discourses on social stratification. In his famous paper entitled 'An Analytical Approach to the Social Stratification' Parsons applied structural functionalism to the study of the maintenance of social stratification. However, his discourses on social stratification go beyond the scope of the paper, Takagi argues. He scrutinized Parsons' unpublished manuscripts and uncovers the central position of social stratification and inequality in his theoretical framework. In Chapter 3 Yoshimichi Sato demonstrates a new methodology for the study of the emergence of inequality: Agent-based modeling. Based on an empirical finding that people with higher incomes are more likely to trust strangers, he points out the possibility that the rich have opportunities to trust strangers in the market to get higher returns, while the poor stay in their neighborhoods without such opportunities, which widens the inequality between the rich and the poor. To test the empirical validity of this possibility, he built an agent-based model with market attractiveness as the manipulating variable. His results demonstrate that the inequality does not necessarily become wider as the market attractiveness becomes higher.

Papers in Part 2 cover social stratification and inequality in Japan from the Edo era till the 21st century. In Chapter 4 Daisuke Sato shows a vivid picture of social stratification in pre-modern Japan. Contrary to a conventional view that there was a solid caste system in pre-modern Japan, he points out that the social networks of rich farmers affected their social statuses and that their social statuses in turn changed their social networks. His paper is a good example of the historical study of social capital and social stratification. In Chapter

5 Yutaka Ginya takes us from the Edo era to the high growth period in Japan. The period started in the mid '50s and ended in 1973 when the oil crisis attacked the world economy. During the period, massive migration from rural areas to large cities occurred in Japan. Ginya focuses on new graduates from junior high and high schools during the period and studies how their migration history interacted with their job history. In Chapter 6 Daisuke Kobayashi analyzed the effect of space on how class identification is determined in contemporary Japan. Applying hierarchical linear models to the Social Stratification and Social Mobility (hereafter: SSM) data sets, he argues that spatial characteristics, which have not been a main topic in the study of social stratification and inequality, play an important role in the process of class identification. In Chapter 7 Yoshimichi Sato studies career images held by Japanese in the 21st century. The long-term employment practice, which used to be an ideal in the Japanese labor market, has been weakening in contemporary Japan. Sato assumes that the weakening employment practice has changed career images held by Japanese. The results of his empirical study show that the weakening of the employment practice has differing effects on workers with different human capital and in different positions in the labor market, rejecting a rough argument that the deterioration in the employment practice would throw all Japanese workers into severe competition for scarce job security. While the papers mentioned above provide snapshots or short movies of social stratification and inequality in Japan, Satoshi Miwa shows long-term trends in status homogamy in Japan in Chapter 8. As status homogamy is a strong driving force for inequality, it is an important topic to see whether status homogamy becomes stronger or weaker. His sophisticated analysis of the SSM data sets indicates that the status homogamy in Japan has shown a trend of very slow decline.

Papers in Part 3 study social stratification and inequality outside of Japan. In Chapter 9 Ki Hun Kim and Satoshi Miwa compare the effects of educational reforms on social class differentials in school transitions over time in Japan and Korea. Although the educational systems in both societies are similar, the educational policies are different between them. Thus this paper exploits an opportunity to study how different educational policies affect education inequality in the same institutional environment of education. In Chapter 10 Guihua Xie explores the effects of China's market oriented reform on urban layoff, re-employment and job rewards. One of her intriguing empirical findings is that both human capital and political capital play important roles in determining layoffs but lose their effects on income in post-layoff jobs. Political capital, such as membership of the Communist Party, still has an effect in the labor market in the process of transition to the market economy. It is an interesting and important topic whether political capital will keep its effects as the transition goes further. In Chapter 11 Yukio Kawano, Katharine M. Donato and Charles M. Tolbert II provide a new aspect of inequality in the U.S: Generational differences in Mexican-American's earnings. They focus on the 2.5th generation of Mexican-Americans. A person in this generation has a foreign-born and a native parent, while a person in the second generation has two foreign-born parents. Their empirical analysis reveals that the 2.5th-generation Mexican-American males have an advantage over the third generation, but the second generation males have a disadvantage. However, the differences are not statistically substantiated in case of females. This suggests interaction between ethnicity and gender, which is another interesting topic in the study of social stratification and inequality.

Readers would be amazed by the wide coverage of the topics in this volume. Astonishing readers, however, is not a purpose of this volume. Rather, deciphering social stratification and inequality from various perspectives is our mission. A long journey of reading the papers in this volume does not end here. I hope that readers will get interested in the topics contained in this volume and join us for the exploration of the mysteries of social stratification and inequality.

The publication of this volume was made possible by a grant offered by the Center for the Study of Social Stratification and Inequality at Tohoku University, whose financial support is gratefully acknowledged. I also thank Airin Izumi, Hiroshi Endo and Hiroaki Ozaki for their excellent secretarial work at the CSSI. Last but not least, I genuinely appreciate the editorial support of Professor Yoshio Sugimoto and Ms. Robyn Mitchell of Trans Pacific Press. Their professional skills as editors of academic books made the publication process of this volume go smoothly.

November 2006
Yoshimichi Sato

List of Contributors

Junsuke Hara	Graduate School of Arts and Letters, Tohoku University
Kazuyoshi Takagi	Faculty of Liberal Arts, Teikyo University
Yoshimichi Sato	Graduate School of Arts and Letters, Tohoku University
Daisuke Sato	Graduate School of Arts and Letters, Tohoku University
Yutaka Ginya	Graduate School of Arts and Letters, Tohoku University
Daisuke Kobayashi	Faculty of Human Studies, Jin-ai University
Satoshi Miwa	Institute of Social Science, The University of Tokyo
Ki Hun Kim	Korea Institute for Youth Development
Guihua Xie	Department of Sociology, Renmin University of China
Yukio Kawano	Faculty of Economics, Daito Bunka University
Katharine M. Donato	Department of Sociology, Rice University
Charles M. Tolbert II	Department of Sociology, Baylor University

Part I
Advancing Theoretical Frontiers

1 Contemporary Japanese Society and the New Inequalities: A Frontier of Social Stratification and Inequality Research

Junsuke Hara

Introduction

Social stratification and inequality have been major issues in the social sciences and have always been linked to the problems of poverty and starvation. Yet in Japan, at least, and in the so-called 'affluent' advanced industrialized societies to which it belongs, problems such as poverty and starvation are no longer the most pressing among issues.

However, this does not mean that social stratification and inequality research has lost its significance. Japanese society is experiencing increasing difficulties and is going through a period of change that has manifested in a variety of ways. Many of the problems which have come to the surface during this period are, in fact, significantly linked to social stratification and inequality. Furthermore, as we will see later in the chapter, over the last decade or so a feeling that socio-economic inequality is once again on the rise has rapidly taken hold and the issue has become a topic of social concern. This occurred against the backdrop of the biggest economic recession since the Second World War.

It is difficult to get to the core of the current inequalities, however, if we rely on the established frameworks for analysis used in the past. We need to understand contemporary inequalities as 'new' inequalities differing to those in the past. The examination of these 'new' inequalities constitutes a major new frontier in contemporary social stratification and inequality research.

The achievement of post-war Japanese society

The 'new' inequalities refer to new features of inequality visible in Japanese society since its attainment of affluence in the wake of the period of high economic growth of the 1960s and 1970s. Before we turn to the details of these 'new' inequalities, however, we need to take an overview of the situation regarding inequality which preceded their emergence. We need, in other words, to consider the new situation by looking at what post-war Japanese society achieved. Thus let us briefly review historical changes in the two aspects of inequality – (1) inequality of possession and (2) inequality of opportunity – using the data of the National Survey of Social Stratification and Social Mobility (hereafter SSM), which has been conducted every ten years since 1955. The high quality of the SSM data is reflected in the fact that social stratification and inequality research in Japan has mainly relied on it to date.

Inequality of possession

'Inequality of possession' refers to inequality in regard to the possession of the tangible and intangible goods that people desire, such as income, assets, information and social prestige. As an example of this kind of inequality let us look at household income disparity.

In Figure 1.1, change in household income disparity is shown using Gini coefficient. Gini coefficient has a value of zero if all household incomes are perfectly equal and, conversely, a value of one if all income is held by just one household. In other words, the greater the numerical value the greater the inequality. In addition to the post-war data, Figure 1.1 shows the situation before the war estimated by Ryōshin Minami (2000) using pre-war tax records from various parts of the country. Compared to the pre-war period, we can see that in the post-war period inequality clearly decreased, and from 1965 to 1975 in particular – in other words during the period of high economic growth – there is a marked decrease in inequality. This certainly does not mean, however, that it has approached zero; we are aware of this fact in our daily lives even if we do not look at the data shown in Figure 1.1.

One more thing that needs to be commented on here is the level of income. As a general indicator of income Figure 1.1 shows change in real per capita GNP, with the 1930 level set at 100. The level of GNP per capita has increased approximately ten-fold in real terms by 1995. If we turn to the SSM survey data we see how this is reflected in annual income levels. Let us focus on real household annual income, which is calculated after controlling for changes in the consumer price level. The comparatively poorer stratum of society is represented at the 25th percentile (that is, those represented by the income level at the level of 25% of society, moving from the poorest

Figure 1.1: Household income disparity and GNP per capita

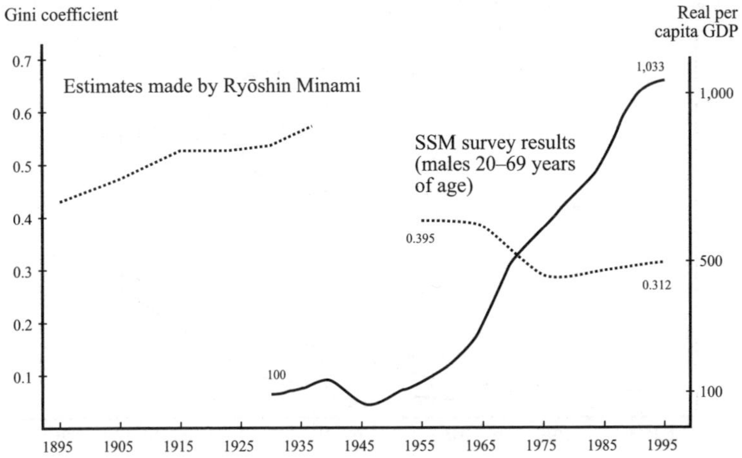

[Chart showing Gini coefficient (left axis, 0.1–0.7) and Real per capita GDP (right axis, 100–1,000) from 1895 to 1995. Estimates made by Ryōshin Minami shown as dotted line rising from ~0.45 to ~0.5. SSM survey results (males 20–69 years of age) showing values of 0.395 and 0.312. Real per capita GDP rising from 100 to 1,033.]

Source: SSM survey results (males 20–69 years of age)

up) and the comparatively richer stratum is at the 75th percentile. If we take the level at the 25th percentile in 1955 (approx. US$1,250) as 100, it is exactly 600 (approx. US$44,000) forty years later in 1995. The level at the 75th percentile, on the other hand, has increased from 260 (approx. US$3,250) in 1955 to 1302 (approx. US$94,000) in 1995. Although the absolute disparity between the two strata has increased, the level of income during this forty year period rose markedly – six-fold at the 25th percentile and approximately five-fold at the 75th percentile. This applies to all occupational strata. Furthermore, if we look at ratios of the 75th percentile to the 25th percentile in the two framing years, 1955 and 1995, there is a reduction from a difference of 2.6 to a difference of 2.2, and this is in keeping with the change in Gini coefficient.

Inequality of opportunity

'Inequality of opportunity' refers to inequality in the extent to which opportunities leading to the possession of goods, such as educational and employment opportunities, can be accessed through individual ability, desire, and effort, regardless of congenital factors such as the status of one's parents, one's gender and so on. As an example of inequality of opportunity, let us examine changes in advancement rates to secondary and higher education. It is well known that advancement

Figure 1.2: University advancement rates by social strata

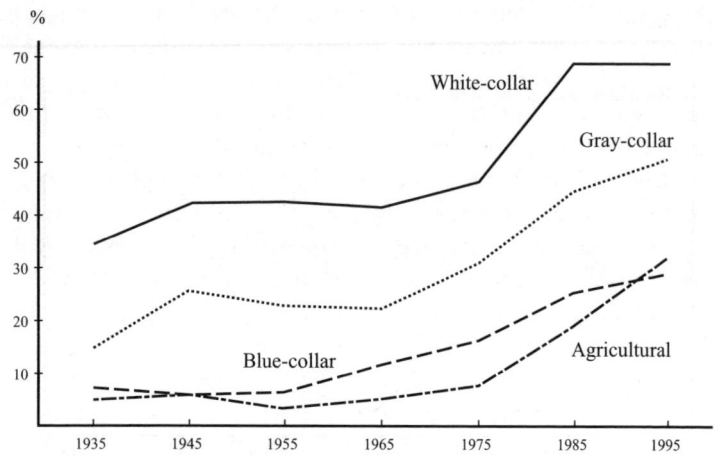

Source: SSM surveys (data for males 25–34 years of age only)

to senior secondary education (junior high school under the old system, senior high school under the new system) had come to include almost everyone by the 1980s. Yet even so, the advancement rate to higher education (university), if we look at a sample of males (25–34 years of age) from the SSM surveys, still remains at 44% in 1995.

Figure 1.2 shows university advancement rates by father's occupation. Values for 1935 and 1945 – before the SSM surveys were begun – shown on Figure 1.2 are estimates based on the SSM survey data. The relative positions of advancement rates amongst the sons of white-collar, gray-collar (retail, service, and security sectors) and manual workers (blue-collar and agricultural workers) have remained the same, and the differences in advancement rates show absolutely no sign of changing.

The achievement of basic equality

The above examples have shown us both a trend toward equality (that is, in changes in Gini coefficient and the secondary school advancement rate) and the persistent inequality (that is, in the absolute value of Gini coefficient and the university advancement rate). Overall, however, we can interpret these examples as indicating a situation in which 'basic equality' has been achieved (Hara and Seiyama 1999).

Basic equality does not mean that all kinds of equality have been achieved. Rather it refers to the fact that, at a minimum, what might be called 'basic goods,' including such things as (1) a sufficient income to avoid poverty and starvation, (2) sufficient clothing, food, housing and durable consumer goods at a level affordable to maintain one's human dignity, and (3) higher secondary education (advancement to senior high school), is in the possession of the vast majority of the people.

Let me take automobiles as an example to make the point clearer. At one time cars were out of the reach of ordinary people and only the very richest members of society were able to own them. Nowadays, however, anyone who wants a car can own one. But if we look at the type of car a person owns, a large disparity (inequality) exists between people, with some only being able to afford cheaper cars produced for the mass-market, whilst others drive around in luxury imported cars. If we focus here on the fact that anyone can own a car in contemporary Japan, the concept of 'basic equality' should be readily understood.

It is interesting here to consider how the situation regarding equality has been understood, not by the researchers but by ordinary people. While the researchers have vehemently emphasized with a variety of indicators that levels of inequality were high, it seems that ordinary people have been particularly conscious of 'equality.' In public opinion surveys conducted during the Showa 30s (1955–1964) the question, 'Which do you feel has been more equal, the pre-war or the post-war period?' was often asked, to which the overwhelming majority of people answered, 'the postwar period.' As well as stemming from the democratization brought about through post-war reforms, this response was also probably due to the sense that most Japanese had become poorer with Japan's defeat in the war (as is shown in the change in Gini coefficient for this period in Figure 1.1).

From the Showa 40s (1965–1974) onwards the fact that as much as 90% of survey respondents regarded themselves as in the 'middle-stratum' became a topic of interest both amongst researchers and amongst the wider public[1]. The author termed this 90% level of self-identification as the 'middle-stratum' a situation of 'saturation' (Hara 1990). Some researchers and journalists have declared it an illusion. However, interpreting it as a sense of affluence backed up by 'basic equality,' we would argue that the figure of 90% is not an illusion but accurately reflects the reality of Japan during the period of high economic growth.

What are the 'new' inequalities?

Simply put, the 'new' inequalities refer to inequalities in a society which has achieved 'basic equality.' In this kind of society the old inequalities take on new features, and therefore a new approach that is different from previous ones is now necessary for studying them. We focus on three aspects of the new inequalities in this section for readers to have a clear understanding of what the new inequalities are.

Greater competitiveness and expanding inequality

Firstly, a situation of greater competitiveness and expanding inequality has been loudly proclaimed over the last decade against the backdrop of the prolonged and biggest recession since the end of the war and of the permeation of the market economy. Books predicting the 'collapse of the middle-stratum' and the return of an 'unequal society' have been widely read and harsh expressions such as 'winners' and 'losers' have become popular. A sense that there is greater inequality has become firmly established in Japanese society. (Tachibanaki 1998; Sato 2000).

However, some of these arguments are exceedingly questionable. Although the data analyses that underlie such arguments show that economic inequality and inequality of opportunity have increased, they have been criticized from a variety of angles (Hara 2002; Hara and Seiyama 2005; Higuchi et al. 2003). The current situation is that opinion on this matter remains divided.

Currently it is white-collar workers in large corporations – workers who have been relatively well off until now – who are most feeling the effects of greater competitiveness and expanding inequality. They constitute the largest group of readers of the books mentioned above. In other words, the basic argument propounded in these books seems to be tailored to the fears and concerns of white-collar workers in large corporations. In addition, the researchers predicting the collapse of the middle-stratum and the return of an unequal society, the journalists giving a wider circulation to the argument being put forward, and the white-collar readers from large corporations consuming it, all share relatively similar backgrounds and socio-economic circumstances.

Thus exists here a situation in which what might be called an 'intellectual community creating a discourse of inequality' can easily take shape. Consequently, caution needs to be taken in generalizing the fears of this intellectual community to society as a whole. The situation of 'basic equality' which has been achieved in post-war Japan is solid and will not easily collapse. However, it is also an undeniable fact that since 1975, Gini coefficient has been on the rise again. What is the cause of this? Seiyama (2001) has pointed out that it is due to an increase in inter-age-group income disparity. Amongst structural factors that have possibility of giving rise to differences in income, such as occupation, educational background and age, in fact the only factor showing a clear increase in inequality from 1975 through 1995 is age based disparity. Figure 1.3 indicates this clearly. It shows intra-age-group and inter-age-group changes in the individual income of workers belonging to the younger age group (25–34 years of age) and the older age group (50–59 years of age). If the increase in income disparity is due to increased competition amongst individuals, then first and foremost, there ought to be an increase in income disparity within the same age group. Yet this is not the case. Figure 1.3 shows that only the disparity between the younger age group and the older age group has, since 1975, been increasing.

Figure 1.3: Intra-age-group and inter-age-group personal income disparity

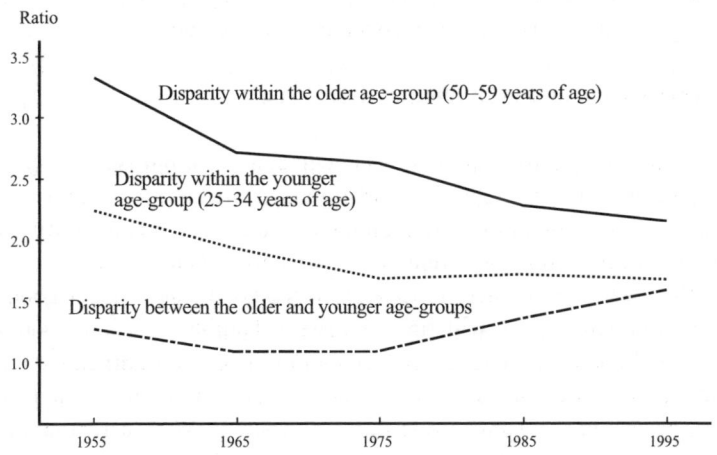

Note: The disparity within age groups is a ratio of the 75th to 25th percentiles. The disparity between age groups is a ratio of the median value of 50-59 age group to 25-34 age group.
Source: SSM surveys (data for males only)

Seiyama gives the following two factors as reasons for the increase in inter-age-group disparity. The first is the increase in college graduates and the expansion of the white-collar sector of the workforce. The two trends indicate an increase in individuals working for organizations with the seniority-based wage system such as large corporations and government ministries and agencies. This is because college-educated white-collar workers are more likely to work for such organizations in Japan than workers in other categories are. Because younger workers are paid less, while older workers earn more under the seniority-based wage system, the increase in workers at organizations with the system leads to an increase in inter-age-group income disparity as a whole.

The second factor is the spread of the seniority-based wage system to the blue-collar sector of the workforce in small to medium sized companies during the period of 'low growth' or 'stable growth' following the period of high economic growth. As a result of this spread the income disparity between different age groups has increased, not only in the case of the more highly educated white-collar workers, but in the case of workers from a variety of educational backgrounds and occupations.

In sum, Japanese society since the period of high economic growth has, whilst restricting competition within age groups, seen an increase in income disparity between different age groups. The social implications of this will be considered in the following section.

A variegation and individualization of goals

A situation of 'basic equality' has been achieved, but inequality in regard to what we might call 'upper goods,' such as a comparatively high income, comparatively high quality assets, or a comparatively higher level of education, remains firmly entrenched.

However, the distinction between 'basic goods' and 'upper goods' is relative and changes with time. A variety of durable consumer goods and the high school (junior high school in the old system) education, for example, were clearly luxury items in the past but have changed into basic items that anyone can desire and pursue. Will current luxury items, then, become basic items at some point? Using the example of automobiles again, will people who are currently satisfied with mass-market cars come to think that they should be driving luxury imported cars? It is possible. However, there are signs that a different trend is also emerging, even though numbers are still small.

People following the trend no longer wish to pursue the same things as everybody else (in the way, for example, that in the past everyone pursued the so-called 'three sacred treasures' or three essential durable consumer goods[2]). Instead, they are pursuing values in areas that have nothing to do with social strata or high status. For example, people may pursue a lifestyle in which one aims for leadership in volunteer groups, hobbies or other groups outside one's work, rather than in his/her corporation or government department (Imada 2000).

A variety of attitudes also seem to be appearing in regard to social stratification and status. One of these is the emergence of a so-called 'de-strata group' from the middle-stratum people. This refers to what appears to be the emergence of a group of people – not as an exceptional existence but as a social stratum – who say that, because they have a sufficient level of basic property, pursuing to be a member of a higher social stratum or attaining a high status does not relate to them and is of no interest to them.

It is an experience in my (author's) own personal life which triggered my awareness of such attitudes. I lived in Yokohama up until a decade ago. Competition for elite junior high schools has been much severer there than in Sendai[3] where I live now. From about the fourth year of elementary school 'every' child starts to attend a cram school in Yokohama. In the evening they set out from home having swapped their schoolbag for the bag of this or that famous cram school. The issue of what I should do for my children when they reached that age really troubled me.

Uncertain as to what I should do I observed the situation in families around me, and it was then I became aware of just how misleading the expression 'every' is. It was certainly not the case that 'every' child was attending cram school. There were many children playing outside in the evening who did not go to cram school. I then thought of their parents to try to get an idea of why they were not sending their children to cram school. The majority of the residents in my condominium complex belong to the sort of intellectual community I mentioned above. The parents who were not sending their children to cram school were certainly not unusual, and it was not because they were financially unable to do so nor because they were anti-intellectual or anti-education. From their general attitudes and behavior, however, I could see why they had made the decision to deliberately not send their children to cram school. They were the model for the 'de-strata group.'

Some issues of schooling and education typically reflect the current situation regarding social stratification and inequality. Problems such as 'declining scholastic ability,' 'differences in the desire to learn' and 'the collapse of classroom order' are currently major issues in education. Fundamental to these issues would be the existence of children and parents who are unable to find meaning in 'studying hard at school.'

Education generally has two types of value in society: (1) the utilitarian value of providing the knowledge and skills for maintaining or advancing social status and (2) the symbolic value of providing social respect due to the inherent value education has in itself.

In a society where basic equality has been achieved, such as contemporary Japan, it is not surprising that people emerge who feel that the utilitarian value of education has gone, particularly if they are not aiming for anything beyond what basic equality provides. For these people school is a place for obtaining the minimum knowledge and skills with which to survive in society, but it is no longer a place for hard study aimed at obtaining a high social status or entry to a good school at a higher level. On the other hand, there are also many people who place an even greater weight on the two types of value of education than in the past. In other words, we observe a differentiation of attitudes toward school education, evidenced in an attitude that still highly evaluates school education and an attitude that does not. Furthermore, what makes the situation more complicated is that many Japanese are vacillating between these two attitudes. Therefore, the elucidation of education consciousness (people's attitudes toward education) is the core of the study of strata consciousness (people's attitudes toward social stratification and inequality) in contemporary Japan (Hara 2000).

New features of 'old' inequalities

The above discussion may have presented a rather sanguine view of the problems of disparity and inequality. This is not, however, the full picture, as disparity, inequality and discrimination, having their roots before the modern period, still clearly exist in contemporary Japanese society. This is to be seen in the case of minorities. Examples can be seen in social status discrimination (discrimination towards the so-called 'burakumin'[4]), gender disparity, discrimination against the disabled, and disparity and discrimination in terms of ethnicity, in the case of foreigners living in Japan and foreign workers. Furthermore, there is also the situation of what might be called a 'peripheral stratum' in society of people who are not included in a formal manner within the Japanese corporation system, such as the unemployed and part-time workers.

What needs to be noted about the continuing existence of these 'old' inequalities is that they have taken on new features in a society with the establishment of basic equality, such as contemporary Japan. These new features refer, first and foremost, to the fact that disparities within minority groups have increased and that it is now difficult to discuss a particular group as one single group. For example, in the past women working as professors or in management positions in corporations were simply exceptions, but now their numbers have risen to a substantial level. This is a change that is clearly evident.

On the other hand, as Figure 1.4 shows, if we compare income by occupation, using the SSM data, a clear disparity still exists between men and women even in 1995. There is, then, a basic disparity (inequality), and protest and law suits in this regard are likely to continue. However, it is far from clear whether inequalities linked to minorities will lead to broader social anger. There is a danger that issues of inequality of this kind will end up becoming obscured in the current situation of a variegation and individualization of goals. That is to say, there is a danger that people will say, 'Those people are unfortunate but the problem involved is their problem. I'm fortunate

Figure 1.4: Personal annual income distribution by social strata and gender

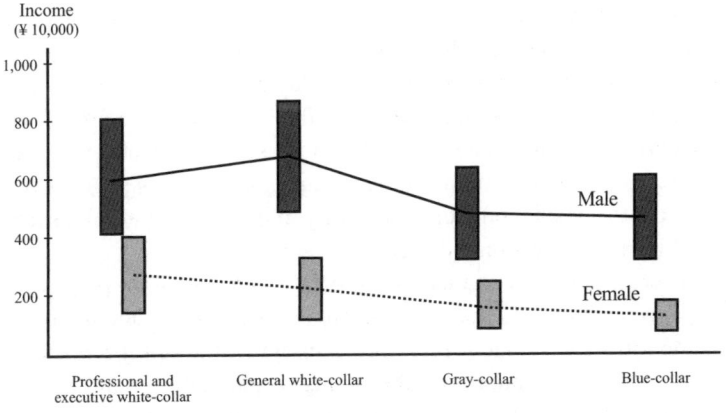

Note: The lines show the median value whilst the bars show the income range from the 25th to the 75th percentile.

Source: 1995 SSM survey (data for 20–59 year-old employees only)

and their problem has nothing to do with me,' and the issue will go no further than this. This too is one of the new features of the 'old' inequalities.

In the previous age of scarcity the problem of poverty concerned the great majority of people in society. It had, one might say, a 'social' nature. The future development of minority issues depends on whether or not they can build a 'publicness' in the same way as the problem of poverty did in the past. On this point I would argue that a different logic should be necessary for the development because the minority issues are located in the new environment.

Tasks for social stratification and inequality research

Theoretical and empirical research into the patterns and structures underlying these new inequalities is the task for us as sociologists. At the same time, however, we are also required to comment publicly on issues related to these inequalities on the basis of our research. Amongst them the following two are examined here.

The difficulty facing the young

In the previous section, it is mentioned that in Japanese society since the period of high economic growth there has been, in conjunction with a restriction on competition within age groups, an increase in income disparity between age groups. In the current economic climate where economic recession does not cease completely, this disparity has taken on the sense of an 'intergenerational disparity' difficult to recover by aging. It is a disparity between the older generation who received the fruits of the high economic growth and the current younger generation who had to start their working lives in the recession which followed the collapse of the bubble economy. If we were to consider only one inequality in the current period it should be this intergenerational disparity.

There is currently an increasing social awareness of the phenomena of *furītā* and *nīto*.[5] In the environment of the recession and increasing competition, permanent full-time employment is being replaced by part-time employment and the young in particular – entering the job market for the first time – are finding it difficult to get full-time employment. In addition, even if they get part-time work for the time being, their employment conditions are not good. Figure 1.5 shows data for female workers, and we can see from it that the proportion of

Figure 1.5: Employment and wage rates for part-time female workers

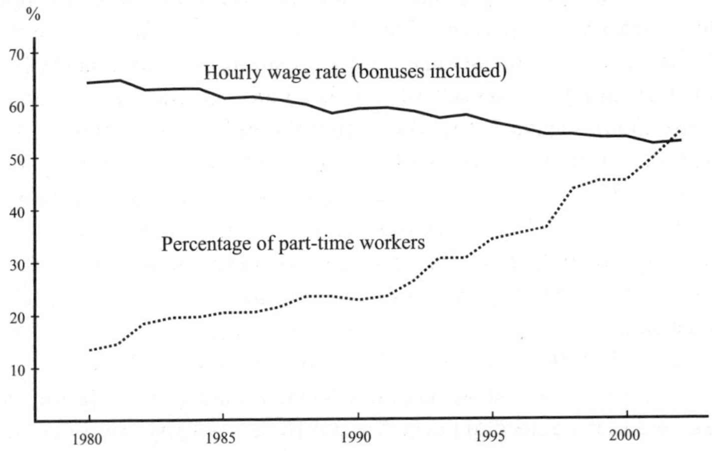

[Chart showing two lines from 1980 to 2000. "Hourly wage rate (bonuses included)" declines slightly from about 65% to 55%. "Percentage of part-time workers" rises from about 15% to over 55%.]

Note: The comparison is in relation to full-time female workers.
Source: Basic Survey on Wage Structure

part-time workers to full-time workers is increasing rapidly and that the hourly wage for part-time workers is decreasing compared to that of full-time workers.

Some commentators argue that the hedonistic attitude of the young is the primary cause of the phenomena of *furītā* and *nīto*. It is certainly true that if one goes overseas he/she finds plenty of happy and relaxed young Japanese travelers who do not seem to be eager to work. Observing these young travelers one might well think 'Is Japan really suffering a recession?' Yet the phenomena of *furītā* and *nīto* need, in the end, to be considered as a structural problem (Genda 2001).

What should we do to solve the situation facing the young? Firstly, work-sharing between age groups needs to be promoted to bring about an increase in regular employment for the young as much as possible. Work-sharing has been considered only for and within the generation in their forties and fifties who are busy with children preparing for matriculation to the next level of schooling. We need to go beyond this and promote work sharing between the older generation and the younger generation. If the inter-age-group disparity decreases through this policy, there is a possibility for the intra-age-group disparity, which has been decreasing, to increase. In such a case we should not see the disparity itself as a bad thing but rather we should aim at securing fair conditions for competition.

Secondly, lifestyles suitable for our contemporary age need to be presented and pursued. In most discussions in recent years regarding the 'disparity of opportunity' and the issue of the 'differences in the desire to learn' there seems to be a presumption that a happy life involves going to good schools and becoming a white-collar worker (Sato 2000; Kariya 2001). But is that the only kind of happy life? Demand for white-collar workers, in actual fact, is not anticipated to increase in the future. Demand for gray-collar workers, rather, is increasing and many young people are pursuing work in that direction, including college graduates. If these young people feel a sense of defeat or unhappiness in undertaking such work, it is a social tragedy.

Takeuchi (2001) has called the desire to go to good schools and become a white-collar worker an 'educated middle-class' desire and asserted that we need to put forward different positive lifestyles and that society needs to value them highly. In addition, however, young people themselves have to acknowledge the fact that there might be different lifestyles from those which have conventionally been regarded as desirable and to pursue them seriously.

A 'fair' society and the idea of equality

Faced with the new inequalities it is important that we indicate the type of society we ought to be aiming at. In this regard there is little disagreement amongst those involved in discussion and debate. Putting aside differences in regard to interpretation of the concept of 'fairness,' it is essentially agreed that what we should be aiming at is a 'fair' society. Needless to say, the problem here is what 'fair' means. This will continue to be a major point of discussion, but one thing that is clear from the debate so far is that 'unequal' is not equal to 'unfair.'

It is interesting that whilst there has been strong criticism of the increasing disparity in Japanese society there has been no mention at all that complete equality should be our ideal aim. Presumably this is because there is a sense that 'basic equality' has already been achieved, and, in addition, because there is a shared understanding that false egalitarianism would cause society to lose its vigor.

This does not mean, however, that all types of inequality can be deemed acceptable. We need to distinguish between acceptable inequality and unacceptable inequality, or between, to put it another way, 'good' inequality and 'bad' inequality. The 'old' inequalities mentioned above, for example, would be typical examples of unacceptable inequality. In regard to acceptable inequality, there is also a necessary precondition that fair conditions for competition have been secured. In addition, the issue of what constitutes fair conditions for competition and the extent to which these have been secured need to be continually pursued.

In addition to focusing on matters such as these involving the arrangements of the distribution of social resources – matters of 'distributive justice' – we also need to look at how these 'arrangements' are decided upon in society or within groups, or matters of 'procedural justice.'

We should also note that aiming for a 'fair' society in this way does not involve casting aside (even partially) the idea of 'equality.' The economist Amartya Sen (1992: 3) has argued as follows in regard to understandings of equality. 'It can be shown that even those theories that are widely taken to be "against equality" (and are often described as such by the authors themselves) turn out to be egalitarian in terms of some focus. The *rejection* of equality in such a theory in terms of some focal variable goes hand in hand with the *endorsement* of equality in terms of another focus.'

The relation between 'fairness' and 'equality' is the same. What makes fairness 'fair' is surely the existence of 'equality' in certain aspect of the matter. Conversely, what makes us feel that something is 'unfair' is an absence of 'equality.' It seems that a re-examination and expansion of the concept of 'equality,' which would subsume the concept of fairness, is necessary, not simply for the maintenance of the idea of equality, but in order to grasp in a unified way inequalities in various societies such as developing societies and advanced industrial societies including contemporary Japan.

Note

This chapter is a substantially revised version of a lecture given at the symposium commemorating the opening of the Center for the Study of Social Stratification and Inequality (CSSI) at Tohoku University on January 31, 2004.

2 Parsons' Discourses on Social Stratification: Some Reflections on Equality and Inequality

Kazuyoshi Takagi

Introduction

In Talcott Parsons' conceptions of social structure, a central and cardinal concept is social stratification. According to Parsons, social stratification means any system of a hierarchical social status that is made by social prestige. Since all societies institutionalize the structure of social esteem, all societies have prestige standards, and therefore social stratification. Parsons had been tackling theoretical and empirical problems of social stratification for 40 years and more. This chapter is an attempt to examine the outline of Parsons' understanding of social stratification and problems of equality and, in doing so, to ensure Parsons' intellectual legacy to the 21st century world remains. What messages, then, did Parsons leave for us?

Yankee City studies and the survey of social mobility

Universally known, the Yankee City Study is a classical work on community stratified structure. It represents six volumes of the Yankee City Series, 1941–1963, by William Lloyd Warner et al. Yankee City is a fictitious name for Newburryport, an old small town in New England. Warner and his colleagues came to grips with the research of this town with a population of 17,000 from 1930 to 1935. They conducted this investigation in an attempt to analyze the typical American local community. 54% of population of this town was WASP (White Anglo-Saxon Protestant) and 23.5% was foreign-born immigrants.

Parsons had the following critical opinions of this survey (Parsons 1938, 1940, 1953). Parsons argued that the upper strata, that was comprised of the upper upper and the lower upper, accounted for only 3% of the population in the city, which suggests that the upper strata,

Figure 2.1: Population composition in Yankee City by social stratification

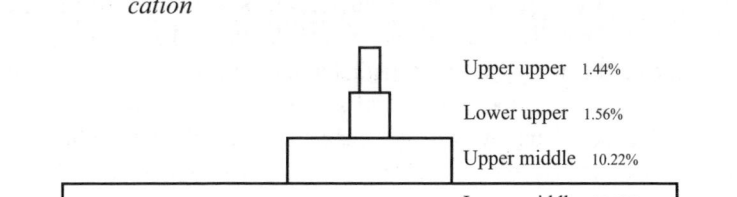

Source: Warner and Lunt (1941: 88)

which is a minority in number, governs the entire population. This means that Yankee City is an area in stagnation or decline. In contrast, growing areas, especially large cities, show different stratification structures from Yankee City. In particular, this study fails to catch the peculiarity of young people moving to large cities.

More generally speaking, in accordance with Parsons, we should not understand local communities as any miniature pictures of the national community structure, but should describe the individual characteristics of local communities as well as the peculiarities of this survey and place them in the national structure.

On the basis of this critique Parsons, along with Samuel Stouffer and Florence Kluckhohn, conducted a social mobility survey in Newton, a Boston metropolitan area, over a ten year period during the 1950s. This investigation was one that attempted to analyze the orientations toward social mobility of 9th grade boys. In this project Parsons attempted to build up huge paradigms and wrote many unpublished memoranda on the socialization of children, hierarchical prestige-ordering of occupational roles, social mobility and the inequality of opportunities based on the sexual division of roles (Parsons grappled with gender problems early in his career). Certainly the study of socialization by Parsons forms a link in the chain of social mobility studies.

In this survey project Stouffer and Kluckhohn also wrote many manuscripts and many graduate students completed and published their Ph.D. dissertations (Toby 1980). This survey itself was not published because of Souffer's sudden death in 1960. Speaking on

Parsons, only two monographs came out in Parsons (1955 Chapter 2 and 3). If we will check the Stouffer and Kluckhohn files in the Harvard University Archives we can understand these surveys by comparing the many materials available with the Yankee City series. Parsons conceptualized social stratification as the system of hierarchical ordering by prestige. 'Since the scale of stratification is a pattern characterized by moral authority which is integrated in terms of common moral sentiments, it is normally part of the institutional pattern of the social system (Parsons 1940 *EST2*: 71).' As all societies have a system of moral evaluation to units, and individuals in the societies ascribe particular kinds of social superiority and inferiority to others, social stratification is seen as an inevitable social structure.

Parsons defined 'a social class as constituting of the group of persons who are members of effective kinship units which, as units, are approximately equally valued (Parsons 1940 *EST2*: 77).' Since all societies have esteem rewards, all societies become class societies. Parsons particularly stressed that even if the prestige is the result of the householder's achievement, the family members who share interests of prestige have inevitably differential advantages. That is, family members are able to share any tangible status symbols acquired, such as a house, furniture, clothes, cars or life style. Therefore there are inherent limits in complete 'equality of opportunities' imposed by kinship solidarity. This is why Parsons insisted that the necessities of warm educational and medical aids be made available to disadvantaged children.

Also, Parsons emphasizes that the allocation of esteem rewards which have diffuse characters must be institutionalized more clearly than any other relational rewards because social stratification constitutes a focal point of serious strains in any social systems. This analysis demonstrates Parsons' recognition of the theoretical importance of Karl Marx. This is further emphasized by Parsons' assertion of the importance of Marx in his centennial celebration lecture of 'Communist Manifesto' at the American Economic Association of 1948 (President at that time was Joseph Schumpeter).

Parsons' reflections on American social stratification

Parsons presented a classification of bases of differential ranking of individuals in American society. In the 1940 article these were six standards: namely, membership in a kinship unit, personal qualities, achievements, possessions, authority and power. In the 1953 article

Parsons reduced them to four standards: qualities, performances, possessions and power.

Of course for Parsons a focus of analysis of stratification structure lies in the common value-pattern of its culture. The paramount American value-pattern, following Parsons, is embodied in universalistic performance values. This value system is institutionalized directly in the occupational roles (Parsons c.1949).

So in American society, 'apart from hereditary groups at the top in certain sections of the country, the main criteria of class status are to be found in the occupational achievements of men (Parsons 1940 *EST2*:.83).' This social stratification is the evaluative ordering of occupational performance measured by achievement and universalism. This is why American society puts such a major emphasis on the value of health and education. In American society, it is considered that without good health or adequate vocational training a person cannot fully realize his potentialities for productive achievement. Under these circumstances instrumental roles were valued higher but in special fields expressive performances valued higher, so there is ambivalence in value standards.

Parsons stresses that in American society class status is not a rigid entity but a fairly loosely institutionalized complex. Above all there is difficulty in the comparison between qualitatively different performance and qualities, of course between many performances of the same occupation. It is essential that the stratification structure is loose and not rigid. Also, we must remember to a considerable extent that value systems are institutionalized only in a relatively rough, broad sense and vague way.

Furthermore, there are many factors that modify the system of stratification built by achievement and universalism. In the first place, Parsons points out the ethnic factor. Because the value-system of ethnic groups may vary from the paramount in the dominant society, the actions of an ethnic group should be interpreted in terms of its own distinctive culture, such as of the case of Italians or East European Jews. Certainly these facts are results and causes of social discrimination. 'The case of the negro, even in the North, is the most conspicuous one (Parsons 1953 *EST2:* 424).'

For Parsons the second factor to modify stratification based on achievement and universalism is kinship solidarity. This is because kinship solidarity is not an individualistic factor. But we should not forget that, according to Parsons, the relation between occupational and family status is relatively loose. Even though there is a tendency, through the consolidation of advantage, for the families of the successful to consolidate their position and perpetuate it as hereditary 'upper class,' this has not been notably effective on a nationwide basis. Again this factor contributes to the looseness of the stratification.

Thirdly, Parsons insists that allocation of possessions is independent of the other components. Inherited wealth plays some part but, compared to other systems, a relatively minor one. In this point it is important that American society does not evaluate inheritance and land ownership and, therefore, institutes a high progressive taxation system. The fourth factor Parsons suggests is the power factor.

Thus Parsons concludes that by accepting and incorporating these factors with the main value pattern, the American system of stratification must maintain its relative looseness, with the absence of a clear-cut hierarchy of prestige.

Moreover, Parsons presented the empirical and concrete pictures of American stratification on the survey of a Boston metropolitan community (Newton). Next we take a brief look at them.

Upper strata

The 'top' is a broad and diffuse category, and undoubtedly its main focus is now on occupational status and occupational earnings. 'Seen in historical as well as comparative perspective this is a notable fact, for the entrepreneurial fortunes of the Civil War, notably failed to produce a set of ruling families on a national scale who as family entities on a Japanese or even a French pattern have tended to keep control of the basic corporate entities in the economy (Parsons 1953 *EST2*: 431).' This was helped by the separation between ownership and management as Berle and Means made clear. Members of these families have retained an elite position but broadly rather through their own occupational or occupation-like achievements rather than on a purely ascriptive basis of family membership.

For Parsons the Warnerian 'upper uppers' hold a secondary, rather than a primary, position in the overall stratification structure. On the whole their 'elite' position is far stronger locally than nationally, and in smaller, rather than in larger communities and least so in metropolitan centers.

Only in a rather loose and insecure way can we speak of the 'business managerial elite,' following Parsons, as the unequivocal top class in occupational status. There is strong competition from the professional elite groups, for example engineers, lawyers, and university professors, which is greatly reinforced by the increasing importance of scientifically based technology and university education.

Middle strata

Parsons stresses there is no clear break between upper elite groups and what is usually called the 'upper middle class' of business and professional people and, increasingly with the expansion of the functions of government and armed forces, of civil servants and professional military officers.

Also, according to Parsons, there is no clear break between upper, upper middle and the next one down (= common middle class). This is because in American society young married couples who are destined by ability or even birth for elite status often start off their married lives with a standard of living which might well be characterized as 'lower middle class.' This is contrasted with the European tradition that a son will follow in his father's footsteps in status if not exact occupation.

Again Parsons emphasizes that the line between the elite, upper middle and common middle is not clear and may be blurred. There is not a clear-cut distinction between the upper middle and general middle in terms of the expectation that children will receive a college and graduate school education. In his last years Parsons regarded the 'educational revolution' in the contemporary world as vital. The educational revolution shows increasingly strong orientations of achievement through capacities and education among all strata. Of course Parsons does not forget to insist that we should not bypass such people caught in a vicious circle of disadvantages, such as African-Americans.

Lower strata

Traditionally the line between 'middle' and 'lower' class status in the Western world has been drawn in terms of the distinction between 'white-collar' and 'labor' occupations. But, Parsons says, development in American society has gone far to blur the distinctiveness of this line. A major contribution to this blurring has been the high income of the elite labor groups who have gone through the assimilation of life styles so that it is difficult to draw clear differentiations. American society, according to Parsons, has relatively little of the traditional 'laboring class' of the European situation.

Following Parsons the occupations consisting of almost sheer drudgery, pick and shovel work, have been enormously diminished. Now technological innovations, especially automatic machinery, are eliminating whole ranges of semi-skilled occupations.

Parsons insists that in the lower levels of the stratification there are some tendencies to deviate from the middle-class pattern which are complementary, to the tendencies near the top toward a shift from predominance of the 'success' goal to that of the 'security' goal. More specifically, it is a loss of interest in achievement, whereby occupational role becomes not the main field for achievement, but simply a means for securing the necessities, or a necessary evil. The basic interest is diverted from the occupational field into the family, amusement, avocations, friendship relations and so on. This makes an excellent contrast to the urban middle classes where competition for class status based on occupational achievement is most severe (Parsons 1940 *EST2*: 80).

Parsons, after presenting the pictures of the American stratification mentioned above, emphasizes the strong tendencies to considerable social mobility in American society. At first he insists the great importance of horizontal mobility, particularly in residential mobility, as well as the shift from one occupation to another. They are most important conditions of vertical mobility. Of course in American society, there is even less continuity of specific occupational status from generation to generation, and significantly less than there has been in Europe.

With the educational revolution, mobility through education has been greatly increasing in importance. Now the economic difficulties of attending college and graduate or professional school are not the main barriers, even for those from relatively low income families, as many kinds of scholarships and financial assistance are available. Rather, the problems relate to the factor of motivation to mobility on the part both of childen and their parents on their behalf, as distinguished from objective opportunity at all class levels. There is no sharp break. So the problem lies in the motivation to mobility of the childern themselves. If the problem focuses on the quality of the personality, then the question is 'how do these qualities develop?' Such qualities are acquired via family structure, community structure, school environments, the situation of peer groups and so on. We cannot forget that Parsons investigates these problems under the clear, strong awareness of the need to create more egalitarian societies. This was a fundamental view Parsons held throughout his entire life.

Stratification in the world social system

Stratification among nations in the world system

Parsons, in his later days, wrote the monographs on the social stratification of the world system in the Encyclopedia of Italy (Parsons 1973). His arguments are as follows.

Along with the Second World War came the rise of the super powers, namely the United States and the Soviet Union. The comparable status of several of such older great European powers as Great Britain, France, Germany and so on have declined. Of course we should remember a notable development has been what we may call European unification. Also a particularly salient scale in the current situation is between what we sometimes call 'developed' and 'underdeveloped,' or 'developing' countries. There have been passionate arguments over the justice of the inequalities which exist between national units.

In turn Japan has enjoyed an unprecedented phase of economic development which has already put it into the position of the third biggest national economy in the world. Also China has begun to re-enter the international political world clearly as a great power. Thus within a short time period 'we have seen a notable recession of talk about the two supper powers to the idea that there is emerging a basic five power constellation (Parsons 1973: 43),' including the United States and the Soviet Union as well as the newly enlarged European community, Japan and the newly-emerging China. This is why we should eagerly seek the new international order of the world.

In adding to this stratification of countries there are dynamic processes that Parsons recognizes, and as Amin said, there is the growing discrepancy of status, resources, and the like, between the affluent elite of the international power system and the underdeveloped or developing countries. The super powers govern the third world, which is sometimes called 'imperialism.' This accelerates the rigid stratification in the developing countries since super powers assist the oligarchy, called the 'dictatorship for development.' Therefore in order to resolve the rigid stratification between developing and advanced countries, namely the huge differentiation of wealth and poverty, it is inevitable that we improve the relationship between them, as well as making changes to policies. This awareness of Parsons is shown clearly in his recommendation to solve the problem of apartheid in South Africa, which we will now consider.

Apartheid in the Republic of South Africa and Parsons

South Africa is an area administrated by Dutch reformists from the middle of 17th century. However, the British conquered the area in the early 19th century and established the Cape colony. Then the Boers, Hollander farmers migrating to north east regions, stole the land of Black people in the middle of the 19th century and established the Transvaal Republic and Orange Free State. But as great mines of gold and diamonds were discovered in these regions, battles between the British and Dutch erupted again (The Boer War), and until the defeat of the Boers (Hollanders) in 1902 the Transvaal Republic and the Orange Free State were changed into the direct control of the British (British imperialism).

Thus in 1910 the Union of South Africa was established, integrating the four regions of Cape, Transvaal, Orange Free State and Natal. This included many Indians who were working at sugar plantations. This made a special kind of 'division of labor,' namely British capital managed the mines of gold and diamonds, while leaving the political sovereignty to Afrikaners who were descendants of the Dutch. It was 1948 when the National Party, the Afrikaners' political party, took power and Afrikaners gained sovereignty. From that time the notorious apartheid system, which racially discriminated against blacks, colored and Indians, was pushed forward and reinforced as the state regime.

Afrikaners failed to challenge the British, but had aspirations to establish the state based on their unity and solidarity. For a while their dream was realized when the Union of South Africa remained a member of the British Commonwealth. It is not an accident that the apartheid system was strengthened by the policy of segregating blacks in various 'homelands' that were treated as 'independent states' as well as of depriving the nationality of the Republic of South Africa from black peoples. Therefore we can conclude that the apartheid system is the transfer system of oppression based on the distorted Afrikaners' nationalism.

Jan Loubser, who was a disciple of Parsons' middle years and became a co-editor of *Festschrift for Parsons* (2 vols.), was a student studying in the United States and had a lineage of Hollanders (Afrikaners). He made an appeal for the democratization of South Africa and for the freedom of black people, while he was the national chairperson of the 'Afrikaner Student Bond' during his student days at the University of Stellenbosch. As a result of these actions, he was ordered to leave the country. Then he went to Harvard University, attained his Ph.D. under Parsons' supervision, after he wrote the dissertation titled *The Development of Religious Liberty in Massachusetts*, comparing Protestantism in Massachusetts with Dutch Calvinism in South Africa.

Parsons, through Loubser, had some strong interests in South Africa's problems and accumulated some knowledge of the situation there. Under these circumstances Parsons, in his last days of May 1977, was invited to attend 'the international conference about racial problems' held at the Cape Town. This occurred just after the large-scale 'Soweto revolt' by blacks. Parsons wrote the memorandum for resolving apartheid problems and sent this to Professor Nicolous J. Rhoodie at Pretoria University who was one of the organizers of this conference. Now I will introduce this memorandum (Parsons 1977). After Parsons stated that 'I am in no ordinary sense an expert on South Africa society,' he presented the following arguments from comparative perspectives.

As a consequence of industrialization in South Africa, today it is impossible to segregate black peoples from whites and to completely exclude blacks from white society. 'The Black working class has developed to a point where the white society had come to be overwhelmingly dependent on its economic contributions and simply cannot bring itself to face the consequences of the radical exclusion of the blacks and their relegation to their own homelands (Parsons 1977: 9).' The apartheid policy has not only been unsuccessful but seems to be quite unpromising. What this seems to mean is that the two bases of diffuse solidarity, namely ethnicity and class, have come to be amalgamated in one aspect of cleavage. This is the most dangerous and explosive element of all for the society's integration.

If the class basis of solidarity is to be broken up in South Africa, it seems imperative that channels of opportunity for socio-economic advancement within the white society must be opened up. The most important mechanisms to facilitate such advancement are 'trade union' support, access to education and higher education in particular, and a variety of different kinds of occupational opportunity. The most immediate pressures are on the political front, with special reference to enfranchisement. Of course there is no reason to believe that either the end result or the process would bear close resemblance to the experience and situation of the United States.

On the basis of these analyses, Parsons recommended more specifically the direction of reformations in South African society. It would be the direction of such examples of the 'columner' model as the Dutch, Belgium, Canada, and Swiss, rather than the American type of pluralistic society, namely the model Arent Lijphart called the 'consociational Democracy.'

In the Dutch case, the main line of division has been on the religious axis between Protestants and Catholics. But it is important that this division has not been primarily geographical. If there was a correspondence to the religious line along with the geographical division, the result would have been much more decisive.

In the case of Belgium the basis has not been religion, but primarily ethnicity, between Waloons who are ethnically French and Flemings who are ethnically considered Dutch. In Belgium this division has also been important territorially. But there have also been other cross currents in Belgium, such as between religious and secularist orientations, for example the University of Brussels is a highly secularized university whereas others are predominantly Catholic.

In the case of Canada the division is between English speaking and French speaking peoples and this also creates a great deal of territorial separateness with the French highly concentrated in the province of Quebec. The great difficulty there has been that the English speaking minority in Quebec has on the whole been dominant in terms of class status and economic status, while the French separatist movement, although it plays with total political separation and national independence, is presumably more oriented in the columner direction.

Among the possible models of decentralization, the example of Switzerland can be adopted in South Africa. However, this model should be the radical one because a federal structure, if it advances pluralization across the racial line, would have to break up what is now white South Africa into several federated units, each of which had a substantial degree of autonomy relative to the others, and to a federal

government. 'Without this, surely white South Africa as an unbroken entity would far too overwhelmingly predominate over other federal units (Parsons 1977: 12).'
Perhaps this division to autonomous units is a way in which the historic difference between the Afrikaners and the English could be built in. Thus two of the Swiss Cantons clearly are much stronger than the rest, especially in economic respects, namely Vaud, which is French-speaking, centering in the city of Geneva, and Zurich, which is German-speaking. If development should take this kind of course, with perhaps Johannesburg as the center of an especially strong 'Canton' and Durban that of the other, it is important that the federal capital should not be too closely associated with one, as Pretoria is now. Thus Bern is in between, and in the United States Washington D.C. is not part of such powerful complexes as New York, Chicago or Los Angeles. Clearly for any pluralization and democratization in South Africa to be achieved, Indians and Coloreds can serve as important spearheads.

Finally, Parsons emphasized that the British and Dutch, two suzerain states, are responsible for the present situations in South Africa, therefore these two advanced governments, as well as societies, must adopt any policies for abolishing the apartheid system. This is the reason why I understand these arguments to be consistent with reflections on developing countries by Parsons.

Paradigm of equality and inequality: Parsons' legacy

Until the time of his death (May 1797) Parsons had been writing a huge book titled *American Societal Community*. In this unfinished and unpublished manuscript, a paradigm called 'Foci of Integrative Balances in the Societal Community' was included (Figure 2.2). The equality, which is a fundamental value in this paradigm, is placed in L-cell (Latent pattern-maintenance and tension management). This means the conversion in burden of proof took place in the contemporary societies. Now the burden of proof is legitimately taken upon the side imposing inequality. On the basis of these situations, recently egalitarian pressures have strengthened greatly in many societies.

For Parsons his ultimate goal was the establishment of 'the Kingdom of God on the earth.' Of course as the Kingdom of God should not be completed on the earth, this goal must be pursued permanently by all human beings. There are so many types of inequality for African-Americans, minorities, women, children, elderly citizens, disabled people, sick people, students and so on. The intellectual legacy Parson left to the 21st century is to continue the pursuit of resolving such massive inequalities.

Figure 2.2: Foci of integrative balances in the societal community

L = Equality   **I = Constraint**

l   Modes of Attribution of Equality in Orientation   i   i   Sources of Constraint (Constraint <u>by</u>)   l

Equality <u>of</u> Basic (human) Rights	Membership Status		Sacrifice[a] ←cost	Moral Authority
Opportunity	'Protection of the Law'		Sanctioned Norms	Facticity (Internal to Social System)

a   (Participatory Democracy)   g   g   (Collegial Association)   a

a   Components of Freedom   g   g   Justifications for Inequality (In treatment of units)   a

Freedom <u>to</u>: Pursue Unit Interests	Freedom <u>of</u>: Participation (in decisions)		Unit Achievement	Givens of the Human Condition (outside social or action system)
Allocation Unit Commitments	Association (in mutuality)		Prestige or Authority	Diachronic Linkage in Solidarity

l   (Market Freedom)   i   i   (Responsibility for Collective Interests)   l

A = Freedom   **G = Inequality**

Note. a: modification by *ASC*, chap. 9, p. 60.
Source: 1979a: *ASC*, chap. 4, p. 49a.

3 Market, Trust and Inequality: An Agent-based Model of Effect of Market Attractiveness on Trusting Behavior and Inequality[1]

Yoshimichi Sato

A dismal society?

It is empirically verified that people with higher income are, on an average, more trustful than those with lower income (Patterson 1999; Yoshimichi Sato 2002: 9, fn. 10), and this finding is theoretically supported by Yoshimichi Sato (2002). He derives an implication from a game-theoretic model that people with higher endowments are more willing to trust their counterpart. In other words, the rich can afford to trust strangers due to the leeway in their incomes. The poor, on the other hand, hesitate to trust strangers because they are afraid of losing their limited endowments.[2]

Sato's model, however, deals with a transaction between only two actors. Thus, it is not clear whether the theoretical argument made by him holds in a society comprising more than two actors. Furthermore, if true, this might lead to the emergence of a dismal society. In society, the rich can trust strangers in the hope of gaining higher returns from them, while the poor are unable to trust strangers. Thus, they miss the opportunities to gain higher returns. Trust of the rich might be betrayed by strangers. Nevertheless, if the rich continue to trust strangers and succeed in gaining higher returns, the difference in the accumulated returns between the rich and the poor increases. In other words, differential endowments establish a self-reinforcing relationship between richness and trustfulness.

The purpose of this chapter is to explore this possibility, that is, to specify the conditions that facilitate or hinder the growth of a dismal society. As will be argued later, the attractiveness of the market, where strangers interact, is an important factor in the growth of an unequal society. Neither Patterson nor Sato mentions this factor;

however, the following scenario appears plausible: If the market is attractive, it is possible that the rich will enter it and exploit the opportunities to gain higher returns from strangers, which results in a wider gap between the rich and the poor; however, if the market is unattractive, they do not enter it, and this gap does not widen.

We built an agent-based model to examine the validity of this scenario. This model is illustrated in Figure 3.1. It is assumed that there are two assurance groups in which agents exchange goods for certain[3]: If an agent offers one unit of the goods to his/her partner, he/she receives three units of the goods from his/her partner.[4] The only difference between groups A and B is marked by the endowments of the members of group A and group B, which range between 50 and 100 and 10 and 20, respectively. In other words, the members of group A are initially richer than those of group B. If a member of group A (B) leaves his/her assurance group and is paired with another agent from group B (A) in the market, one of the following two possibilities is observed. He/she receives X (≥ 3) units of the goods from his/her partner if the partner is trustworthy. He/she, however, receives nothing from the partner and loses one unit of the goods if the partner is not trustworthy. The variable X reflects the attractiveness of the market. The increasing value of X results in an increase in the agent's payoff provided his/her partner is trustworthy. The market, however, is risky in that the partner may not be trustworthy.[5] As will be shown, we manipulate the value of X in order to examine the above-mentioned self-reinforcing mechanism. With the terminology of the model we formulate it in the following way:

> *Hypothesis*: The attractiveness of the market, X, promotes the trusting behavior of the members of group A in the market, which results in a wider gap of the accumulated payoffs between the members of group A and those of group B.

We examine this hypothesis by building an agent-based model and conducting simulation based on it. In addition to testing the hypothesis, this study reexamines the relationship between trust and assurance. Yamagishi (1998) argues that being embedded in an assurance group hinders the development of trustfulness. Putnam (1993), however, shows that the civic intermediate groups promote the level of trust in society. Macy and Sato (2002) demonstrate in keeping with his argument that neighborhoods with moderate mobility of newcomers are a springboard for trust. In this chapter, we add a third

Figure 3.1: Trusting game

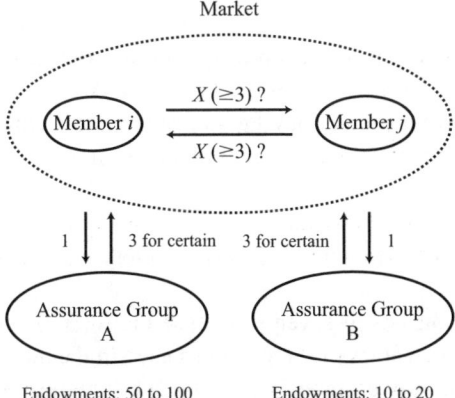

variable – market attractiveness – to the relationship between trust and assurance and analyze its effect on the relationship. It is assumed in the above hypothesis that the attractiveness of the market draws in agents who have developed a high level of trustfulness by interacting with other members of their assurance group.

This study also contributes to the study of social capital. Trust is an important aspect of social capital; however, its emergence between strangers is still under investigation. The model in this chapter analyzes the transformation of differential financial capital – initial endowments – into social capital and how social capital in turn is converted into financial capital – accumulated payoffs. Although a large body of literature has studied social capital, its emergence and its consequences, the self-enforcing mechanism of social capital, to the best of my knowledge, has not been fully explored.

The chapter has been organized as follows: In the next section, we describe the steps of the model; in the third section, we analyze the results of the simulation using the model; in the fourth section, we apply the findings of the simulation to a broader context of the studies related to trust.

The Steps of the agent-based model

The mathematical structure of the model used in this chapter is based on the game-theoretic model proposed by Yoshimichi Sato (2002). As shown in the above section, his model captures the essence of the trust relationship: An agent receives a higher payoff in the trust relationship than in the assurance relationship if his/her partner is trustworthy; however, he/she receives a lower payoff if the partner is not trustworthy.

The model used in this chapter can be treated as an extension of Sato's model on the basis of the following two points: First, the model deals with a society having more than two agents; second, it is a dynamic model in which agents learn to modify their actions over time. These modifications of the original model allow us to analyze the effect of the attractiveness of the market on the decision-making ability of the agents in a large society with less restrictive assumptions.[6]

The model consists of seven steps (see Figure 3.2). The first step is to initialize the values of the variables used in the model. First, the agents are randomly assigned values for the three propensities that they will learn to modify over time: The propensity to leave their assurance group, the propensity to cooperate with their counterpart

Figure 3.2: Steps of the agent-based model

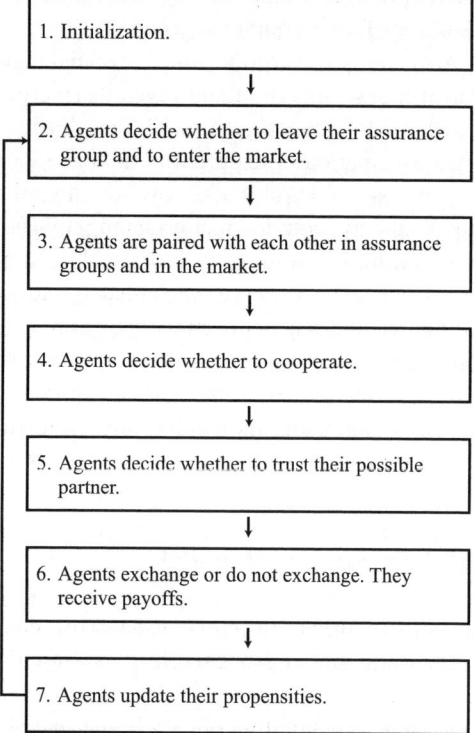

and the propensity to check the trustworthiness of their counterpart.[7] Second, the agents are randomly placed in two assurance groups such that each group, on an average, has nearly half of the agents as its members. Initially, there is no agent in the market. Third, the endowments of a member of group A randomly range between 50 and 100, while those of a member of group B randomly range between 10 and 20. These endowments are the initial accumulated payoffs of the agents.

In the second step, agents decide whether or not they should leave their assurance group. We assume a stochastic decision-making rule in this case. In other words, an agent leaves his/her assurance group if his/her propensity to leave his/her assurance group is greater than or equal to a random number, which is uniformly distributed between 0 and 1 exclusive.[8] An agent with a higher propensity to leave his/her assurance group tends to do that. However, he/she may incidentally continue to be a member of the group.

In the third step, the agents are paired with each other. An agent in group A (group B) is randomly paired with an agent in group A (group B). An agent in the market is randomly paired with another agent in the market if they belong to different assurance groups. If the strength of the agents in an assurance group sums up to an odd number, one agent in the group is left unpaired and has to 'sit out' one iteration. This also occurs when the number of the members of one assurance group in the market is larger than that of the members of the other assurance group in the market.

In the fourth step, agents decide whether or not they should cooperate, that is, offer one unit of the goods in the exchange in the sixth step. This decision-making is also stochastic: An agent decides to cooperate if his/her propensity to cooperate is greater than or equal to a random number.

In the fifth step, agents decide whether or not they should trust their potential partner. Two conditions must be satisfied for an agent to trust his/her potential partner. First, his/her propensity to check the trustworthiness of his/her potential partner must be greater than or equal to a random number. Second, his/her potential partner's propensity to cooperate must be greater than or equal to a random number. In other words, an agent's potential partner must be sufficiently trustworthy to signalize his/her goodwill to the agent, and the agent should be adequately able to receive these signals from his/her potential partner. Note that the agent's potential partner may fail to signalize his/her goodwill to the agent even though he/she has decided to cooperate in the fourth step. This is because we assume that signals agents send to each other are not necessarily reliable under uncertainty.

In the sixth step, agents receive different payoffs depending on their situations. If an agent has to refrain from participating in an exchange, he/she is unable to exchange goods. Thus, his/her payoff is 0. If an agent continues in his/her assurance group and exchanges goods with another member in the group, his/her payoff is 2.[9] Two possibilities exist for an agent who leaves his/her assurance group, enters the market and is paired with another agent. First, if the agent does not trust his/her potential partner and/or his/her potential partner does not trust him/her, the agent's payoff is 0. Second, if the agent and his/her potential partner trust each other, they participate in the Prisoner's Dilemma game, as shown in Figure 3.3. With mutual cooperation, agent i (j) offers one unit of the goods to agent j (i) and receives X units of the goods from agent j (i). Thus, their payoffs become $X - 1$. If agent i cooperates and agent j defects, agent i offers one unit of the goods to agent j but does not receive anything from agent j; agent j does not offer anything to agent i and yet receives X units of the goods from agent i. Thus, agent i's payoff is -1, while agent j's payoff is X. The same logic is applicable to the case in which agent i defects and agent j cooperates. If both agents i and j defect, they neither offer nor receive anything from their partner; therefore, their payoffs are 0. The payoff received by an agent per round is added to his/her accumulated payoff.

In the seventh step, agents learn to modify their propensities. This model assumes two types of learning: learning from one's own experience and vicarious learning. If an agent gains the highest accumulated payoff among the members of his/her assurance group,

Figure 3.3: Prisoner's dilemma game

		Agent j	
		C	D
Agent i	C	$X-1, X-1$	$-1, X$
	D	$X, -1$	$0, 0$

Note. $X \geq 3$

he/she modifies his/her propensities based on the Bush-Mosteller algorithm with the ratio of his/her payoff per round to his/her accumulated payoff as reinforcement. Alternatively, he/she emulates the propensities of that member of his/her assurance group who has the highest accumulated payoff in the group.[10] The mathematical formula for the Bush-Mosteller algorithm is as follows. Suppose p_t is an agent's propensity to take an action such as cooperation in the tth round. If the agent cooperates and his/her payoff is positive or if the agent defects and his/her payoff is negative, his/her propensity to cooperate increases by the following formula:

$$p_{t+1} = p_t + |r_t| (1 - p_t),$$

where r_t is the ratio of his/her payoff in the tth round to his/her accumulated payoff.[11] On the other hand, if the agent cooperates and his/her payoff is negative or if the agent defects and his/her payoff is positive, his/her propensity to cooperate decreases by the following formula:

$$p_{t+1} = p_t - |r_t| p_t.$$

After the seventh step, the system regresses to the second step and enters the next round.

Results of the simulation

Simulation was conducted for the model described in the previous section. The design of the simulation is summarized in Table 3.1. For statistical analysis, we recorded the information on the system for the second half of the 1,000 rounds in order to avoid startup anomalies.

In order to examine the validity of the hypothesis proposed in the first section, we calculated the average correlation coefficient between endowments and the accumulated payoff at each value of X, that is, the attractiveness of the market. We conducted 50 runs at each value

Table 3.1: Design of the simulation

The number of the agents	500
X (The attractiveness of the market)	Increasing from 3 to 20 by 1
The number of runs at each value of X	50
The number of iterations per run	1000
Total Runs	900 (= 50 × 18)
Recording of the data	Second half of 1000 iterations

Figure 3.4: Correlation between endowments and accumulated payoff

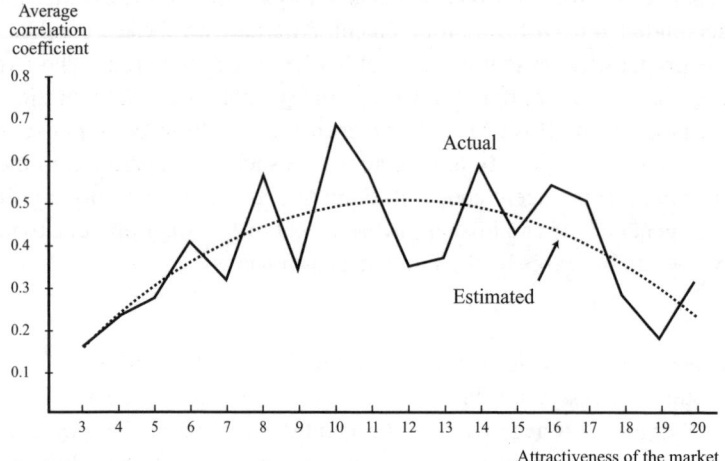

of X and hence obtained 50 correlation coefficients at each value of X. The 50 coefficients are added and divided by 50. We then obtained the average coefficient at each value of X. If the hypothesis is valid, the average correlation coefficient monotonically increases with the value of X.

However, the result of the simulation does not support the hypothesis. Figure 3.4 shows the relationship between the average correlation coefficient and the attractiveness of the market. The average predictor of a curvilinear regression analysis is added to the figure.[12] The graphs evidently indicate an inverted U-shaped pattern, which is contradictory to the hypothesis.[13]

Given this result, we attempt to explain the inverted U-shaped pattern. For this purpose, we examine the following variables: the difference in the average accumulated payoff between those members of group A and group B who are in the market (Figure 3.5), the difference in the average accumulated payoff between those members of group A and group B who are in their assurance groups (Figure 3.5), the average percentage of agents in the market (Figure 3.6), the average percentage of trusting behavior in the market (Figure 3.7) and the average percentage of cooperating behavior in the market (Figure 3.8). These statistics are calculated by 1) calculating the average (or the percentage) at each iteration, 2) adding the average (or the percentage) for the second half of 1,000 iterations and dividing it by

Figure 3.5: Difference in accumulated payoff between members of group A and members of group B

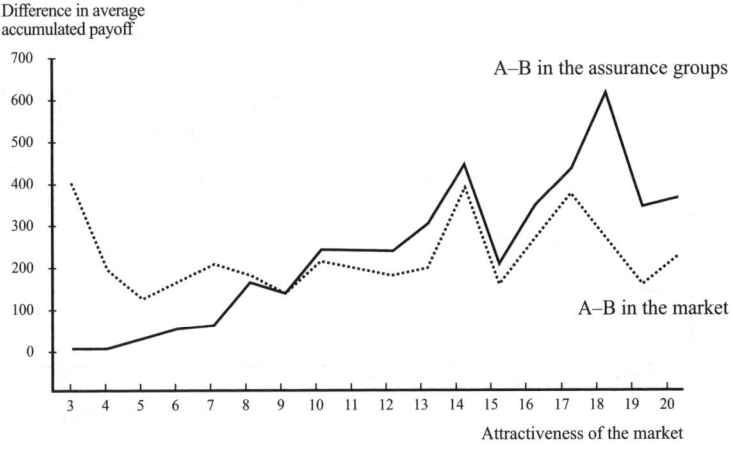

Figure 3.6: Percentage of agents in the market

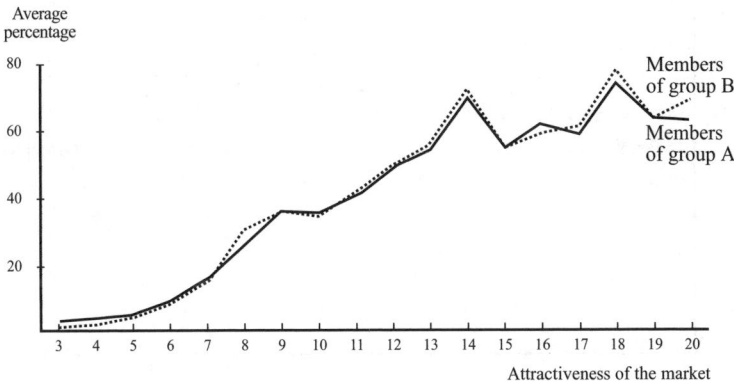

500 and 3) adding the divided number for 50 runs and dividing it by 50. Table 3.2 summarizes the findings in the figures.

As shown in Figure 3.5, the members of group A earn higher accumulated payoffs in the market as well as in their assurance group than those of group B do. I argue that this is the key factor for the inverted U-shaped pattern in Figure 3.4. This factor, however, does

Figure 3.7: Percentage of trusting behavior in the market

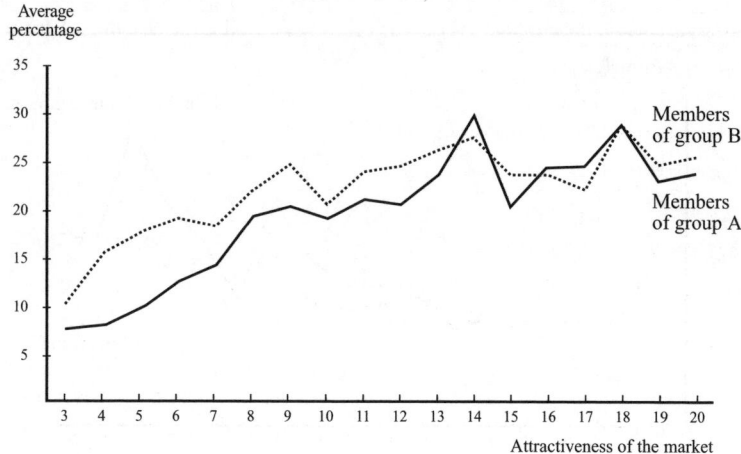

Figure 3.8: Percentage of cooperating behavior in the market

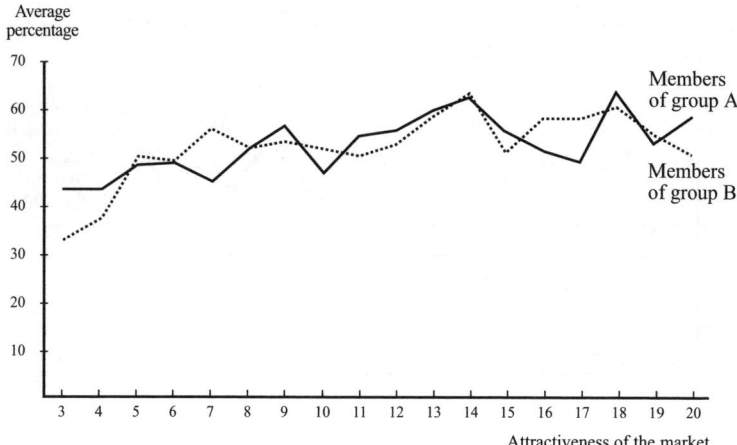

not solely produce the pattern. Rather, it interacts with other factors to produce the pattern. This interaction between the key factor and other factors is summarized as follows.

When the market is unattractive, the difference in the average accumulated payoff between the members of group A and those of group B in the market is large (Figure 3.5), but the percentage of the agents in the market are very small (Figure 3.6). Thus the dif-

Table 3.2: Summary of the findings

Attractiveness of the market		Low	Middle	High
Correlation between endowments and accumulated payoff	Fig. 3.4	Low	High	Low
Accumulated payoff in the market: A vs. B	Fig. 3.5	A >> B	A > B	A > B
Accumulated payoff in assurance groups: A vs. B	Fig. 3.5	A = B	A > B	A >> B
% of agents in the market	Fig. 3.6	Low	Middle	High
% of trusting behavior in the market	Fig. 3.7	Low	Middle	High
% of cooperating behavior in the market: A vs. B	Fig. 3.8	Low	Middle	Middle (Saturated)

ference does not have a substantial effect on the average correlation coefficient in Figure 3.4. In addition, the difference in the average accumulated payoff between the members of group A and those of group B in their assurance groups is substantially null (Figure 3.5), although most of the agents stay in their assurance groups. Thus, the difference in endowments between the members of group A and those of group B diminishes as agents steadily accumulate payoffs in their assurance groups. Therefore, the average correlation coefficient becomes low.

In the case of a moderately attractive market, the members of group A earn higher average accumulated payoffs in the market as well as in group A than those of group B do. Furthermore the gap between the level of trusting behavior of members of group A and that of group B becomes narrower as market attractiveness becomes higher (Figure 3.7). This means that market attractiveness encourages the members of group A, who learn slower than those of group B do, to trust strangers in the market. These factors result in higher correlation coefficients for the moderately attractive market.

In the case of a highly attractive market, the difference in the average accumulated payoff between the members of group A and those of group B in the assurance groups is large (Figure 3.5), but the percentage of agents in the assurance groups are less than around 40 % (Figure 3.6). The difference in the market, on the other hand, does not increase as the market becomes more attractive (Figure 3.5), even though the market attracts more than 60 % of the agents (Figure 3.6). A reason for that, I argue, is that the market is in turmoil. That is, although the percentage of trusting behavior increases with the attractiveness of the market (Figure 3.7), the percentage of cooperating behavior saturates or decreases slightly in the case of a highly attractive market (Figure 3.8). In other words, the attractive market entices some defectors to enter it, which leads to lesser efficiency of the market. Thus, the correlation coefficient becomes lower. The hypothesis proposed in the first section does not acknowledge this perverse effect of the attractiveness of the market.

Conclusions

The analysis of the simulation data reveals that the attractiveness of the market has an inverted U-shaped effect on the correlation between endowments and the accumulated payoff. This provides an answer to our original question – what conditions facilitate or hinder the emergence of a dismal society that makes the rich even richer and the poor even poorer. This can be explained as follows: A dismal society emerges only if the market is moderately attractive. If the market is unattractive, the rich do not risk entering the market and exchanging goods with strangers. If the market is highly attractive, defectors enter it and prove to be a hindrance to the rich who wish to accumulate higher payoffs. Although the effect of the market attractiveness on trusting behavior in Figure 3.7 is different than that stated in the hypothesis, the interactions between the effect and other factors produce the inverted U-shaped pattern.

This explanation contributes to the studies of trust in that trusting behavior and its results are affected by macro factors such as the attractiveness of the market. Macy and Sato (2002) point out another macro factor – geographical mobility. They argue that geographical mobility has an inverted U-shaped effect on the trusting behavior. In the case of low geographical mobility, agents continue in their neighborhoods – assurance groups – and do not have opportunities to interact with strangers. Thus, they do not learn to trust strangers. In the case of high mobility, every agent becomes a stranger and moves around. Thus, the agents lose the stable base that teaches them to trust strangers. If the mobility is modest, however, neighbors have opportunities to interact with newcomers to their neighborhood and learn to trust them, following which they begin to enter the market and to trust strangers.

These analyses bring the studies of trust back to sociologists. Although psychological studies of trust such as Yamagishi and Yamagishi (1994) and Yamagishi (1998) have revealed the intriguing psychological mechanism of trust, they tend to ignore the above-mentioned sociological macro factors. The model in this chapter and that proposed by Macy and Sato (2002) point out that the interaction between the psychological mechanism of trust and sociological macro factors deserves to be explored. In addition, they also demonstrate the importance of assurance groups for the development of trust. This line of research would promote a productive dialogue between sociologists and psychologists in the studies of trust.

Part II:
Exploring Realities in Japan

4 Local Leaders' Network Structure in the Edo Period: The Case of 'Busyu-gi Bo' of the Suzukis in Ushu Area

Daisuke Sato

Introduction

This chapter examines surviving documents of the family of Suzuki Gorobee in the village of Obanazawa, Murayama-gun (part of present day Yamagata prefecture), in the feudal domain of Dewa, in an attempt to establish the family's social standing through the analysis of its network structure. The author previously studied the family's New Year greeting card exchanges in the year 1866 and analyzed the structure and characteristics of the family's network as at the end of the Edo period (Sato 2003). The present study will address some of the shortcomings of the previous analysis: the family's relationship with neighbors in their home village and how the network's structure changed over time. Drawing on the findings from the previous analysis, this study will aim to picture the personal and social grid of this particular locality as seen from the Suzuki family.

The historical documents analyzed for this chapter are the so-called 'funeral record (*bushūgi bo*)': descriptions of the proceedings, distribution of duties and condolence gift exchanges of the funerals of family members. The documents provide detailed information on the nature of the family's relationship with the persons involved in the funeral, so they present excellent material for network analysis. The existing twenty-seven volumes of 'funeral records' in the Suzuki family documents cover the period from the pre-modern (Edo) period (1615–1868) through to the Shōwa era (1926–89). This study will focus on the funeral records of the family heads and their wives over a half century: Waki (wife of Sōfuku, the Second Suzuki Gorobee) in 1821; Kin (wife of Sōei, the Third) in 1837; Sōei in 1857; Sana (wife of Sōin, the Fifth) in 1866; and Sōto, the Fourth Suzuki Gorobee.[1] These five funerals were selected on the assumption that deaths of the family heads and their wives involve the widest possible range of people connected to the family.

Before beginning the analysis, I will briefly describe the geographical and social features of Obanazawa village and environs (see Figure 4.1). The village was located in the northern part of Murayama-gun, an area called 'lower villages' as opposed to 'upper villages' which refer to the southern part, the castle town of Yamagata and its surroundings. Murayama-gun was known for its cash crops such as safflower and *aoso* (a plant cultivated for its fiber). In the 'lower villages,' however, no cash crops were grown and rice was its major crop. On the other hand, it was located on the main thoroughfare connecting the north-western coastal domains of the region such as Akita, Shōnai and Shinjō with the domains of Nanbu in the north and Sendai in the east.

The village of Obanazawa, the home of the generations of Suzuki Gorobee, was a local governor's posting site from 1659, when the Shogunate set it up, until 1855. During this period the post oversaw about forty villages under its administration. After 1855 the office remained, governing thirteen villages belonging to the Matsumae domain. It had a population of 2,274 (1,149 male, 1,125 female) in

Figure 4.1: Location of Obanazawa village and seven other villages and areas

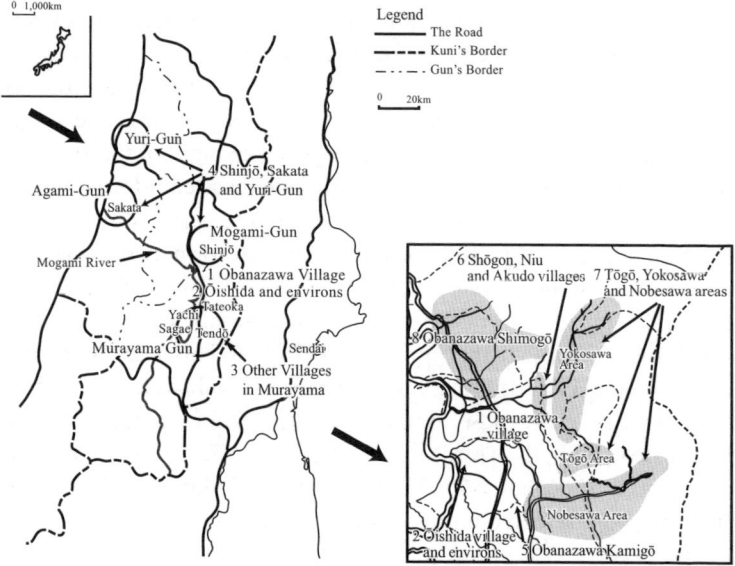

1858.[2] The village was divided into three *kumi* units for taxation purposes: upper *kumi*, middle *kumi* and lower *kumi*, each of which was further divided into *machi* (towns). They were: Nanoka-machi, Jūnanoka-machi and Nijūnanoka-machi (upper *kumi*); Tsuitachi-machi (middle *kumi*); Jūichinichi-machi and Nijūichinichi-machi (lower *kumi*). In addition, another town called Shin-machi developed along the highway leading to Sendai. Suzuki Gorobee lived in Tsuitachi-machi in the middle *kumi*.

The family of Suzuki Gorobee was established when Suzuki Dōsei, the first generation Gorobee, founded a branch family from Suzuki Gonzaemon in 1742. Gonzaemon had also branched from the family of wealthy merchant Suzuki Hachiemon, whose head was Suzuki Seifū, known for his association with the haiku master Matsuo Bashō (1644–94). The Gorobee family was thus an offshoot family, but enjoyed respectability in its home village. The family wealth reached its height in the first half of the nineteenth century, when its land tax and farm rental (used as estimates of the value of the estate) totalled 2,056 rice sacks (*hyō*) in 1827. Although the details of the family's business activities are not known, it is likely that it sold the rice to the Sakata region and purchased clothing from the Osaka area for sale. The official 1873 record[3] shows that in the following fifty years this figure was reduced down to a quarter – just over 446 rice sacks. But even then, in Obanazawa village the Suzuki family business was only second to Shibazaki Yazaemon's over 2,000 sacks.

Changes in the family status and gift exchanges

Geographical spread of the network

In the Suzuki family's 'funeral records,' individuals who brought gifts to funerals are divided into groups according to their geographical origins, and each entry shows the name, address and gift content. The geographical divisions vary slightly over the years, but they can be adjusted to the eight groups that were adopted since 1857. The divisions and their descriptions are as follows (see Figure 4.1 for locations):

① **Obanazawa village**
This is the home village of the Suzuki Gorobee family. I have not taken into account the above *machi* subdivisions and treated the whole village as one group.

② **Ōishida village and environs**
This area is centred around Ōishida, located approximately 3km west of Obanazawa village, on the Mogami River. In the pre-modern period, the Mogami was a distribution artery, linking the port of Shōnai Sakata, the northern regions' gateway to Osaka/Kyoto via the western coastal route, and the inland Murayama-gun. The village of Ōishida was an important river port. This area includes Yokoyama village at the opposite bank, Kaiya village and Fukabori village (all part of the present day Ōishida).

③ **Other villages in Murayama**
This area was called Kamigō of Murayama-gun. However, in order not to confuse this with Obanazawa Kamigō below, I will call it 'other villages' in Murayama. This area includes: Tateoka (part of present day Murayama-city); Tendō (present day Tendō-city); Yachi (present day Kahoku town); and Yamagata (present day Yamagata-city). These villages played an important part in the pre-modern economy of this region.

④ **Shinjō, Sakata and Yuri-gun**
This area includes: Shinjō (present day Shinjō-shi), an old castle town in Mogami-gun and the northern neighbour to Obanazawa; Shimizu (present day Ōkura-machi) on the bank of the Mogami River; and Sakata (Sakata-shi), at the mouth of the Mogami River and one of the largest ports along Japan's west coast at the time. Also in this area is Yuri-gun (present day Akita prefecture), which was north of Sakata and part of its economic zone.

⑤ **Obanazawa Kamigō**
This area includes adjacent villages on the south of Obanazawa, such as Oboroge, Yokouchi and Isazawa (all part of present day Obanazawa-city).

⑥ **Shōgon, Niu and Akudo villages**
The three villages are located to the northeast of Obanazawa. They were part of Yokosawa (see below), but the Suzuki family treated the three villages as a distinct group. They were said to have produced high quality rice and were a kind of 'rice district' in this area.[4]

⑦ **Tōgō, Yokosawa and Nobesawa areas**
Yokosawa here refers to an area close to the Ōu mountain ranges, including Takahashi, Namesawa and Nakajima villages. Tōgō and

Nobesawa are to the southeast of Obanazawa. Nobesawa village is closer to Obanazawa and Tōgō further towards the Ōu ranges. They were located on the highway to other regions: the former led to Sendai and Nanbu domains through Sabusawa and Senasaka Passes, while the latter was en route to Ginzan Pass, which linked Murayama with Sendai.

⑧ Obanazawa Shimogō

The Shimogō area consisted of five neighboring villages in the north: Oginofukuro, Ashizawa, Nogurozawa, Terauchi and Minamizawa.

Thus, the Suzuki Gorobee family had established a wide network, which spread far beyond its own village. I will analyze the nature of the family's activities that were basis of this network in each area in the next section.

Gift contents

Various people from the above areas sent condolence gifts to the Suzuki family at the funerals. For convenience, I have divided these gifts into eight categories according to their perceived values:

A. Cooked foods: *sekihan* (glutinous rice cooked with *azuki* beans), boxed dishes and Soba noodles

B. Luxuries: sweets and tea

C. Dried noodles and foods: dried noodles such as *udon* (thick wheat noodles) and *sōmen* (wheat vermicelli) and *fu* (wheat gluten bread)

D. Rice: rice and glutinous rice

E. Perishable foods: tofu, fried tofu and vegetables

F. Funeral goods: candles, lamps and incense

G. Money: monetary gifts (where their use is specified, such as '*sekihan* money,' they are treated as goods)

H. Others: condolence letters; goods outside the above categories (such as paper)

For the purpose of simplifying the classification, quantitative variations of gifts are not taken into account. Also, where more than one category of gifts was presented, they are included in the higher of the categories: for example, if the gifts fell into categories A and F, they are counted as A. Likewise, categories F and G are classified as F. This is because the presence of items of higher value is more indicative of the status and/or means of the gift bearer than the accompanying lower value items. Preparation of cooked foods would involve a good amount of manpower, and only privileged households could afford these or expensive B, luxuries. However, ranking of the other categories is not as straightforward. Considering the time it took to travel in those days, it would have been impossible for visitors from distant areas to bring cooked or perishable foods. Thus gift categories for distant visitors would have been limited, which causes problems in ranking C and F, which occupy the largest portion of gifts. I have ranked C, dried noodles and foods, higher than F, funeral goods, here for two reasons: first, a large number of people brought the latter, suggesting that funeral goods were more common, and second, prior to deaths some visitors brought dried *sōmen* alongside cooked foods and sweets as get-well gifts. Furthermore, category C included some Wajima *sōmen*, a specialty of Wajima on the western coast and a known brand. In the following analysis of stratification of the gift bearers, gift categories A/B, C and F are given a special focus.

Gift goods reflect the strength of the relationship between the sender and the recipient as well as the economic means of the former, and thus are indicative of the stratification of those who brought them. Table 4.0 shows the total of these categories according to the geographical groups for each of the five funerals between 1821 and 1869. According to this table, the largest category across all the groups is F, funeral goods, suggesting that it is the general choice of gift to funerals. C, dried noodles and foods, are also common. E, perishable foods, is also a popular choice in Obanazawa village. After 1866, G, money, increased in proportion. It is known that the Murayama region was hit by rising prices from that year, and people in the lower social strata could no longer afford to purchase goods, so they brought money instead.

Structure and changes in the Suzuki family network

This section will examine the changes in funeral gifts and their numbers over the years and analyze the structure of the Suzuki family's network. I will take the oldest record, that of 1821, as the basic data and look at changes that occurred over the subsequent years in the funeral attendants and their gifts as shown in two kinds of tables.

Tables A (4.1.A–4.8.A) aim to show the continuity of relationships between the Suzuki family and those who brought funeral gifts over the years from each of the geographical groups. The first row in Table 4.1.A (1), for example, indicates the number of returning gift bearers on subsequent occasions and their proportions to the number

Local Leaders' Network Structure in the Edo Period

Table 4.0: Total gifts by category and locality

	A	B	C	D	E	F	G	H	Total
1821 (Bunsei 4)									
① Obanazawa village	35	56	24	4	45	54			218
② Ōishida village and environs	2	15	10				7	1	35
③ Other villages in Murayama		16	13				7		36
④ Shinjō, Sakata and Yuri-gun	12		1	7	10	5	17		52
⑤ Obanazawa Kamigō	1	11		1	1	4	3	1	22
⑥ Shōgon, Niu and Akudo villages		11	9	8		12			40
⑦ Tōgō, Yokosawa and Nobesawa areas	6	14	7	7	1	23	1		59
⑧ Obanazawa Shimogō		7	7	3	3	2	1		23
Total	56	130	71	30	60	100	36	2	485
1837 (Tenpō 6)									
① Obanazawa village	19	23	9	3	60	79			193
② Ōishida village and environs	2	8	5		1	11	2		29
③ Other villages in Murayama		7	4		2	13	2		28
④ Shinjō, Sakata and Yuri-gun	1	5	2		13	12	5		38
⑤ Obanazawa Kamigō	1	1	1		6	8			17
⑥ Shōgon, Niu and Akudo villages		5	6	6	1	12	3		33
⑦ Tōgō, Yokosawa and Nobesawa areas	2	11	7		4	19	4		47
⑧ Obanazawa Shimogō		6	5	1	3	4			19
Total	25	66	39	10	90	158	16		404
1857 (Ansei 4)									
① Obanazawa village	22	2	33	3	67	102	8		237
② Ōishida village and environs	3	3	9		3	18	3		39
③ Other villages in Murayama	1	2	8			7	8		26
④ Shinjō, Sakata and Yuri-gun		2	6		2	9	5		24
⑤ Obanazawa Kamigō			2	1	2	9	3		17
⑥ Shōgon, Niu and Akudo villages			4	7		9	1		21
⑦Tōgō, Yokosawa and Nobesawa areas	7	1	4	4	11	2			29
⑧ Obanazawa Shimogō			4	3	3	6	3		19
Total	33	10	70	18	88	162	31		412
1866 (Keiō 2)									
① Obanazawa village	17	5	26	8	39	90	21	5	211
② Ōishida village and environs	5		6	2	1	17	1		32
③ Other villages in Murayama		3			1	7	22	3	36
④ Shinjō, Sakata and Yuri-gun		4	3		2	5	11		25
⑤ Obanazawa Kamigō			2	1		1	1	1	6
⑥ Shōgon, Niu and Akudo villages			6		2	3	7		18
⑦ Tōgō, Yokosawa and Nobesawa areas	1	1	10	2	3	10	5		32
⑧ Obanazawa Shimogō			5		6	6	3		20
Total	23	13	58	13	54	139	71	9	380

Table 4.0: continued...

	A	B	C	D	E	F	G	H	Total
1869 (Meiji 2)									
① Obanazawa village	20	3	17	3	51	32	27	37	190
② Ōishida village and environs	4		6		3	7	5	1	26
③ Other villages in Murayama			1	2		5	14		22
④ Shinjō, Sakata and Yuri-gun			1	1		2	19	2	25
⑤ Obanazawa Kamigō			2	1		2	1		6
⑥ Shōgon, Niu and Akudo villages			8	5		4		2	19
⑦ Tōgō, Yokosawa and Nobesawa areas	2		15	2	1	6	3	1	30
⑧ Obanazawa Shimogō		2	7	1	4	2	2	2	20
Total	26	7	58	12	59	60	71	45	338

A: Cooked foods; B: Luxuries; C: Dried noodles and foods; D: Rice; E: Perishable foods; F: Funeral goods; G: Money; H: Other.

in Obanazawa village in 1821. The second row of the second column shows the number of new names that appear in the 1837 record and the columns to the right indicate how many of them returned in later occasions. Thus each column after 1821 shows the percentages of returning and new gift bearers indicating the continuing and newly entered associates with the family. Table 4.1.A (2) shows the breakdown of those gift bearers according to the ranking of the gifts in order to indicate continuity of these associates according to their social standing.

Tables B (4.1.B–4.8.B) focus on the gift items and observe the changes with each of the funerals. Table 4.1.B (1), for example, indicates multiple categories of gifts in Obanazawa village. The underlying assumption here is that more than one kind of gift would reflect stronger ties between the bearer and the family, and one may be able to observe the strength in the areas covered by this network. Tables 4.1.B after 1821 have an added section (2) to indicate the changes in the gift contents from the preceding occasion in Obanazawa village; an increase in higher-ranking gifts (such as A, cooked foods) would suggest that the family had deepened its ties with the people in the area, while movements towards lower-ranking gifts (such as F, funeral goods) indicate that their relationship became weaker.

The basis for ascertaining the 'continuity' of association is the recorded names. In pre-modern Japan, the name of the head of the family, such as Suzuki Gorobee, was handed down to the following generations (for example, Suzuki Sōfuku is the Second

Suzuki Gorobee). However, the records cannot detect generational changes within a family where the name was not succeeded by new generations. This means that the same family line could have entered the data as different families. However, the resultant inaccuracies are considered small, while the number of visitors and their gift contents provide a good source for the present analysis.

The Suzuki family's network within Obanazawa village

See Tables 4.1.A; 4.1.B

The Suzuki family received the largest number of funeral gifts from the people in its home village. Although the number decreased from the highest at 237 in 1857 and the lowest in 1869 by forty-seven, the number of gift bearers was around 200 on average. The decrease in 1837 may be results of the population decline due to the famine during the Bunsei era (1818–30), and the increase in 1857 of the population inflow following the lifting of restrictions on the ports. As the population of Obanazawa was 2,038 in 1856,[5] the number of gift bearers in 1857 constitutes 11.6% of the whole population. In reality, however, the names in the record are only those of the family heads, so if we include their family members, the extent of the family's association would have been much larger.

Table 4.1.A (1) shows that almost 40% of the gift bearers in 1869 had been continuing family associates since 1821. On the other hand, with intervals of approximately twenty years, new gift bearers were recorded. From 1857, 1866 and 1869 where the intervals were shorter, of the new 123 names that appear in 1857 only fifty-six (26.5%) returned in the next occasion, and of the new names that appear in 1857 only twenty-eight (47.4%) returned in 1869. As mentioned above, one cannot tell from the list of gift bearers whether the new head of a family succeeded the name or took up a new name. Thus it is unclear whether the name changes reflect those of different families or the same families in different names. Nevertheless, considering the fact that changes in family heads do not occur every several years, and at the time there was a trend of population shift in local towns, those figures reflect at least a degree of population shift in Obanazawa village.

As for the gift contents, general increase in A, cooked foods, E, perishable foods, and F, funeral goods, can be observed.

With A, cooked foods, after 1837 more people brought them with other goods. Also, of the thirty-five families that brought A, cooked

Table 4.1.A: Number of gift bearers and return rates/Continuity of gifts by category – ① Obanazawa village

	1821	(%)	1837	(%)	1857	(%)	1866	(%)	1869	(%)
1. New and returning gift bearers after 1821										
1821 (Bunsei 4)	218	100	103	53.4	85	35.9	74	35.1	73	38.4
1837 (Tenpō 8)			90	46.6	29	12.2	22	10.4	15	7.9
1857 (Ansei 4)					123	51.9	56	26.5	44	23.2
1866 (Keiō 2)							59	28	28	14.7
1869 (Meiji 2)									30	15.8
Total	218	100	193	100	237	100	211	100	190	100
2. Gift categories and return rates										
A 1821	35	100	24	68.6	21	60	22	62.9	22	62.9
1837			1							
1857					3		2		2	
1866							2		2	
1869										
B 1821	56	100	28	50	22	39.2	17	30.3	19	33.9
1837			7	100	1	14.3	1	14.3	1	14.3
1857					2	100	2	100	1	50
1866							3	100	1	50
1869									2	100
C 1821	24	100	14	58.3	12	50	10	41.7	10	41.7
1837			4	100	2	50	2	50	2	50
1857					13	100	8	61.5	6	46.1
1866							7	100	3	42.9
1869									1	100
D 1821	4	100	4	100	4	100	3	75	2	50
1837			2	100	1	50	1	50	1	50
1857										
1866							1	100		0
1869									1	100
E 1821	45	100	16	35.6	13	28.9	12	26.7	9	20
1837			28	100	9	32.1	6	21.4	4	14.3
1857					45	100	19	42.2	14	31.1
1866							9	100	4	44.4
1869									6	100
F 1821	54	100	17	31.5	16	29.6	13	24.1	12	22.2
1837			48	100	16	33.3	12	25	7	14.6
1857					56	100	23	41.1	19	33.9
1866							27	100	14	51.9
1869									6	100
G 1821										
1837										
1857					4	100	2	50	2	50
1866							7	100	2	28.6
1869									4	100
H 1821										
1837										
1857										
1866							3	100	2	66.7
1869									10	100

A: Cooked foods; B: Luxuries; C: Dried noodles and foods; D: Rice; E: Perishable foods; F: Funeral goods; G: Money; H: Other.

foods, in 1821, at least twenty-two (62.3%) remained at the time of the 1869 funeral, representing the strongest ties with quality of the gifts and continuity of association. They include influential families such as the members of the Suzuki clan in the village (the main family was headed by Suzuki Yachiemon) and Shibazaki Yazaemon, one of the most prominent business families in Murayama-gun. Those who brought other gifts alongside A, cooked foods, were ten out of nineteen (52.6%) in 1837, and twenty out of twenty-two (approx. 91%) in 1857. This group of people must have also played a seminal role in the funeral proceedings. The shift from other goods to A, cooked foods, shown in Table 4.1.B (2) also seems to have occurred among those who were either related to or branched from the family or who had brought A, cooked foods, on previous occasions. New names among the bearers of these status gifts only appear in three instances in 1857, three in 1866 and one in 1869. This implies that it was uncommon for the people in Obanazawa village to rise in status and to become able to afford such gifts by means such as association with prominent families through marriage.

The most common gifts recorded are E, perishable foods and F, funeral goods. Particularly the latter is the largest group of all the gifts brought to the family in all occasions. On four occasions from 1821 to 1866, F, funeral goods, such as candles and lanterns were the largest number of items among the single gifts and those presented by new names on the list. This suggests that they were most common funeral gifts in Obanazawa. Another characteristic of the bearers of the two gift groups is that almost half were replaced by new names in the following occasion (Table 4.1.B (2)), suggesting that this group of gift bearers were fluid. On the other hand, the total number of bearers remains fairly steady. One can surmise from these that their relationship with the family was mainly geographical association, rather than the length of their residency in the village.

As a summary, the Suzuki Gorobee family's associations in its home village can be roughly divided into long-term associations with relatives and influential families who brought A, cooked foods, to funerals, and a fluid group of residents who brought F, funeral goods, and other common single gifts.

The Suzuki family's network in other areas

② **Ōishida**
See Tables 4.2.A; 4.2.B.

Table 4.1.B: Single/multiple gift categories and changes in subsequent occasions – ① Obanazawa village

	A	B	C	D	E	F	G	H	Total
1821 (Bunsei 4)									
1. Number of categories									
One category	26	46	23	3	43	54			
Two categories	9	10	1	1	2				
≥ Three categories									
Total	35	56	24	4	45	54			218
%	16.1	25.7	11	1.8	20.6	24.8			
Actual figure	35	56	26	7	48	69			
1837 (Tenpō 8)									
1. Number of categories									
One category	9	16	2	2	36	79			
Two categories	9	7	4		23				
≥ Three categories	1		3	1	1				
Total	19	23	9	3	60	79			193
%	9.8	11.9	4.7	1.6	31.1	40.9			
2. Previous categories									
A	15	9	2		7	2			
B			1		3	14			
C	1	4	1		4	3			
D	1			1	2				
E		2	2		9	3			
F	1				7	9			
G									
H									
New	1	8	3	2	28	48			
Total	19	23	9	3	60	79			193
Actual figure	19	23	9	3	66	126			
1857 (Ansei 4)									
1. Number of categories									
One category	2	2	16		39	100	8		
Two categories	14		15		24	2			
≥ Three categories	6		2	3	4				
Total	22	2	33	3	67	102	8		237
%	9.2	0.8	13.9	1.2	28.2	43	3.3		
2. Previous categories									
A	13		1	1					
B			3			9			
C	1		3		1	3			
D	1		1	2	1	1			
E			7		12	8			
F	3 (1ª)		4		4	22			
G									
H									
New	4	2	14		49	59	8		
Total	22	2	33	3	67	102	8		237
Actual figure	22	5	34	4	76	163	13		

Table 4.1.B: Continued...

	A	B	C	D	E	F	G	H	Total
1866 (Keiō 2)									
1. Number of categories									
One category	5	1	20	2	28	74	21	5	
Two categories	7	3	6	2	11	16			
≥ Three categories	5	1		4					
Total	17	5	26	8	39	90	21	5	211
%	8	2.3	12.3	3.8	18.5	42.7	10	2.4	
2. Previous categories									
A	11			3		3	3		
B		1			1				
C	2	1	6	2	4	8	2	1	
D				2			1		
E			3		15	13	3		
F	1		6		8	35	4		
G						2	1	1	
H									
New	3	3	11	1	11	29	7	3	
Total	17	5	26	8	39	90	21	5	211
Actual figure	17	9	32	10	45	122	37	13	
1869 (Meiji 2)									
1. Number of categories									
One category	4	2	15	1	42	23	26	37	
Two categories	11		2		7	9	1		
≥ Three categories	5	1		2	2				
Total	20	3	17	3	51	32	27	37	190
%	10.5	1.6	8.9	1.6	26.8	16.8	14.2	19.5	
2. Previous categories									
A	11		2		1	2		1	
B		2					1		
C			5		9	3	1	1	
D	4			3					
E			1		16		3	3	
F	4 (1ª)		8		13	17	10	10 (4ª)	
G	1				1	1	5	5	
H					1	1	1	1	
New			1	1	10	8	6	16	
Total	20	3	17	3	51	32	27	37	190
Actual figure	20	6	17	6	56	59	40	45	

A: Cooked foods; B: Luxuries; C: Dried noodles and foods; D: Rice; E: Perishable foods; F: Funeral goods; G: Money; H: Other.

Note. Figures marked 'a' denote gift bearers to the funeral before last.

Table 4.2.A: Number of gift bearers and return rates/Continuity of gifts by category – ② *Ōishida village and environs*

		1821 (%)		1837 (%)		1857 (%)		1866 (%)		1869 (%)	
1. New and returning gift bearers after 1821											
1821 (Bunsei 4)		35	100	15	51.7	13	33.3	9	29	8	30.8
1837 (Tenpō 8)				14	48.3	5	12.8	4	12.9	3	11.5
1857 (Ansei 4)						21	53.8	5	16.1	4	15.4
1866 (Keiō 2)								13	41.9	3	11.5
1869 (Meiji 2)										8	30.8
Total		35	100	29	100	39	100	31	100	26	100
2. Gift categories and return rates											
A	1821	2	100	2	100	2	100	2	100	2	100
	1837										
	1857										
	1866										
	1869										
B	1821	15	100	7	46.7	5	33.3	4	26.7	3	20
	1837			3	100	1	33.3	1	33.3	1	33.3
	1857					2	100		0		
	1866										
	1869										
C	1821	10	100	4	40	3	30	1	10	1	10
	1837			3	100	2	66.7	2	66.7	2	66.7
	1857					6	100	3	50	2	33.3
	1866							3	100	2	66.7
	1869									2	100
D	1821										
	1837										
	1857										
	1866										
	1869										
E	1821										
	1837			1	100		0				
	1857					4	100	2	50		0
	1866										
	1869									1	100
F	1821										
	1837			7	100	2	28.6	2	28.6	1	14.3
	1857					11	100	2	18.2	3	27.3
	1866							11	100	2	18.2
	1869									2	100
G	1821	7	100	1	14.3	2	28.6	2	28.6		
	1837			1	100		0				
	1857					1	100		0		
	1866										
	1869									2	100
H	1821	1	100	1	100	1	100		0	1	100
	1837										
	1857										
	1866										
	1869										

A: Cooked foods; B: Luxuries; C: Dried noodles and foods; D: Rice; E: Perishable foods; F: Funeral goods; G: Money; H: Other.

Names of the Suzuki family's business associates are found among the gift bearers from the Mogami River port of Ōishida; eleven out of the eighteen names registered in the Cargo Stations Guild as at 1814 appear as gift bearers of the 1821 funeral, and fifteen out of thirty-two of the Cargo Merchants' Guild as at 1836 appear in the list of the 1837 funeral. The Suzuki family's business was at its height during those years, and the gifts reflect their strong and extensive ties with the riverbank merchants. Particularly noticeable are the family of Nitobe Heiemon and its branch family Nitobe Heizō: the former was the largest river cargo merchant in the pre-modern period in the region whose business peaked at the beginning of the nineteenth century. Both families brought A, cooked foods, to all of the Suzuki family funerals. The Suzuki Gorobee and Nitōbe Hyōzō families are also related by marriage: Miwa, sister of the Third Gorōbee, married into the Nitobe family. The other people who brought A, cooked foods, to the Suzuki funerals after 1837 were all family relations with exception of Terasaki Niemon, a prominent family in Shinjō domain.

Among the cargo merchants, only three families other than Nitobe continued to bring condolence gifts to the three funerals from 1837. They were Tsuchiya Gihei, Takakuwa Kōsuke and Nishizuka Yōichirō. The Tsuchiyas were related to the Suzukis after a sister of the Fifth Gorobee married into the Tsuchiya family. All three were merchants who quickly expanded their businesses from the Tenpō era (1830–44) to the end of the Edo period (1868). Togashi Kyūbee, whose name appears in all lists except in 1837, and Shōji Seikichi, whose name appears from 1837 onwards, are said to have developed their businesses in similar manner (Yokoyama 1980). From the Tenpō era, Suzuki Gorobee began contracting their land administration. It seems that he perceived the increasing prosperity among Ōishida merchants and sought alliance with promising families in the area, including marriage connections.

Table 4.2.B shows that from the mid nineteenth century the proportion of F, funeral goods, increased. Many of the names in this group appear only once, which suggests that the family also formed short-term relationships with a substantial number of people, as it did in its home village. This group seems to include river administration officials of the Shogunate as well as families related to the above merchants (judging from surnames). In addition there were a plasterer (one in 1837), a blacksmith (one in 1857) and several carpenters (three in 1857 and two in 1869). Ōishida is known for

Table 4.2.B: Single/multiple gift categories and changes in subsequent occasions – ② Ōishida village and environs

	A	B	C	D	E	F	G	H	Total
1821 (Bunsei 4)									
1. Number of categories									
One category	1	15	9				7	1	
Two categories	1		1						
≥ Three categories									
Total	2	15	10				7	1	35
%	5.7	42.9	28.6				20	2.9	
Actual figure	2	15	10				7	1	
1837 (Tenpō 8)									
1. Number of categories									
One category	2	5	5			10	2		
Two categories		3			1	1			
≥ Three categories									
Total	2	8	5		1	11	2		29
%	6.9	27.6	17.2		3.4	37.9	6.9		
2. Previous categories									
A	2								
B		4	1			2			
C		1	1			1	1		
D									
E									
F									
G							1		
H		1							
New		2	3		1	7	1		
Total	2	8	5		1	11	2		29
Actual figure	2	8	5	1	1	15	2		
1857 (Ansei 4)									
1. Number of categories									
One category	2	1	3		2	17	3		
Two categories		2	4		1	1			
≥ Three categories	1		2						
Total	3	3	9		3	18	3		39
%	7.7	7.7	23.1		7.7	46.2	7.7		
2. Previous categories									
A	2								
B			2			4	1		
C		1	1						
D									
E									
F			1			3			
G							1		
H									
New	1	2	5		3	11	1		
Total	3	3	9		3	18	3		39
Actual figure	3	3	9		3	28	3		

Table 4.2.B: Continued...

	A	B	C	D	E	F	G	H	Total
1866 (Keiō 2)									
1. Number of categories									
One category			3			15	1		
Two categories	4		3	1	1	2			
≥ Three categories	1			1					
Total	5		6	2	1	17	1		32
%	15.6		18.8	6.3	3.1	53.1	3.1		
2. Previous categories									
A	3								
B	2								
C			2	1					
D									
E					1	1			
F						5	1		
G				1					
H									
New			4			11			
Total	5		6	2	1	17	1		32
Actual figure	5		7	2	1	26	4		
1869 (Meiji 2)									
1. Number of categories									
One category	1		2		3	3	5	2	
Two categories	3		4			4			
≥ Three categories									
Total	4		6		3	7	5	2	27
%	15.3		23.1		11.5	26.9	19.2	3.8	
2. Previous categories									
A	3		1			1			
B									
C			1		1	2			
D	1							1	
E									
F			2		1	1	3		
G									
H									
New			2		1	3	2	1	
Total	4		6		3	7	5	2	27
Actual figure	4		6		3	13	10	2	

A: Cooked foods; B: Luxuries; C: Dried noodles and foods; D: Rice; E: Perishable foods; F: Funeral goods; G: Money; H: Other.

Note. Figures marked 'a' denote gift bearers to the funeral before last.

its artisans, so the Suzuki family must have associated with them through business dealings such as house repairs and extensions.

③ Other villages in Murayama

See Tables 4.3.A; 4.3.B.

As Table 4.3.A (1) shows fewer people from this area were returning visitors: new names constitute 68% of the gift bearers in 1837 and 67% in 1866.

Those who brought condolence gifts to all five funerals were three families: Harada Kichiemon, Tsujimura Ichirōbee and Kisō Iemon, all prominent merchants of Tateoka town. The Suzuki family took the wife of the Fifth Gorobee's son Tomojirō from the Tsujimura family, and there is evidence that the Suzuki family attempted to align themselves with the Haradas who were powerful landowners. As for the Kisō family, there were financial ties between the families from the Bunka/Bunsei eras (1804–30) to the end of the Edo period (Sato 2003).

Suzuki Sōin, the Fifth Suzuki Gorobee, married Sana from the Hoshino family, a vassal of the Akimoto clan of Yamagata domain. In the 1840 record of Sōin's visit to the Hoshino family in Yamagata, there are names of Murai Seishichi (an influential safflower and clothes merchant), Makiya Shinbee (clothes merchant) and Kobayashi Shichiemon (herb medicine merchant). These three names also appear in the funeral gift bearers' list: Murai in 1837 with gift category E; Makiya in 1837 with gift category E, 1857, 1866 and 1869 with category G; and Kobayashi in 1837 with category B, 1857 and 1866 with category G. The Kobayashi family seemed to have a close relationship with the Suzukis: a number of names bearing the Kobayashi surname, which suggests they were related, brought gifts to the Suzukis.

The shift in gift categories is shown in Table 4.3.B (2): gifts from this area had a higher proportion of C, dried noodles and foods, and F, funeral goods, in the earlier occasions (1821 and 1857). From 1866, G, money, increased. Combined with the information in Table 4.3.A, the implication is that the Suzuki family, through the established associations with particular families in Tateoka and Yamagata area, formed a secondary network that was short-term and fluid. Exceptions to this general network were Ishikara Tsugishirō of Yamabe, who brought 'cooked foods' in 1821, and Shimaya Isuke of Sagae who upgraded gift from low-ranking F, funeral goods, in 1866 to B, luxuries, in 1869. The two were prominent merchants in the area. The

Table 4.3.A: Number of gift bearers and return rates/Continuity of gifts by category – ③ Other villages in Murayama

		1821	(%)	1837	(%)	1857	(%)	1866	(%)	1869	(%)
1. New and returning gift bearers after 1821											
1821 (Bunsei 4)		36	100	9	32.1	7	26.9	4	11.1	4	18.1
1837 (Tenpō 8)				19	67.9	4	15.4	3	8.3	3	13.7
1857 (Ansei 4)						15	57.7	5	13.9	3	13.7
1866 (Keiō 2)								24	66.7	12	54.5
1869 (Meiji 2)										0	
Total		36	100	28	100	26	100	36	100	22	100
2. Gift categories and return rates											
A	1821	1	100	1	100	1	100	1	100	1	100
	1837										
	1857										
	1866										
	1869										
B	1821	11	100	2	18.2	1	9.1		0		
	1837										
	1857										
	1866										
	1869										
C	1821	8	100	3	37.5	3	37.5	1	12.5	1	12.5
	1837										
	1857					1	100		0		
	1866							1	100		0
	1869										
D	1821	1	100		0						
	1837										
	1857										
	1866										
	1869										
E	1821	1	100								
	1837			3	100	1	33.3				
	1857										
	1866							4	100		
	1869										
F	1821	4	100	1	25	2	50	0	0	2	50
	1837			4	100	1	25	1	25	1	25
	1857					3	100		0		
	1866							2	100		0
	1869										
G	1821	4	100	3	75	2	50	1	25	1	25
	1837										
	1857					2	100	1	50	1	50
	1866							2	100		
	1869										
H	1821	1	100								
	1837										
	1857										
	1866										
	1869										

A: Cooked foods; B: Luxuries; C: Dried noodles and foods; D: Rice; E: Perishable foods; F: Funeral goods; G: Money; H: Other.

Table 4.3.B: Single/multiple gift categories and changes in subsequent occasions – ③ Other villages in Murayama

	A	B	C	D	E	F	G	H	Total
1821 (Bunsei 4)									
1. Number of categories									
One category		11	10				7		
Two categories		5	3						
≥ Three categories									
Total		16	13				7		36
%		44.4	36.1				19.4		
Actual figure		16	13				11	3	
1837 (Tenpō 8)									
1. Number of categories									
One category		6	4		1	13	2		
Two categories		1			1				
≥ Three categories									
Total		7	4		2	13	2		28
%		25	14.3		7.1	46.4	7.1		
2. Previous categories									
A									
B		2	2			2			
C						2			
D									
E									
F									
G									
H							1		
New		5	2		2	8			
Total		7	4		2	13	2		28
Actual figure		7	4		3	14	3		
1857 (Ansei 4)									
1. Number of categories									
One category		2	7			5	8		
Two categories	1		1			2			
≥ Three categories									
Total	1	2	8			7	8		26
%	3.8	7.7	30.8			26.9	42.3		
2. Previous categories									
A									
B							1		
C			1						
D									
E							1		
F			3			3	1		
G									
H									
New	1		4			4	5		
Total	1	2	8			7	8		26
Actual figure	1	2	8			7	11		

Table 4.3.B: Continued...

	A	B	C	D	E	F	G	H	Total
1866 (Keiō 2)									
1. Number of categories									
One category		2				5	22	3	
Two categories		1			1	1			
≥ Three categories						1			
Total		3			1	7	22	3	36
%		8.3			2.8	19.4	61.1	8.3	
2. Previous categories									
A									
B							1		
C						1			
D									
E							1		
F						1	3	1	
G							4		
H									
New		3			1	5	13	2	
Total		3			1	7	22	3	36
Actual figure		3			2	8	26	3	
1869 (Meiji 2)									
1. Number of categories									
One category			2			2	12		
Two categories		1				3	2		
≥ Three categories									
Total		1	2			5	14		22
%		4.5	9.1			22.7	63.6		
2. Previous categories									
A									
B							1		
C			1^b					1^a	
D									
E						1			
F		1	1^a			2	2		
G						1		1	
H						1			
New							9		
Total		1	2			5	12	2	22
Actual figure		1	2			6	17	2	

A: Cooked foods; B: Luxuries; C: Dried noodles and foods; D: Rice; E: Perishable foods; F: Funeral goods; G: Money; H: Other.

Notes. Figures marked 'a' denote gift bearers to the funeral before last. Figures marked 'b' denote those who offered gifts three funerals ago.

Suzuki family seem to have used the general contacts for occasionally developing closer ties with some of them as their business required.

④ **Shinjō, Sakata and Yuri-gun**
See Tables 4.4.A; 4.4.B.

The number of funeral gift bearers from this area in 1821 was fifty-two; outnumbering thirty-six from the other Murayama villages (see Table 4.0). The breakdown is: fifteen from Shinjō, ten from Shimizu and ten from Sakata. The Suzuki family's network in this area was stronger than that of villages in its home region of Murayama. The Fourth Suzuki Gorobee was adopted from the family of Saitō Ichirōbee of Mitsumori, Yuri-gun, which explains that five Saitōs including Ichirōbee are listed in the 1821 funeral. Also, most of the new names in the lists from 1857 onwards were retainers of the Ikoma clan, a direct vassal of the Shogun from the Shogunate land of Yashima in Yuri-gun. The relationship between the two families seemed to have been established during the early nineteenth century when the Suzuki family's business activities were at its peak and were deeply involved in people in those trading bases.

However, the number declines to thirty-eight in 1837, then to twenty-five in 1857. Table 4.0 and Table 4.4.A show that guests from Sakata shrank from ten in 1821 to two in 1837, then zero in 1857; those from Shinjō from ten in 1837 to three after 1857; those from Shimizu were reduced to seven in 1837, to two in 1857, three in 1866 and four in 1869. Table 4.4.A indicates another characteristic of the area: about a half of the gift bearers kept returning, and the new names that appeared in 1866 and 1869 were definitely changeover retainers of the Ikoma clan. What is observed here is consolidation of networks centred on the above-mentioned relationship.

As for the gift categories, E, perishable foods, and F, funeral goods, were largely replaced by G, money, after 1866. In the days of severe price hikes, the people in this area shifted their funeral gifts to the Suzuki Gorobee family from goods to money. On the other hand, the family reduced its ties with Sakata, which is directly connected to the nationwide market, while retaining a small network in the neighboring Shinjō and Shimizu.

⑤ **Obanazawa Kamigō**
See Tables 4.5.A; 4.5.B.

Table 4.5.A shows that thirty gift bearers visited the Suzuki family in 1821 but the number decreased to nine in 1837. No new names were

Table 4.4.A: Number of gift bearers and return rates/Continuity of gifts by category – ④ Shinjō, Sakata and Yuri-gun

	1821	(%)	1837	(%)	1857	(%)	1866	(%)	1869	(%)
1. New and returning gift bearers after 1821										
1821 (Bunsei 4)	52	100	23	60.5	10	41.7	11	44	11	44
1837 (Tenpō 8)			15	39.5	2	8.3	1	4	2	8
1857 (Ansei 4)					12	50	5	20	1	4
1866 (Keiō 2)							8	32	6	24
1869 (Meiji 2)									5	20
Total	52	100	38	100	24	100	25	100	25	100

2. Gift categories and return rates

		1821	(%)	1837	(%)	1857	(%)	1866	(%)	1869	(%)
A	1821			1	100		0				
	1837										
	1857										
	1866										
	1869										
B	1821	12	100	4	33.3	2	16.7	2	16.7	2	16.7
	1837			1							
	1857										
	1866							1	100	1	100
	1869										
C	1821										
	1837			1	100						
	1857					4	100	1	25		
	1866							1	100	1	100
	1869										
D	1821	1									
	1837										
	1857										
	1866										
	1869										
E	1821	7	100	3	42.9	1	14.3	1	14.3	1	14.3
	1837			4	100	2	50	1	25	2	50
	1857					1	100		0		
	1866							1	100	1	100
	1869										
F	1821	10	100	3	30	1	10	1	10	1	10
	1837			4	100		0				
	1857					4	100	2	50		0
	1866							1	100	1	50
	1869										
G	1821	5	100	4	80	3	60	3	60	2	40
	1837			2	100		0				
	1857					3	100	2	66.7	1	33.3
	1866							4	100	2	50
	1869									4	100
H	1821	17	100	9	52.9	3	17.6	3	17.6	3	17.6
	1837										
	1857										
	1866										
	1869										

A: Cooked foods; B: Luxuries; C: Dried noodles and foods; D: Rice; E: Perishable foods; F: Funeral goods; G: Money; H: Other.

Table 4.4.B: Single/multiple gift categories and changes in subsequent occasions – ④ Shinjō, Sakata and Yuri-gun

	A	B	C	D	E	F	G	H	Total
1821 (Bunsei 4)									
1. Number of categories									
One category		6			4	10		16	
Two categories		5		1	3		5	1	
≥ Three categories		1							
Total		12		1	7	10	5	17	52
%		23.1		1.9	13.5	19.2	13.5	32.7	
Actual figure		12		1	7	13	7	25	
1837 (Tenpō 8)									
1. Number of categories									
One category	1	4	1		6	11	5		
Two categories			1		6	1			
≥ Three categories		1			1				
Total	1	5	2		13	12	5		38
%	2.6	13.2	5.3		34.2	31.6	13.2		
2. Previous categories									
A									
B					2		1		
C			1						
D									
E		2			1	1			
F					1	2			
G					1	1			
H		1			3	4	2		
New	1	2	1		5	4	2		
Total	1	5	2		13	12	5		38
Actual figure	1	5	2		13	20	9		
1857 (Ansei 4)									
1. Number of categories									
One category		2	3		2	5	5		
Two categories			2			4			
≥ Three categories			1						
Total		2	6		2	9	5		24
%		8.3	25		8.3	37.5	20.8		
2. Previous categories									
A									
B		1	1ª						
C			1						
D									
E		1			1	3	1		
F						2			
G									
H							1		
New			4		1	4	3		
Total		2	6		2	9	5		24
Actual figure		2	6		2	12	10		

Table 4.4.B: Continued...

	A	B	C	D	E	F	G	H	Total
1866 (Keiō 2)									
1. Number of categories									
One category		2	1		2	1	11		
Two categories		1	1			4			
≥ Three categories		1	1						
Total		4	3		2	5	11		25
%		16	12		8	20	44		
2. Previous categories									
A									
B							1		
C		1				1			
D									
E					1				
F		1	2			1	3		
G		1				1	2		
H									
New			1		1	2	5		
Total		4	3		2	5	11		25
Actual figure		4	3		2	7	14		
1869 (Meiji 2)									
1. Number of categories									
One category			1			1	19	2	
Two categories						1			
≥ Three categories		1							
Total		1	1			2	19	2	25
%		4	4			8	76	8	
2. Previous categories									
A									
B			1				1		
C						1	1		
D									
E							2		
F		1				1	2		
G							7		
H									
New							6	2	
Total		1	1			2	19	2	25
Actual figure		1	1			3	21	2	

A: Cooked foods; B: Luxuries; C: Dried noodles and foods; D: Rice; E: Perishable foods; F: Funeral goods; G: Money; H: Other.

Note. Figures marked 'a' denote gift bearers to the funeral before last.

added after 1866. From 1857, 50–60% of the names were returnees since 1821, indicating that the family's relationship with people in this area was static.

In terms of gift contents, in 1821 one visitor brought A, cooked foods, and eleven brought B, luxuries, indicating closeness of their relationship. However, while the 'A' gift bearer returned at all the later funerals, only one of the eleven 'B' gift bearers returned in 1837, while the proportion of C, dried noodles and foods, increased.

The reason for the large drop in the number of gift bearers between 1821 and 1837 was possibly the famine, which must have hit the area badly. The lack of movement in names suggests that the Suzuki family's network in this area was limited to people with steady economic means, who could ride out bad times. Similar patterns can be found in the next geographical group.

⑥ **Shōgon, Niu and Akudo villages**
See Tables 4.6.A; 4.6.B.

As with the previous group, the number of the names from this area declined over the years. However, the decrease was greater in later years with twelve between 1837 and 1857 compared to seven between 1821 and 1837. Also noticeable is that after 1837 the rate of returning gift bearers in this group is higher than any other group.

Tables 4.6.B (1) and (2) indicate that the dominant gifts shifted from F, funeral goods, to C, dried noodles and foods. In other words, while the range of association shrank and became fixed, the gift values increased. This implies that the Suzuki family's networks in this area changed so that they consisted mainly of families with stable economic conditions.

In his diary, the Fifth Suzuki Gorobee notes that this area was central to the family's land management.[6] As mentioned above, towards the mid nineteenth century the family reduced the scale of land management, and the decline in gift bearers can be seen as a result of the family's land sell-off. It is possible to think that the family decided to concentrate on a core of steady tenant farmers and thus rationalized its land operation.

⑦ **Tōgō, Yokosawa and Nobesawa areas**
See Tables 4.7.A; 4.7.B.

Gift bearers from this area gradually declined from the maximum of fifty-nine in 1821, but turned around to increase slightly after 1857.

Table 4.5.A: Number of gift bearers and return rates/Continuity of gifts by category – ⑤ Obanazawa Kamigō

		1821	(%)	1837	(%)	1857	(%)	1866	(%)	1869	(%)
1. New and returning gift bearers after 1821
1821 (Bunsei 4)		30	100	9	52.9	9	52.9	3	50	5	62.5
1837 (Tenpō 8)				8	47.1	2	11.8	2	33.3	2	25
1857 (Ansei 4)						6	35.3	1	16.7	1	12.5
1866 (Keiō 2)								0		0	
1869 (Meiji 2)										0	
Total		30	100	17	100	17	100	6	100	8	100
2. Gift categories and return rates
A	1821					1	100		0		
	1837										
	1857										
	1866										
B	1821	16	100	6	37.5	4	25	2	12.5	1	6.2
	1837			5		1		1			
	1857					2		1			
	1866							3		1	
C	1821	13	100	2	15.4	2	15.4	1	7.7	2	15.4
	1837			2	100					1	50
	1857					8	100	2	25	3	37.5
	1866										
D	1821										
	1837										
	1857										
	1866										
E	1821	1	100		0						
	1837			3	100	1	33.3		0		
	1857										
	1866							4	100		
	1869										
F	1821	4	100	1	25	2	50	0	0	2	50
	1837			4	100	1	25	1	25	1	25
	1857					3	100		0		
	1866							2	100		
	1869										
G	1821	4	100	3	75	2	50	1	25	1	25
	1837										
	1857					2	100	1	50	1	50
	1866							2	100		0
	1869										
H	1821	1	100		0						
	1837										
	1857										
	1866										
	1869										

A: Cooked foods; B: Luxuries; C: Dried noodles and foods; D: Rice; E: Perishable foods; F: Funeral goods; G: Money; H: Other.

Table 4.5.B: Single/multiple gift categories and changes in subsequent occasions – ⑤ *Obanazawa Kamigō*

	A	B	C	D	E	F	G	H	Total
1821 (Bunsei 4)									
1. Number of categories									
One category		11	5		1	3	3	1	
Two categories	1		3	1		1			
≥ Three categories									
Total	1	11	8	1	1	4	3	1	30
%	3.3	36.7	26.7	3.3	3.3	13.3	10	3.3	
Actual figure	1	11	9	1	1	5	3	1	
1837 (Tenpō 8)									
1. Number of categories									
One category					5	8			
Two categories	1	1	1		1				
≥ Three categories									
Total	1	1	1		6	8			17
%	7.7	7.7	7.7		46.2	61.5			
2. Previous categories									
A	1		1			1			
B					1	1			
C		1							
D									
E									
F					1	2			
G									
H						4			
New					4				
Total	1	1	1		6	8			17
Actual figure	1	1	1		6	9			
1857 (Ansei 4)									
1. Number of categories									
One category			1		2	9	3		
Two categories			1						
≥ Three categories				1					
Total		2	1	2	9	3			17
%		11.8	5.9	11.8	52.9	17.6			
2. Previous categories									
A				1					
B					2[a]	1			
C			1						
D									
E						2			
F						2	1		
G									
H									
New			1			4	2		
Total		2	1	2	9	3			17
Actual figure		2	1	3	10	4			

Table 4.5.B: Continued...

	A	B	C	D	E	F	G	H	Total
1866 (Keiō 2)									
1. Number of categories									
One category	2					1	1	1	
Two categories				1					
≥ Three categories									
Total	2		1	1		1	1	1	6
%	33.3		16.7	16.7		16.7	16.7	16.7	
2. Previous categories									
A									
B									
C			1						
D				1					
E								1[a]	
F			1			1			
G							1		
H									
New						1			
Total			2	1		2	1		6
Actual figure			2	1		2	1	1	
1869 (Meiji 2)									
1. Number of categories									
One category	2					2	3		
Two categories									
≥ Three categories				1					
Total	2			1		2	3		8
%	25			12.5		25	37.5		
2. Previous categories									
A									
B									
C			1				1		
D				1					
E							1[a]		
F						1 (1[a])			
G							1		
H				1					
New									
Total			2	1		2	3		8
Actual figure			2	1		1	2		

A: Cooked foods; B: Luxuries; C: Dried noodles and foods; D: Rice; E: Perishable foods; F: Funeral goods; G: Money; H: Other.

Note. Figures marked 'a' denote gift bearers to the funeral before last.

A (cooked foods) was presented at all five funerals from this area. According to the loan certificates in the Suzuki family documents, Ōyama Shirōbee and Ōyama Kyūhachi, both of whom brought cooked foods to the family in 1821 and 1857 were related to each other and worked as a kind of intermediary for the Suzuki family in dealing in land and financial matters with villages away from them.[7] Other bearers of A, cooked foods, include Ōnuki Kan'emon of Nakazawa, Takahashi village and Ishiyama Matsunosuke of Namesawa village, both of whom were prominent landowners in their respective villages. Ōnuki, who had continued to send A, cooked foods, since 1837, became a close financial partner with the Suzuki family from the mid nineteenth century. Yagihashi Kanbee of Hosono village, who sent cooked foods in 1869, also had a large loan from Suzuki Gorobee in relation to lacquer trading (Sato 2003). The above three men were closely associated in business with the Suzuki family, and the relationship was reflected in their funeral gifts.

Gift contents from this area, as seen in Table 4.7.B, reveal that in 1821 and 1837, F, funeral goods, formed the largest portion of 39% and 40.4% respectively. In 1857 A, cooked foods, and E, perishable foods, increased to 24.1% and 37.9% respectively. In 1869, the largest component was C, dried noodles and foods, with 50%. There was no noticeable shift to F, money, from this area, which suggests that the Suzuki family's associates from this area were financially stable.

The background to this trend is the fact that trading between both sides of Ōu ranges became very active from the beginning of the nineteenth century: Safflower and horses were traded in from Sendai and Nanbu domains; new and old clothing from Kyoto/Osaka area were sent to those domains through this region. Although the gift bearers between 1837 and 1857 wildly fluctuated, some associates in this region rode out the waves with steady economic management. The number of gift bearers and the quality of the gifts seem to reflect that the Suzuki family, while reducing their land in Shōgon and Niu villages, actively strengthened its relationship with this border area.

⑧ Obanazawa Shimogō
See Tables 4.8.A; 4.8.B.

No noticeable changes are observed in the gift bearers from this area throughout the five funerals. Table 4.8.A (1) shows that ten new people were added in 1857, but by and large about 40–50% of the names remain since 1821.

Table 4.6.A: Number of gift bearers and return rates/Continuity of gifts by category – ⑥ Shōgon, Niu and Akudo villages

		1821	(%)	1837	(%)	1857	(%)	1866	(%)	1869	(%)
1. New and returning gift bearers after 1821											
1821 (Bunsei 4)		40	100	26	78.8	15	71.4	13	72.2	10	52.6
1837 (Tenpō 8)				7	21.2	3	14.3	3	16.7	3	15.8
1857 (Ansei 4)						3	14.3				
1866 (Keiō 2)								2	11.1	2	10.5
1869 (Meiji 2)										4	21.1
Total		40	100	33	100	21	100	18	100	19	100
2. Gift categories and return rates											
A	1821					1	100		0		
	1837										
	1857										
	1866										
B	1821	16	100	6	37.5	4	25	2	12.5	1	6.3
	1837			5		1		1			
	1857					2		1			
	1866							3		1	
C	1821	13	100	2	15.4	2	15.4	1	7.7	2	15.4
	1837			2	100		0		0	1	50
	1857					8	100	2	25	3	37.5
	1866										
D	1821										
	1837										
	1857										
	1866										
E	1821										
	1837			2	100	1	50	1	50	1	50
	1857										
	1866							1	100	1	100
F	1821										
	1837			13	100	7	53.8	3	23.1	2	15.4
	1857					7	100	5	71.4	4	57.1
	1866							7	100	7	100
G	1821	7	100	1	14.3	1	14.3	1	14.3	1	14.3
	1837										
	1857					8	100	4	50	2	25
	1866							12	100	7	58.3
H	1821										
	1837										
	1857										
	1866							2	100		0

A: Cooked foods; B: Luxuries; C: Dried noodles and foods; D: Rice; E: Perishable foods; F: Funeral goods; G: Money; H: Other.

Table 4.6.B: Single/multiple gift categories and changes in subsequent occasions – ⑥ Shōgon, Niu and Akudo villages

	A	B	C	D	E	F	G	H	Total
1821 (Bunsei 4)									
1. Number of categories									
One category		8	7	4		11			
Two categories		3	2	4		1			
≥ Three categories									
Total		11	9	8		12			40
%		27.5	22.5	20		30			
Actual figure				10	9		16	4	
1837 (Tenpō 8)									
1. Number of categories									
One category		2	5	3	1	9	3		
Two categories		3	1	3		3			
≥ Three categories									
Total		5	6	6	1	12	3		33
%		15.2	18.2	18.2	3	36.4	9.1		
2. Previous categories									
A									
B		2	2	1		2			
C		2	1			3	1		
D			2	4			1		
E									
F			1	1		2	1		
G									
H									
New		1				5			
Total		5	6	6	1	12	3		33
Actual figure		5	7	6	1	14	5		
1857 (Ansei 4)									
1. Number of categories									
One category			3	1		9	1		
Two categories			1	6					
≥ Three categories									
Total			4	7		9	1		21
%			19	33.3		42.9	4.8		
2. Previous categories									
A									
B			1			2[a]			
C			1	1		1			
D				1			1		
E									
F			1	1		5			
G			1	1		1			
H									
New				3					
Total			4	7		9	1		21
Actual figure			4	7		14	1		

Table 4.6.B: Continued...

	A	B	C	D	E	F	G	H	Total
1866 (Keiō 2)									
1. Number of categories									
One category			5			3	7		
Two categories			1		2				
≥ Three categories									
Total			6		2	3	7		18
%			33.3		11.1	16.7	38.9		
2. Previous categories									
A									
B									
C			1 (1ª)			1			
D			2				3		
E									
F			1		2	2	1 (1ª)		
G									
H									
New			2				2		
Total			6		2	3	7		18
Actual figure			6		2	6	7		
1869 (Meiji 2)									
1. Number of categories									
One category			6	5		4		2	
Two categories			2						
≥ Three categories									
Total			8	5		4		2	19
%			42.1	26.3		21.1		10.5	
2. Previous categories									
A									
B									
C			3	1					
D									
E			1						
F			1				2 (2ª)		
G				4				2	
H									
New			3						
Total			8	5		4		2	19
Actual figure			8	5		6		2	

A: Cooked foods; B: Luxuries; C: Dried noodles and foods; D: Rice; E: Perishable foods; F: Funeral goods; G: Money; H: Other.

Note. Figures marked 'a' denote gift bearers to the funeral before last.

Table 4.8.B shows that C, dried noodles and foods, E, perishable foods, and F, funeral goods, take up high proportions of the gifts from this area. Also, like the above-mentioned Tōgō, Yokosawa and Nobesawa area, few swapped to G, money. The family's network in this area was also steady with financially solid people.

Like Obanazawa Kamigō area, the family's ties with this area are unclear. A noticeable feature is that Ōrui Kyūbee of Ashizawa village, who brought F, funeral goods, in 1821, has upgraded his gift to B, luxuries, in 1866. He became a close financial and business associate of the Suzukis from around this time, which was clearly reflected in the change in funeral gifts.

Conclusions

This study has examined funeral documents of the Suzuki Gorobee family of Murayama gun, Dewa domain, and used the family as an example of prominent local figure in the late Edo period to see how its network was structured and how it changed over the years. From the examination of the family's record of funeral gift bearers, the following conclusions can be drawn:

1. The total number of the people associated with the family declined over the years. This was particularly true in distant areas and Ōishida region, which was a main trade post. This change is in line with the contraction of family business after its peak in the early nineteenth century.
2. The family maintained a strong network of relatives and prominent families in its home village Obanazawa. On the other hand, there was also a section of fluid and short-term associates who would bring single gifts, mainly funeral goods.
3. As for the surrounding areas, while the scope of network in the areas related to the family's land management contracted, relationship with villages and towns along the border with other regions became stronger. One of the reasons for this change is probably that the family shifted its main economic activity from land management to businesses closely tied to the regional economy.
4. Judging from the changes and continuity of gift contents, it seems to have been difficult for the temporary associates to become part of the family's network. The distinction between the families with strong and lasting association with the Suzuki family and those with general association was very clear-cut.

Table 4.7.A: Number of gift bearers and return rates/Continuity of gifts by category – ⑦ Tōgō, Yokosawa and Nobesawa areas

	1821	(%)	1837	(%)	1857	(%)	1866	(%)	1869	(%)
1. New and returning gift bearers after 1821										
1821 (Bunsei 4)	59	100	30	0.64	19	0.66	14	0.52	13	0.43
1837 (Tenpō 8)			17	0.36	0		0		0	
1857 (Ansei 4)					10	0.34	7	0.26	4	0.13
1866 (Keiō 2)							11	0.22	6	0.2
1869 (Meiji 2)									7	0.23
Total	59	100	47	100	29	100	32	100	30	100
2. Gift categories and return rates										
A 1821	6	100	6	100	5	83.3	5	83.3	4	66.7
1837										
1857										
1866										
1869										
B 1821	14	100	8	57.1	3	21.4	2	14.3	2	14.3
1837			3	100		0				
1857					1	0				
1866										
1869										
C 1821	7	100	5	71.4	4	57.1	3	42.9	3	42.9
1837			1							
1857										
1866							4	100	2	50
1869									3	100
D 1821	7	100	6	85.7	4	57.1	2	28.6	2	28.6
1837					2	100	1	50	1	50
1857										
1866							1	100	1	100
1869										
E 1821	1	100		0						
1837			1	100		0				
1857					6	100	5	83.3	3	50
1866							3	100	2	66.7
1869									1	100
F 1821	23	100	5	21.7	3	13	2	8.7	2	8.7
1837			12	100		0				
1857					1	100	1	100		0
1866							3	100	1	33.3
1869									1	100
G 1821	1	100		0					1	
1837										
1857										
1866										
1869										
H 1821										
1837										
1857										
1866										
1869										

A: Cooked foods; B: Luxuries; C: Dried noodles and foods; D: Rice; E: Perishable foods; F: Funeral goods; G: Money; H: Other.

Table 4.7.B: Single/multiple gift categories and changes in subsequent occasions – ⑦ Tōgō, Yokosawa and Nobesawa areas

	A	B	C	D	E	F	G	H	Total
1821 (Bunsei 4)									
1. Number of categories									
One category	5	9	5	6	1	22	1		
Two categories	1	5	1	1		1			
≥ Three categories			1						
Total	6	14	7	7	1	23	1		59
%	10.1	23.7	11.9	11.9	1.7	39	1.7		
Actual figure	6	14	8	8	1	31	1		
1837 (Tenpō 8)									
1. Number of categories									
One category	1	7	3		1	18	4		
Two categories	1	3	4		3	1			
≥ Three categories		1							
Total	2	11	7		4	19	4		47
%	4.3	23.4	14.9		8.5	40.4	8.5		
2. Previous categories									
A		1	4		1				
B		3			1	4			
C	2	1	2						
D					1	1	4		
E									
F		3				2			
G									
H									
New		3	1		1	12			
Total	2	11	7		4	19	4		47
Actual figure			9	1	5	28	7		
1857 (Ansei 4)									
1. Number of categories									
One category	7		2	2	6	1			
Two categories	4	1	2	2	5	1			
≥ Three categories	3								
Total	7	1	4	4	11	2			29
%	24.1	3.4	13.8	13.8	37.9	6.9			
2. Previous categories									
A	2								
B			2		2				
C	4		1						
D									
E	1								
F					2	1			
G			1	2	1				
H									
New		1		2	6	1			
Total	7	1	4	4	11	2			29
Actual figure	7	1	4	4	18	6			

Table 4.7.B: Continued...

	A	B	C	D	E	F	G	H	Total
1866 (Keiō 2)									
1. Number of categories									
One category			4	1		6	5		
Two categories	1	1	6	1	3	2			
≥ Three categories						2			
Total	1	1	10	2	3	10	5		32
%	3.1	3.1	31.3	6.3	9.4	31.3	15.6		
2. Previous categories									
A	1	1	4			1			
B									
C			1			1	1		
D							1		
E			1			5	3		
F				1	1				
G					1				
H									
New			4	1	1	3			
Total	1	1	10	2	3	10	5		32
Actual figure	1	1	10	2	4	18	7		
1869 (Meiji 2)									
1. Number of categories									
One category			13	1		2	3	1	
Two categories	2		2	1	1	4			
≥ Three categories									
Total	2		15	2	1	6	3	1	30
%	6.7		50	6.7	3.3	20	10	3.3	
2. Previous categories									
A	1								
B									
C			8						
D				1					
E			1			1	1		
F	1		1	1		3			
G			2			1	1		
H									
New			3		1	1	1	1	
Total	2		15	2	1	6	3	1	30
Actual figure	2		15	2	1	9	8	1	

A: Cooked foods; B: Luxuries; C: Dried noodles and foods; D: Rice; E: Perishable foods; F: Funeral goods; G: Money; H: Other.

Note. Figures marked 'a' denote gift bearers to the funeral before last.

Due to the limits inherent in the material itself such as the identification of the names as well as problems in ranking of gifts, the findings of this study are not conclusive. Also, the network as shown in the form of gift bearers is the result, rather than the process, of the family's economic and political activities.[8] The restructuring of family network through the shift from distant lands to home village and its surroundings, and the interchange between the above network and the general public through the Suzuki family are areas that need future research.

Table 4.8.A: Number of gift bearers and return rates/Continuity of gifts by category – ⑧ Obanazawa Shimogō

		1821	(%)	1837	(%)	1857	(%)	1866	(%)	1869	(%)
1. New and returning gift bearers after 1821											
1821 (Bunsei 4)		21	100	10	52.6	6	31.6	7	35	8	40
1837 (Tenpō 8)				9	47.4	3	15.8	2	10	1	5
1857 (Ansei 4)						10	52.6	3	15	3	15
1866 (Keiō 2)								8	40	4	20
1869 (Meiji 2)										4	20
Total		21	100	19	100	19	100	20	100	20	100
2. Gift categories and return rates											
A	1821										
	1837										
	1857										
	1866										
	1869										
B	1821	7	100	3	42.9			1	14.3	1	14.3
	1837			3	100	1	33.3				
	1857										
	1866										
	1869									1	
C	1821	6	100	3	50	2	33.3	3	50	3	50
	1837			3		1	33.3	1	33.3	1	33.3
	1857					1					
	1866							1		1	100
	1869										
D	1821	3	100	1	33.3	1	33.3		0	1	33.3
	1837			1	100	1	100	1	100		0
	1857					1	100	1	100		0
	1866										
	1869										
E	1821	2	100	1	50	1	50	1	50	1	50
	1837			1							
	1857					1		1	100	1	100
	1866							4		2	50
	1869									1	
F	1821	2	100	1	50	1	50	1	50	1	50
	1837			1		0	0				
	1857					6	100	1	16.7	2	33.3
	1866							2	100		0
	1869									1	100
G	1821	1	100	0	0						
	1837										
	1857							1	100		
	1866							1	100	1	100
	1869										
H	1821										
	1837										
	1857										
	1866										
	1869									1	100

A: Cooked foods; B: Luxuries; C: Dried noodles and foods; D: Rice; E: Perishable foods; F: Funeral goods; G: Money; H: Other.

Table 4.8.B: Single/multiple gift categories and changes in subsequent occasions – ⑧ Obanazawa Shimogō

	A	B	C	D	E	F	G	H	Total
1821 (Bunsei 4)									
1. Number of categories									
One category		5	5	3	2	2	1		
Two categories		2	1						
≥ Three categories									
Total		7	6	3	2	2	1		21
%		33.3	28.6	14.3	9.5	9.5	4.8		
Actual figure		7	7	3	3	2	1		
1837 (Tenpō 8)									
1. Number of categories									
One category		5	4		2	4			
Two categories		1	1	1	1				
≥ Three categories									
Total		6	5	1	3	4			19
%		31.6	26.3	5.3	15.8	21.1			
2. Previous categories									
A									
B		5				1			
C		1			1	1			
D					1				
E			1						
F						1			
G			1						
H			3						
New				1	1	1			
Total		6	5	1	3	4			19
Actual figure		6	5	1	4	7			
1857 (Ansei 4)									
1. Number of categories									
One category		4		1	6	3			
Two categories			3	2					
≥ Three categories									
Total		4	3	3	6	3			19
%		21.1	15.8	15.8	31.6	15.8			
2. Previous categories									
A									
B		1							
C		1		1		1			
D				1					
E				1	1				
F		1				1			
G									
H		1							
New			1	1	6	1			
Total		4	3	3	6	3			19
Actual figure		4	3	4	9	4			

Table 4.8.B: Continued...

	A	B	C	D	E	F	G	H	Total
1866 (Keiō 2)									
1. Number of categories									
One category			3		1	4	3		
Two categories			2		5	2			
≥ Three categories									
Total			5		6	6	3		20
%			25		30	30	15		
2. Previous categories									
A									
B			1a						
C			2						
D			1				1		
E					1	1	1		
F					1				
G							2		
H									
New			1		4	3	1		
Total			5		6	6	3		20
Actual figure			5		6	10	7		
1869 (Meiji 2)									
1. Number of categories									
One category	1	7			3	2	2	2	
Two categories	1			1	1				
≥ Three categories									
Total	2	7		1	4	2	2	2	20
%	10	35		5	20	10	10	10	
2. Previous categories									
A									
B				4					
C									
D				1			1a		
E				2		3			
F							1 (1a)		
G		1						1	
H									
New		1			1	1		1	
Total		7			4	2	2	2	20
Actual figure	2	7		1	5	3	3	2	

A: Cooked foods; B: Luxuries; C: Dried noodles and foods; D: Rice; E: Perishable foods; F: Funeral goods; G: Money; H: Other.

Note. Figures marked 'a' denote gift bearers to the funeral before last.

5 Migration and Status Attainment during the High Growth Period

Yutaka Ginya

Introduction

In contemporary society moving from one's original place of residence has become a feature of many people's lives. For example, some people move away from their hometowns to large cities in order to pursue studies at university, while others do so to seek employment. Many life events, such as advancing to higher education or gaining employment, trigger migration. Such events can also lead to the achievement of, or change in, social status. In other words, migration is closely linked to social mobility.

The disparity in available opportunities between regions is an important factor that needs to be considered when examining the relationship between migration and social mobility. This is because a lack of opportunities frequently promotes migration. Demographers point out that regional disparity in wages, as well as in opportunity for employment, triggers migration and migration from non-metropolises to metropolises in particular (Ishikawa 1994). Lipset and Bendix (1959) also point out that, in comparison with other areas, large cities provide greater opportunities for changing jobs, offer greater numbers of high-status jobs and necessitate population inflow from other areas due to their comparatively low birth rates. When we locate this in the context of social mobility study, we can say that the search for employment drives people in areas lacking in opportunities to migrate to urban areas where they are plentiful. Naturally, some people do not migrate to urban areas but instead remain in their hometowns. However their employment prospects will be limited to opportunities available locally. In other words, regional disparity in opportunity caused by macro factors, such as differences in industrial structure, affects social mobility, and the effect of regional disparity varies with one's place of origin and his/her migration that follows. Therefore, these two factors play an important role in status attainment.

With the above argument as the motif, this chapter will study the relationship between migration and status attainment during Japan's high growth period (from the mid 1950s to the oil crisis in 1973). An examination of inter-regional migration after the war reveals that in 1955, when the high growth period took off, more than 2 million people changed their residences, crossing borders of prefectures. This number continued to rise throughout the high growth period, peaking at 4 million a year in 1973. Inter-regional migration then settled and, despite subsequent minor changes, has been maintained at around 3 million. The major part of this massive migration involved moves to metropolises from other areas (Yukiko Araragi 1994). The well-known and representative phenomenon of 'mass employment'[1] describes the vigorous migration that occurred at that time. Consequently, the phrase 'landslide-like migration' was coined to exemplify the massive migratory changes that took place during the high growth period.

The major upheaval in industrial structure due to rapid economic growth forms the background of migration. This upheaval did not spread uniformly throughout Japan but advanced while creating regional gaps in labor supply and demand. Social mobility studies, however, have not paid proper attention to this social change. They divide occupational mobility into 'forced mobility,' generated by changes in job structure, and 'pure mobility,' generated by other factors. The latter is interpreted as an indicator of social openness (Yasuda 1964). However, we argue that the change in industrial structure also prescribes opportunities for individuals and has differing effects on the status attainment process, depending on the place of origin and the migration history of individuals.[2]

Based on these empirical findings, this chapter focuses on new graduates, junior high and senior high school graduates in particular, during the high growth period. We analyze the relationship between their status attainment, place of origin and migration history. Furthermore, through this analysis, we examine how the place of origin and migration affected the status attainment process and what consequences these factors produced under macro-structural constraints, such as social change and regional disparities in opportunities, during the high growth period.

Japan's high growth period and migration

'Japan is no longer in the Postwar Period' – this phrase was used in the Economic White Paper of 1956 and became a popular catchphrase.

The phrase clearly proclaims the recovery of the Japanese economy based on the fact that major economic indicators surpassed pre-war standards in 1955, following the immediate post-war period, when GDP per capita had fallen to 55% of pre-war levels. This occurred alongside the period of the buoyant economy, or the 'special procurement boom,' generated by the Korean War (1950 to 1953) as well as the 'Jinmu boom' (1954 to 1957).

In the same Economic White Paper, the statement 'Japan is no longer in the Postwar Period' was followed by these words: 'We are now about to confront a different situation. Growth through recovery has now ended. From now, growth will be supported by modernization. Progress in modernization will only be possible with rapid and at the same time stable economic growth.' As predicted by this statement, Japan went on to propel a period of rapid modernization that ushered in the high growth period. This was followed by a capital investment boom in heavy industries such as the steel, petrochemical and shipbuilding industries, when state-of-the-art factories and plants incorporating American and European technology were constructed. On the consumer side, huge demand for durable goods emerged. In particular, this included the 'three sacred treasures' – black-and-white television sets, electric washing machines, and electric refrigerators – in the early 60s, and the '3C's' – *c*olor television sets, *c*ars, and *c*oolers (air conditioners) – in the late 60s. These streams merged into the high economic growth based on massive and heavy industries, mass production and mass consumption. Consequently, Japan experienced a rapid economic growth with an annual growth rate of 10% [3] until the oil crisis signaled the end of the high growth period in 1973.

How did these short-term and rapid changes in economic conditions change Japan's industrial structure? The following is an overview of these changes. Figure 5.1, based on the national census, shows the changes in worker ratios by industry. 1955 marked the beginning of the high growth period. At this point, primary industry, which was largely represented by the agricultural sector, accounted for around 40% of the workforce. Thereafter, this figure continued to fall, so that by 1975, after the end of the high growth period, the share of workers in primary industry had fallen to just over 10%. Secondary industry, representing the industrial sector, accounted for just over 20% of the workforce in 1955. By 1975, however, it had grown to a 30% share. In contrast, tertiary industry, which accounted for 36% of the workforce in 1955, had increased significantly to 52%

Figure 5.1: Changes in worker ratios by industry

Source: The National Census

of the workforce by 1975. In other words, the high growth period was a time in which the agricultural sector which had represented Japan's key industry went into a decline. This was replaced by the prospering secondary and tertiary industries that supported massive and heavy industries, mass production and mass consumption.

In terms of labor supply and demand, this shift from primary industry to secondary and tertiary industries had differing effects in urban and rural areas. That is, because of the obviously large number of farmers in rural areas, a decline in primary industry – with its focus on agriculture –generated a large excess population that could not be absorbed by the local labor market in the areas. Meanwhile, as the agricultural population had always been small in urban areas, the effect of the decline in agriculture was also small. However, the rapid growth of secondary and tertiary industries increased labor demand in urban areas. It was this labor supply and demand – an excess of labor in rural areas and insufficient labor in urban areas – that resulted in the so-called 'landslide-like' migration from rural to urban areas.[4]

I shall now examine migration at the time, with a focus on migration amongst new graduates (junior high and senior high school graduates). The reason for this focus is that new graduates who are about to enter the labor market are most keenly affected by the labor market during the above-mentioned high growth economic period.

The cross-prefecture employment rate of junior and senior high school graduates (the rate of those finding employment in prefectures other than where they were born and raised) shows that 14.3% of new graduates (13.7% of junior high school graduates and 15.9% of senior high school graduates) or around 150,000 graduates found employment outside their own prefectures in 1953, immediately prior to the high growth period.[5] This is probably because post-war reconstruction had not been completed even in urban areas at that time. Thereafter, however, the rate had increased to 29.5% (31.8% of junior high school graduates and 27.8% of senior high school graduates) or around 420,000 graduates to reach a peak by 1966, in the middle of the high growth period. The numbers of graduates then began to taper off due to the popularization of higher education but this rate continued to be high, and in 1973, the end of the high growth period, 32.4% (34.4% of junior high school graduates and 31.9% of senior high school graduates) or more than 260,000 graduates sought employment outside their prefectures. This may have been a result of the relocation of factories and plants to rural areas, once the high growth period had ended, which led to the establishment of employment opportunities in those regions. Consequently, this rate began to fall. By the 1980s, the figures had stabilized to a rate of 20 to 25%, or around 150,000 graduates (23.4% in 1983 – 16.8% junior high school graduates and 24.2% senior high school graduates). This stable pattern continued until the early 1990s when the university entrance rate began to rise again. These trends in the cross-prefecture employment rate clearly show that, in terms of both scale and possibilities, the practice of new graduates finding first jobs through migration was extremely pronounced during the high growth economic period.

Let us now examine the geographical mobility of graduates seeking employment through migration during the high growth period, based on data by prefecture. Table 5.1 represents the number of graduates who found employment in other prefectures, i, the number of graduates who moved from other prefectures and found employment, j, and the difference, $j - i$, and ratio, j/i, of high school graduates in 1966 by prefecture. This difference indicates the number of excess jobs in the local labor market of a prefecture, assuming that all graduates found employment within the prefecture. (A negative number means a shortage of jobs in the local labor market.)

In other words, the difference indicates the extent to which the size of the local labor market of a prefecture determines the inflow rate of new graduates from other prefectures, or the outflow rate to other prefectures. The ratio also indicates how strong the inflow or outflow tendency is: The higher the figure over 1, the higher the inflow tendency; and lower the figure below 1, the higher the outflow tendency. Table 5.1 indicates that Tokyo, Aichi and Osaka – in comparison to other prefectures – represent a strong inflow tendency. The outflow figures from these three areas are extremely low while the inflow numbers are extremely high and therefore these areas are clearly intake centers. Kanagawa has a complicated character. It has a significant outflow, partly because it lies next to Tokyo. However, it also has a high rate of inflow that places it in the fourth place after the above three areas. Looking at the difference between its inflow and outflow figures, we eventually understand that it is clearly more of an intake center. Kyoto and Hyogo display a similar tendency to Kanagawa. However, because the difference between outflow and inflow numbers is much smaller than that in Kanagawa, they are intake as well as outlet centers. Prefectures other than those mentioned above are essentially outlet prefectures[6], although the migration tendencies of Chiba, Shizuoka, Gifu and Hiroshima differ depending on the level of education. Consequently, during the high growth period, it is the metropolitan areas of Tokyo, Osaka and Aichi, cities that house the three major industrial areas, which dominated the rural to urban migration figures of new graduates from other prefectures who were seeking their first jobs.

Determinant factors behind migration

Does anyone born in a rural area then become involved in migration towards urban areas when they enter the labor market, as examined in the preceding section? We argue that the decision of whether or not to migrate is affected by the individual's characteristics and social environments as well as his/her intention. The first factor that either restricts or promotes migration is the costs involved in the actual migration. There are many more costs involved in seeking employment in another region compared to seeking employment in one's own area. These include the cost of gathering information related to a prospective employer, the costs related to the move itself and the cost of living once leaving home. It would have been difficult to make the move unless there was a high possibility of finding

Table 5.1: Outflow and inflow numbers of new graduates by prefecture

	Junior High School Graduates			Senior High School Graduates			Total		
	(i)	(j)	(j)-(i)	(j)/(i)	(i)	(j)	(j)-(i)	(j)/(i)	(i)	(j)	(j)-(i)	(j)/(i)
Hokkaido	5157	848	(4309)	0.16	5027	269	(4758)	0.05	10184	1117	(9067)	0.11
Aomori	5865	226	(5639)	0.04	4322	136	(4186)	0.03	10187	362	(9825)	0.04
Iwate	6136	68	(6068)	0.01	4993	277	(4716)	0.06	11129	345	(10784)	0.03
Miyagi	4950	414	(4536)	0.08	5033	1380	(3653)	0.27	9983	1794	(8189)	0.18
Akita	5294	53	(5241)	0.01	5522	97	(5425)	0.02	10816	150	(10666)	0.01
Yamagata	4007	44	(3963)	0.01	5875	67	(5808)	0.01	9882	111	(9771)	0.01
Fukushima	8206	210	(7996)	0.03	10279	411	(9868)	0.04	18485	621	(17864)	0.03
Ibaraki	7188	392	(6796)	0.05	7812	646	(7166)	0.08	15000	1038	(13962)	0.07
Tochigi	4574	767	(3807)	0.17	5925	762	(5163)	0.13	10499	1529	(8970)	0.15
Gunma	2497	583	(1914)	0.23	4796	949	(3847)	0.20	7293	1532	(5761)	0.21
Saitama	2341	5472	3131	2.34	10764	5530	(5234)	0.51	13105	11002	(2103)	0.84
Chiba	4315	1922	(2393)	0.45	9949	2610	(7339)	0.26	14264	4532	(9732)	0.32
Tokyo	606	47348	46742	78.13	2625	106526	103901	40.58	3231	153874	150643	47.62
Kanagawa	542	10980	10438	20.26	5050	15590	10540	3.09	5592	26570	20978	4.75
Niigata	7395	123	(7272)	0.02	8848	285	(8563)	0.03	16243	408	(15835)	0.03
Toyama	864	825	(39)	0.95	2848	198	(2650)	0.07	3712	1023	(2689)	0.28
Ishikawa	1535	1001	(534)	0.65	2067	561	(1506)	0.27	3602	1562	(2040)	0.43
Fukui	1455	570	(885)	0.39	2597	71	(2526)	0.03	4052	641	(3411)	0.16
Yamanashi	1409	189	(1220)	0.13	4815	141	(4674)	0.03	6224	330	(5894)	0.05
Nagano	3075	347	(2728)	0.11	7359	473	(6886)	0.06	10434	820	(9614)	0.08
Gifu	2912	5212	2300	1.79	4915	1650	(3265)	0.34	7827	6862	(965)	0.88
Shizuoka	1703	3846	2143	2.26	8829	2618	(6211)	0.30	10532	6464	(4068)	0.61
Aichi	722	27656	26934	38.30	1887	19861	17974	10.53	2609	47517	44908	18.21
Mie	2840	2599	(241)	0.92	4840	823	(4017)	0.17	7680	3422	(4258)	0.45
Shiga	1244	1510	266	1.21	3738	644	(3094)	0.17	4982	2154	(2828)	0.43

Table 5.1: Continued

	Junior High School Graduates				Senior High School Graduates				Total			
	(i)	(j)	(j)-(i)	(j)/(i)	(i)	(j)	(j)-(i)	(j)/(i)	(i)	(j)	(j)-(i)	(j)/(i)
Kyoto	745	3409	2664	4.58	3842	6926	3084	1.80	4587	10335	5748	2.25
Osaka	130	31368	**31238**	**241.29**	1499	57418	**55919**	**38.30**	1629	88786	**87157**	**54.50**
Hyogo	2590	5804	3214	2.24	8467	8944	477	1.06	11057	14748	3691	1.33
Nara	832	1211	379	1.46	3939	1127	(2812)	0.29	4771	2338	(2433)	0.49
Wakayama	2260	471	(1789)	0.21	3522	337	(3185)	0.10	5782	808	(4974)	0.14
Tottori	1418	145	(1273)	0.10	3597	150	(3447)	0.04	5015	295	(4720)	0.06
Shimane	4422	41	(4381)	0.01	6556	78	(6478)	0.01	10978	119	(10859)	0.01
Okayama	1754	3078	1324	1.75	6448	1072	(5376)	0.17	8202	4150	(4052)	0.51
Hiroshima	1262	2277	1015	1.80	4037	3638	(399)	0.90	5299	5915	616	1.12
Yamaguchi	3550	421	(3129)	0.12	6209	1403	(4806)	0.23	9759	1824	(7935)	0.19
Tokushima	3600	41	(3559)	0.01	4519	40	(4479)	0.01	8119	81	(8038)	0.01
Kagawa	1613	343	(1270)	0.21	4186	453	(3733)	0.11	5799	796	(5003)	0.14
Ehime	5498	183	(5315)	0.03	6071	470	(5601)	0.08	11569	653	(10916)	0.06
Kochi	3820	52	(3768)	0.01	2584	48	(2536)	0.02	6404	100	(6304)	0.02
Fukuoka	5248	2886	(2362)	0.55	8479	4426	(4053)	0.52	13727	7312	(6415)	0.53
Saga	2878	156	(2722)	0.05	4599	206	(4393)	0.04	7477	362	(7115)	0.05
Nagasaki	8810	197	(8613)	0.02	5760	440	(5320)	0.08	14570	637	(13933)	0.04
Kumamoto	6905	134	(6771)	0.02	6590	669	(5921)	0.10	13495	803	(12692)	0.06
Oita	3464	235	(3229)	0.07	6774	389	(6385)	0.06	10238	624	(9614)	0.06
Miyazaki	5895	129	(5766)	0.02	4318	316	(4002)	0.07	10213	445	(9768)	0.04
Kagoshima	12424	62	(12362)	0.00	13527	201	(13326)	0.01	25951	263	(25688)	0.01

Note. (i) represents the outflow numbers, (j) the inflow numbers, while figures in brackets from (j)−(i) indicate negative values. The bold figures indicate significantly high inflow numbers in comparison to outflow numbers.

Source: School Basic Survey

employment that would in turn enable the costs to be defrayed, while there was also the need to consider one's ability to cover these costs when making the move. Consequently, there is a possibility that migration is affected by the ability of the job seeker's family to bear the costs involved. That is, by the family's socio-economic status.

Another factor that impacts on socio-economic status and migration is the 'issue of the second and third sons of farmers.' This was raised as a social problem during Japan's post-war restoration period. Because the farming business would become too small to be viable if a farmer were to allow multiple children to inherit the farm, the farm was essentially passed on to the eldest son.[7] As a result, the second and third sons of a farmer had to find alternative sources of employment, with some 'moving from the agricultural village to the city, where they settled and became modern workers employed by factories' (Tominaga 1990). At a time when post-war restoration had not fully progressed, however, many second and third sons of farmers found themselves part of a surplus population (Nakayasu 1983), which was described as the 'issue of the second and third sons of farmers.' This issue was solved during the high growth period by the 'landslide-like' migration from agricultural villages to cities, which was caused by an increase in labor demand in urban areas attracting the inheritors of the family farm, along with a simultaneous decline in the number of farmers overall (Kase 1997). In this way, migration during the high growth period has been being discussed within the context of rural exodus based on the 'issue of the second and third sons of farmers.'

Moreover, an institutional mechanism existed that had strong links to migration during the high growth period. This is the search for employment via employment agencies. During this period the government utilized employment agencies to manage labor demand and supply between different regions. Although the employment agencies were under the jurisdiction of each prefecture, employment agents from throughout the country attended 'National Supply and Demand Management Meetings' where information and communication on job offers and applications were exchanged so that, in effect, labor supply and demand was adjusted through so-called 'wide-area placements' over jurisdictions. As a result, many of the high school graduates (in particular junior high school graduates) left their prefectures via the employment agency, or via their school in cooperation with the local employment agency (Kariya 2000). This section examines the effect of employment through employment agencies on migration, together with the effect of individual characteristics, including socio-economic background. The focus on employment through employment agencies is based on the following reason. Obtaining information on job offers, work environment and work conditions in distant places is normally a difficult and costly process. If, however, the process of finding employment with migration through employment agencies is institutionalized, the cost of obtaining the information is reduced, which in turn reduces the restrictions on migration imposed by socio-economic background. This is because one's ability to bear the cost depends on his/her socio-economic background.

Microdata on individuals will be used to identify who migrated and whether there were restrictions on them based on socio-economic background. The data to be used is the A dataset of the 1995 Social Stratification and Social Mobility Survey (henceforth the SSM Survey). This survey was held in 1995 and targeted men and women aged 20 to 69 from throughout Japan and includes questions about the respondent's and his/her family's socio-economic background, such as occupation and education and questions about the respondent's residential history. Because the target of our analysis is new graduates from junior high and high schools during the high growth period, we focus on male respondents born from 1940 to 1955 whose highest educational level is junior high or high school and who lived in prefectures other than Tokyo, Kanagawa, Aichi and Osaka when they finished their schooling ($N = 262$). (Henceforth the four prefectures are called 'the metropolitan areas,' while the other prefectures are called 'the non-metropolitan areas.') They represent a cohort who obtained their first jobs during the high growth period from 1955 to 1973.

Table 5.2 represents the results of logistic regression analysis of the determinant factors for migration. The dependent variable is a dummy variable, with 0 representing those who have not experienced inter-prefectural migration during the transition from school to work, and 1 representing those who moved to the metropolitan areas.[8] The independent variables are whether the respondent is the eldest son or not (henceforth 'non-eldest son'), father's occupation (self-employed, upper white-collar employee, lower white-collar employee, blue-collar employee, and agriculture), whether or not the first-time employment was found through an employment agency or school and the interaction effect between non-eldest son and agriculture as father's occupation. Model 1 with non-eldest son and father's occupation shows that non-eldest son and upper white-collar background have

Table 5.2: Logistic regression analysis with migration as the dependent variable

	Model 1		Model 2		Model 3	
	B	Exp(B)	B	Exp(B)	B	Exp(B)
Father's occupation (Reference category: Blue-collar workers)						
Self-employed	0.882	2.416	0.994^c	2.703	1.002^c	2.724
Upper white-collar workers	1.646^b	5.184	1.538^c	4.656	1.470^c	4.348
Lower white-collar workers	0.782	2.186	0.963	2.619	1.017	2.764
Agriculture	0.509	1.663	0.621	1.860	1.171	3.225
Non-eldest son	0.753^b	2.123	0.878^b	2.406	1.217^b	3.377
Utilized employment agency			1.067^a	2.905	1.149^b	3.156
Agriculture × Non-eldest son					−0.814	0.443
Constant	−2.451^a	0.086	−3.046^a	0.048	−3.314^a	0.036
Nagelkerke's R^2	0.077		0.136		0.143	
−2LL	225.728		216.280		215.138	

Note. a: $p < 0.01$; b: $p < 0.05$; c: $p < 0.10$

significant positive effects. In other words, the eldest son tends not to migrate, while migration tends to be easier for those from upper white-collar backgrounds. Certainly, 40% of migrants came from farming backgrounds at the societal level, but having an agricultural background does not necessarily promote migration at the individual level. Rather, people from other backgrounds were equally involved in migration, and those from upper white-collar families with a high socio-economic status found it easier to migrate. In other words, migration during the high growth period was not unique to those from agricultural backgrounds and was undertaken by a broad spectrum of those living in non-metropolitan areas. The key factor that determined migration was whether or not the individual came from a background that enabled him to bear the costs of migration. Let us now examine Model 2, in which information on whether individuals sought work through employment agencies and schools has been added. First-time employment through employment agencies and schools had a considerable effect on migration. Therefore, the use of employment agencies can be seen as an important channel in the process of finding employment that accompanies migration. Moreover, when examining the effect of the father's occupation, a significant and positive effect was seen when the father's occupation was upper white-collar or self-employed, and we can see the dominance in migration amongst those from higher socio-economic backgrounds even after controlling for the effect of the employment agencies. Although the interaction effect between non-eldest son and agriculture was added to Model 3, the interaction did not have a significant effect. In other words, although migrants included many 'second and third sons of farmers,' this simply indicates that there were many males in this category from non-metropolitan areas, but their background was not significantly different from others when seen from the perspective of possibility of migration. However, as is evident in Models 1 and 2, it is clearly difficult for the eldest son to migrate, but this is not a tendency seen only in agriculture, in which direct succession has an important impact.

In this section, an analysis was carried out on the determinant factors of migration. As a result, it is clear that finding one's first job through an employment agency represents an important trigger to migration. The employment agency appears to have succeeded in reducing the costs incurred in migration and enabled a smooth transfer of work forces between regions. Although the institutional mechanism of migration weakened the restrictions to migration caused by individual characteristics, the effect of socio-economic background still remains a significant factor affecting migration. This is in contrast to the decline in primary industry, which resulted in a structural tendency for second and third sons of farmers and those who left their villages to move to metropolitan areas in search of employment, as found in the macrodata. Rather, this is a tendency in which the ability to bear the costs that accompany migration makes it easier for individuals from higher socio-economic backgrounds to migrate.

Finding first jobs

What, then, is the relationship between migration to metropolitan areas – which takes place when junior high and high school graduates enter the labor market – and the achievement of occupational status? Let us examine this by comparing status attainment of migrants with the status attainment of those who remained in non-metropolitan areas or who were originally from metropolitan areas.

As in the preceding section, we use the SSM survey data to classify patterns of geographical mobility with details on the respondent's place of residence at the time when one's education ended and the place of residence when finding the first job. By combining the place of residence at two points (when the highest level of education was achieved and when finding first-time employment) with whether migration took place between these two points, three migration patterns are defined: (1) those who remained in non-metropolitan areas, (2) those who moved from non-metropolitan areas to metropolitan areas and (3) those who remained in metropolitan areas.[9] By comparing these patterns, I have attempted to analyze the effect of place of origin and migration on status attainment.

First we shall look at the process of getting the first job, a direct consequence of migration. For this purpose, we classify occupations into nine groups: Self-employed white-collar workers, self-employed blue-collar workers, professionals, managers, white-collar workers at large companies, white-collar workers at small and medium companies, blue-collar workers at large companies, blue-collar workers at small and medium companies and farmers.[10]

Table 5.3 represents the distribution of first job by migration pattern. As a general tendency, blue-collar workers at small and medium companies represent over 30% of each migration pattern, representing the primary source of employment. This finding reflects the popular image of 'mass employment' that the people involved in it embarked on their working lives as part of the lower socio-economic

Table 5.3: Distribution of first jobs by migration pattern

	Non-metropolitan non-migrants		Migrants		Metropolitan non-migrants		Overall
	%	Adjusted residuals	%	Adjusted residuals	%	Adjusted residuals	%
Self-employed white-collar	2.9	0.27	0.0	−1.32	4.2	0.85	2.7
Self-employed blue-collar	6.8	−0.94	1.9	−1.74[c]	15.3	2.64[a]	7.9
Professionals	2.4	−2.64[a]	7.7	1.04	9.7	2.18[b]	4.8
White-collar workers at large companies	14.1	0.51	15.4	0.47	9.7	−1.02	13.3
White-collar workers at small and medium companies	15.0	−0.26	15.4	−0.02	16.7	0.32	15.5
Blue-collar workers at large companies	7.3	−1.47	17.3	2.25[b]	8.3	−0.25	9.1
Blue-collar workers at small and medium companies	39.8	0.34	42.3	0.52	34.7	−0.86	39.1
Agriculture	11.7	3.61[a]	0.0	−2.25[b]	1.4	−2.24[b]	7.6

Note. a: $p < 0.01$; b: $p < 0.05$; c: $p < 0.10$.

group of workers such as live-in shop assistants and manual workers in small factories. However, the finding points out that this process also applies to junior and senior high school graduates in general at the time.

Let us now examine in more detail the differences in finding the first job by migration pattern, focusing on the adjusted residuals. The occupations with significant adjusted residuals are farmers, self-employed blue-collar workers, professionals and blue-collar workers at large companies. Many non-migrants who were living in non-metropolitan areas when they found their first jobs obviously did so in the agricultural sector. However, 43% of the fathers of the migrants worked in the agricultural sector, which means that there was a considerable and growing exodus from the agricultural sector and into employment in other sectors even in non-metropolitan areas. As for self-employed blue-collar workers, metropolitan non-migrants are very likely to find the first job in this occupational category. This is because of a strong tendency to inherit the family business, as found in the agricultural sector. As for professionals, there are higher numbers of metropolitan non-migrants than other migration patterns in this sector. This is because of two factors. First, a significant demand for professionals was yet to emerge at that stage in non-metropolitan areas. Second, employment agencies, through which many migrants found their first jobs, provided them with information on occupations that could not be filled by people in metropolitan areas (Kase 1997). Thus there is a possibility that professional occupations with good working conditions were not offered to people from non-metropolitan areas. For these reasons, one can argue that metropolitan non-migrants, in comparison to those from other migration patterns, found themselves in a situation that facilitated finding work in professional occupations. However, even amongst metropolitan non-migrants, the actual share of professional occupations was insubstantial and was not a major source of employment. Finally, a significant number of migrants entered the large company blue-collar sector.

Migrants tend to get the first job in other sectors than agriculture and self-employment. Thus the same analysis as for Table 5.3 was applied to employees in the large company white-collar, the small and medium company white-collar, the large company blue-collar and the small and medium blue-collar sectors (see Table 5.4). The result shows that, as in Table 5.3, migrants are more likely to find the first job as blue-collar employees in large companies (although the

Table 5.4: Distribution of first jobs amongst employees only

	Non-metropolitan non-migrants		Migrants		Metropolitan non-migrants		Overall
	%	Adjusted residuals	%	Adjusted residuals	%	Adjusted residuals	%
White-collar workers at large companies	18.5	0.62	17.0	−0.06	14.0	−0.69	17.32
White-collar workers at small and medium companies	19.7	−0.17	17.0	−0.58	24.0	0.77	20.08
Blue-collar workers at large companies	9.6	−1.42	19.1	1.73[a]	12.0	0.05	11.81
Blue-collar workers at small and medium companies	52.2	0.58	46.8	−0.60	50.0	−0.12	50.79

Note. a: $p < 0.10$

level of significance is 10%). These results conflict with the results of previous research indicating that, in comparison to those born in large cities, migrants flowing from non-metropolitan areas to large cities found themselves in inferior work environments in small companies and family companies (Namiki 1960; Kase 1997). Let us therefore examine, in more detail, the relationship between the size of company and migration patterns.

Table 5.5 represents the results of multiple regression analysis with the size of the company of the first job[11] as the dependent variable, migration pattern (a dummy variable) and whether the first job was found through an employment agency or school (a dummy variable) as the independent variables, and the father's schooling years, the father's occupational prestige score and the respondent's educational level (a dummy variable with junior high school at the baseline category) as the control variables. Model 1 represents a model in which the migration pattern and the control variables are used, and indicates the significant effect of the migration pattern, the father's occupational prestige and the respondent's educational level. In other words, even after controlling for the respondent's socio-economic background and educational level, migrants have achieved an advantageous status in terms of the size of the company. Therefore, this indicates that people were not only able to access the abundance of employment opportunities found in metropolitan areas through migration, but the results also reflect that people migrated because there was a likelihood of being able to make use of these opportunities. When the use of employment agencies is added to Model 1 (Model 2), the results indicate the significantly positive benefits of using employment agencies. These results

Table 5.5: *Multiple regression analysis with the size of the company where first employed as the dependent variable*

	Model 1		Model 2	
	B	β	B	β
Migration pattern				
(Reference category: Migrants)				
Non-metropolitan non-migrants	−1.623	−0.281[a]	−1.105	−0.191[b]
Metropolitan non-migrants	−1.589	−0.241[a]	−1.202	−0.182[b]
Utilized employment agency			1.682	0.280[a]
Control variables				
Father's education	−0.109	−0.102	−0.084	−0.079
Father's occupational prestige	0.103	0.235[a]	0.092	0.209[a]
Respondent's education	1.675	0.249[a]	1.733	0.258[a]
Constant	1.471		0.836	
R^2		0.177		0.250
Adjusted R^2		0.157		0.228

Note. a: $p < 0.01$; b: $p < 0.05$

probably reflect the larger numbers of job openings in large companies offered through employment agencies in the 1960s. During the period, job vacancies dramatically increased, and employment agencies, in response to this increase, tightened the standard of working conditions of job openings they dealt with. As a result, they were able to offer job openings in large companies with relatively good working conditions (Sugayama and Nishimura 2000). Moreover, the effects of the migration pattern are reduced when use of employment agencies is added to Model 1 (Changes in the coefficient are as follows: −.281 → −.191 for non-migrants in non-metropolitan areas; −.241 → −.182 for non-migrants in metropolitan areas). This indicates that the reason for the competitive edge of some migrants lies in the fact that many of these were users of employment agencies. However, because the effects are still significant, we would argue that migration functioned advantageously to access opportunities, independent of employment agencies.

In this section, an analysis was carried out on getting the first job as a direct consequence of migration. As a result, it became clear that migrants were more advantaged in comparison to non-migrants in terms of the size of the company when finding the first job. This is probably because people actively migrated in search of good opportunities, rather than because they were forced to migrate because of the lack of employment opportunities in their home towns.

Job changes and careers

The preceding section focused on the first jobs found by migrants. Regional differences in employment opportunities are believed to not only have an effect at the time of finding one's first job but continue to have an effect on career change opportunities during an individual's working life. Therefore, in this section, we examine job changes and careers that follow the first job. This section examines how, and to what extent, the decision to move (or not) when looking for first-time employment affects socio-economic consequences.

Let us first examine those leaving their first jobs. Based on data on those who left their jobs in 1962 and 1963, Kase (1997: 181) claims that 'there was a considerably high rate of job turnover amongst younger workers' at the time. Leaving aside the issue of whether the indicated job turnover rate of 25% (at businesses employing 30 to 99 people) within a year of finding work is high or not, what is of interest here is whether there is a difference in the ease of leaving a job, depending on whether one was living in one's own area or whether migration took place. It is assumed, naturally, that job turnover would differ depending on the occupation that the individual is engaged in and therefore event history analysis has been carried out to control for the effect of the first job on job turnover.

Table 5.6 represents the results of the event history analysis with leaving one's first job as the dependent variable. First job in some occupations lowers the hazard rate of job change. They are self-employed white-collar and blue-collar workers with little occupational mobility, professionals – a so-called 'destined occupation' (Hara 1986) – and white-collar workers at large companies whose working conditions are relatively good. However, even after controlling for first job, there is a significantly higher hazard rate of job change amongst migrants in comparison to non-metropolitan as well as metropolitan non-migrants. This means that there is a greater tendency amongst migrants to leave their first jobs. Furthermore, in contrast to the average job change rate of 2.65 amongst migrants, the rate amongst non-metropolitan non-migrants was 1.84 and metropolitan non-migrants 2.29, also indicating a greater tendency amongst migrants to change jobs more often ($df = 2, 331$, $F = 5.58$, $p = .004$). Kase (1997) gives the following three reasons why those involved in 'mass employment' tend to leave their jobs more

Table 5.6: Event history analysis with leaving the first job as the dependent variable

	B	Exp(B)
Migration Pattern		
(Reference category: Migrants)		
Non-metropolitan non-migrants	−0.603[a]	0.547
Metropolitan non-migrants	−0.468[b]	0.626
First job		
(Reference category: Blue-collar workers at small and medium companies)		
Self-employed white-collar	−1.090[a]	0.336
Self-employed blue-collar	−0.967[a]	0.380
Professionals	−0.611[b]	0.543
White-collar workers at large companies	−0.364[b]	0.695
White-collar workers at small and medium companies	0.160	1.174
Blue-collar workers at large companies	−0.296	0.744
Agriculture	−0.023	0.977
−2LL	2882.327	

Note. a: $p < 0.01$; b: $p < 0.05$

often. The first is the discrepancy between the information provided at the time of employment and the real situation, with working conditions significantly worse than anticipated in many cases. The second reason is that the employment agency often played an intermediary role in migration, as described in the third section. Depending on how prospective employees were allocated to companies by a particular employment agency, many were persuaded to join a company that they had no desire to join, after being given reasons such as 'suitability' or being criticized for having 'unrealistic expectations.' The third reason is that, in an environment where there was a shortage of young workers, employees were head-hunted by other companies. The first two reasons are based on negative reasons unique to migrants, including the limited information available on prospective employers in remote areas and job seekers having to rely on the employment agency for information. These reasons are consistent with the results of the analysis. However, determining whether leaving one's job had a negative effect would require an examination of the type of job found after leaving the first job.

We shall therefore examine the type of job found immediately after leaving the first job. Because the number of samples is limited, jobs are classified into two groups – white-collar jobs and blue-collar jobs (The latter includes agriculture).

Figure 5.2: Occupational mobility from first job to second job by migration pattern

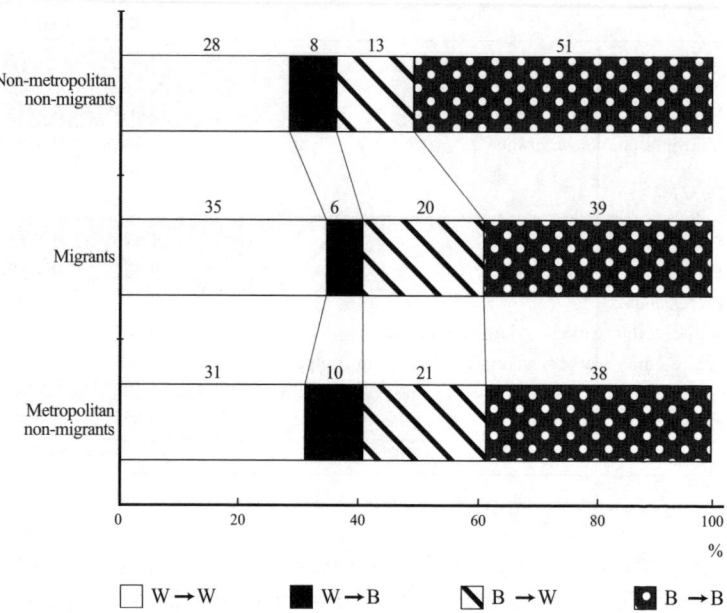

Note: Figures represent percentages. W stands for white-collar workers; B stands for blue-collar workers.

Figure 5.2 shows the percentage of four patterns of intragenerational mobility from the first job to the second job by the migration pattern. This indicates that, amongst both migrants and metropolitan non-migrants, upward mobility to white-collar jobs took place amongst approximately one third of those whose first job was blue-collar (20% of the overall figure). In contrast, the rate amongst non-metropolitan non-migrants is approximately 20% (13% of the overall figure). As a result, approximately half of the non-metropolitan non-migrants who left their blue-collar jobs once again found blue-collar jobs. It can be seen that residents in metropolitan areas, including metropolitan non-migrants and non-metropolitan migrants, enjoyed the benefits of the growth in the service industry that continued even after the high growth period. Although there may have been negative reasons behind early job changes amongst migrants, one can argue that such job changes offered greater opportunities to them than to those who remained in the non-metropolitan areas.

Figure 5.3: Occupational mobility from first job to current job by migration pattern

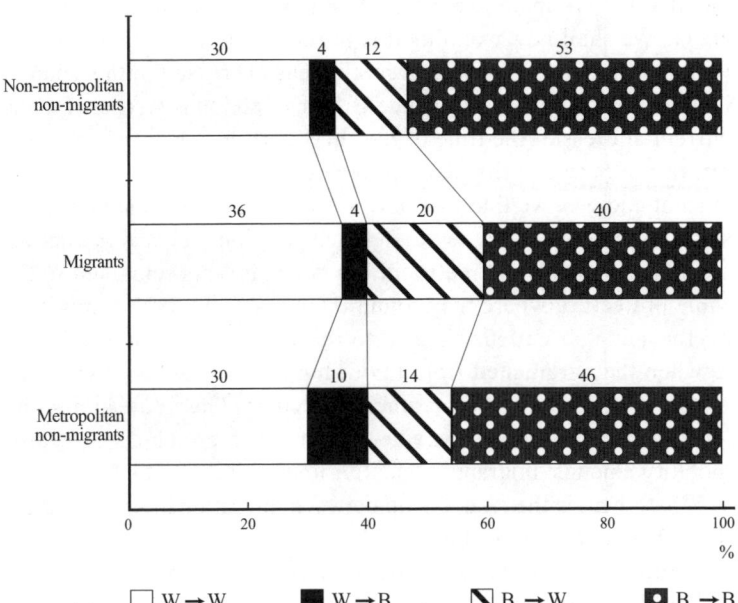

Note: Figures represent percentages. W stands for white-collar workers; B stands for blue-collar workers.

For a more general overview of the relationship between place of origin and migration and career, we shall now look at intragenerational mobility between first job and current job.

Figure 5.3 shows the association between first job and current job by the migration pattern. The competitive edge of migrants is even more prominent in this figure. The mobility rate from blue-collar jobs to white-collar jobs amongst migrants is also approximately a third (20% of the overall figure), and the rates for non-migrants in metropolitan and non-metropolitan areas are lower. Meanwhile, the ratio of those who moved from white-collar jobs to blue-collar jobs is the largest amongst metropolitan non-migrants, with a quarter of metropolitan non-migrants in white-collar jobs when first employed (10% of the overall figure). We could argue that, in contrast to the large opportunities for upward mobility amongst migrants, there is a high possibility of downward mobility amongst metropolitan non-migrants.[12]

What is the reason behind this disparity in opportunities for job change between migrants and metropolitan non-migrants, despite the fact that both of them found their first jobs in the same metropolitan areas? We shall now examine this in relation to migration after the first job. In the 1995 SSM data set that has been used in this chapter, information on place of residence after the first job is restricted to the current address at the time of the survey. If, however, we examine migration between the place of residence at the first job and the current address, we find that only 19% of migrants remained in the same prefecture where they found their first job. (This is in contrast to the fact that 71% of metropolitan non-migrants remained in the same prefecture where they found their first job.) 58% of migrants performed a so-called 'U-turn' to return to the region they lived in when they graduated from junior high or high school, while the remaining 27% moved to another prefecture. The figures therefore indicate a strong tendency, when U-turners are included, towards mobility amongst migrants even after finding their first job.

What, then, is the relationship between migration after finding the first job and occupational mobility?

Figure 5.4 shows occupational mobility from first job to current job by the migration pattern – those moving to other prefectures, non-movers and U-turners (only in the case of migrants). (We added migrants and metropolitan non-migrants samples to create the figure.) When the results are examined, U-turners who moved up from blue-collar to white-collar jobs make up approximately 25% of the total, a figure that is quite high in comparison to other migration patterns. The upward mobility rate amongst those moving to other prefectures is not substantially different from that amongst non-movers, but this is because first jobs of many of those moving to other prefectures are white-collar jobs. Therefore, if we consider the outflow from blue-collar to white-collar jobs, upward mobility took place in approximately 35% of those moving to other prefectures who were first employed in blue-collar jobs, a figure similar to that amongst U-turners (approximately 39%). As it is not possible to ascertain from the data exactly when migration from the place of residence at the time of the first job to the current address actually took place, it is not possible to vouch for whether this upward mobility took place alongside migration. However, in many cases a change in one's place of residence accompanied job change, and therefore we can safely assume that migration following the first job is linked to upward mobility.

Figure 5.4: Occupational mobility from first job to current job by mobility pattern after first job

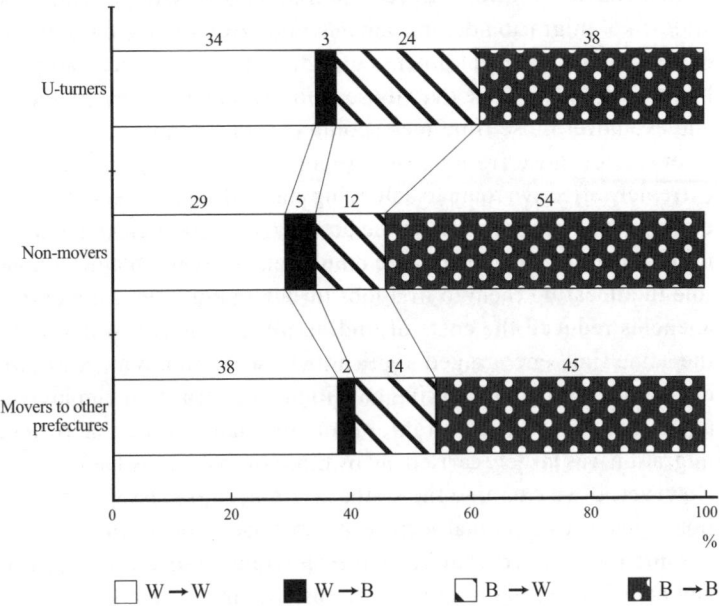

Note: Figures represent percentages. W stands for white-collar workers; B stands for blue-collar workers.

Lying in the background of this relationship between migration and occupational mobility was a situation in which the rapid concentration of population in large cities during the high growth period 'even influenced the location of companies, enhanced external diseconomies such as statutory regulations in response to soaring land prices and environmental deterioration, *promoted the establishment and the relocation of industries in rural areas and, as a result, made a massive contribution to employment opportunities in rural areas*' (Shinzō Araragi 1994: 184–185). In other words, with the development of employment opportunities in regional hub cities in the years following the high growth period, it was migrants – who had already left their places of origins and who could easily migrate to other prefectures, or who could easily migrate back to their place of origin – who found it easy to access newly created job opportunities in non-metropolitan areas.

Conclusion

In this chapter, I have analyzed the role played by large scale 'landslide-like' migration during Japan's high growth economic period in the status attainment process of individuals. In general, migrants had a competitive edge over those who remained in their prefecture and even over those from metropolitan areas in status attainment in a sense. For those from non-metropolitan areas, migration was an extremely effective route to achieving status through overcoming the disparity in opportunities that lie between metropolitan and non-metropolitan areas. In addition the employment agency played a major role in allocating them to first jobs through migration. Employment agencies reduced the costs of finding jobs in distant places and at the same time encouraged applicants to seek employment in large companies with good working conditions. It is true that employment agencies reduced costs in migration and that, on the macro level, migration was largely carried out by those from farming backgrounds. However, if we examine the status attainment process of via migration, it becomes clear that socio-economic backgrounds of those from non-metropolitan areas affected their migration process and (directly and/or indirectly via migration) status attainment. Thus the interaction between the disparity in opportunity between regions and that between family backgrounds determines status attainment.

Lastly, I would like to mention another aspect of the regional disparities that I was unable to refer to in this chapter. This chapter focused on migration in first-time employment amongst new graduates, which was a typical phenomenon during the high growth period. Thus the analysis was restricted to junior and senior high school graduates. Naturally, however, college graduates also existed and represented 17% of those originating from non-metropolitan areas, with the ratio increasing to 44% of those originating from metropolitan areas. This means that while the analysis carried out here covered more than 80% of people born in non-metropolitan areas, only 50% of those born in metropolitan areas were covered at most. Because of the strong link between education and occupation, and with the popularization of higher education and college graduates forming the backbone of the work force in contemporary society, the regional disparities in educational opportunities and migration to attend university will no doubt become increasingly significant factors in status attainment.

Acknowledgement

Permission was received from the 2005 SSM Research Committee for use of the SSM survey data.

6 The Effects of Spatial Characteristics on the Determinants of Class Identification

Daisuke Kobayashi

Introduction

This chapter argues that spatial characteristics are an intervening factor between objective class and subjective perception. It is natural that we have to focus on the distributions of economic, social and human resources among people in order to consider inequality or justice in society. However, if people's actions depend on the perception of difference more than on the actual situation of distribution, it is also important to study the perceptions of distribution or class. In short, it is important for class research to study the difference between objective class and subjective perception.

In this point, spatiality is one of the interesting factors. This is because spatial factors might affect people's perceptions as a result of a limitation of comparison or because spatial characteristics might have an effect on the elements of class consciousness. This chapter examines the effects of spatial characteristics such as social context on the determinants of class consciousness in Japan, focusing on class identification. Class identification is the most controversial question among class researchers in Japan, because it clearly shows the gap between objective class situation and subjective perception. Class identification was simply considered as subjective position or rank in macro society. However, previous studies show class identification does not simply reflect the objective situation of social stratum. Some scholars have even said that the study of class identification is meaningless.

Rather, we think that the results of previous studies mean that there is room for another approach to study the relation between objective class and subjective identification. Therefore, more work needs to be done to study how people identify their own class. This chapter proposes that it is important to take spatial characteristics into consideration as an intervening factor between objective class situation and subjective perception.

Previous studies

Class identification is one of the class consciousnesses. In Japan, class identification has been an interesting topic for sociologists. To date, data about class consciousness that use similar questions is available only from surveys conducted through the postwar period. These academic surveys by Japanese class researchers are entitled 'Statistical Research of the Japanese National Character' and 'the national survey of Social Stratification and Social Mobility (SSM).'

However, Tomoeda and Kojima (1987) who used the SSM survey data reported that objective socio-economic situation has not strongly correlated with class identification. This resulted in various reactions from class researchers. Mamada (1990) concluded that there is little connection between class identification and objective social class, and that study of class identification is meaningless for class researchers. Kosaka and Miyano (1990) insisted that the distribution of class identification could not be explained by the metric approach and that using mathematical models would be a better alternative.

In spite of these doubts, some scholars have tried to explain the gap positively. On one hand, Kikkawa (1999) claimed that determinants of class identification had been changing through the 1970s–90s. He proposed that this trend was the result of the process of enthusiasm in the age of rapid economic growth. On the other hand, some scholars questioned the assumption that determinants of class identification are uniform at the macro level, such as studies that focused on social networks (Hoshi 2000) and region (Tomoeda 1988).

From the same point of view, Kobayashi (2004) also showed that it is important to take into consideration the effect of spatial characteristics as determinants of class identification. In that paper, a quantitative analysis was performed, testing the two hypotheses that (1) people compare their income with national levels in their residential areas, and that (2) the urban and the rural areas have different effects on the causal relationship between explanatory variables and class identification. As a result, hypothesis (2) is adopted, because it was observed that the effect of income is stronger and the explanatory power of the model is also higher in more urbanized areas. It means that the assumption that determinants of class identification are uniform at the macro level is not true and that there is the possibility that spatiality intervenes between objective status and subjective perception. If class consciousness is regarded as a product of comparison with others, it is essentially contextual. Therefore, it is natural that the analyses conducted only by individual-level variables will have limitations.

Issues of previous study and hypotheses

However, my former study (Kobayashi 2004) has two remaining issues. Firstly, as a substantial issue, it is not clear what characteristic of urban spatiality has effects on class identification. For example, if we focus on the demographic aspect of urban area, it is unclear whether a density as stock of population, or a population change as flow of population has an effect on determinants of class identification. To answer this question, we need to use more elaborate factors that indicate spatial characteristics, and to attempt time serial analysis to interpret precisely the obtained tendency.

Secondly, treatment of macro-level factors is questioned as a technical issue. In that study, macro-level factor is a spatial factor. The data which social scientists use are usually nested, not collected by simple random sampling. If data structure is nested, macro-level variance should be taken into consideration in order to estimate macro-level factors precisely.

On the basis of these issues, the purposes of this chapter are as follows. Firstly, other variables of spatial characteristics are adopted to examine whether a density of population or a population change has an effect on determinants of class identification. Secondly, we examine whether the same tendencies can be observed or not, using past data to analyze this. Finally, the method that can adequately treat nested data and macro-level factors is applied to estimate the effect of spatial characteristics more precisely.

According to the above issues, two hypotheses are proposed. H1 hypothesis is that the effect of income is stronger and the explanatory power of the model is also higher in the region where the population increases more rapidly, focusing on the migration characteristics of urban area. H2 hypothesis is that the characteristics of urban area consistently affect the determinants of class identification, focusing on trend in time series.

Data and methods

We estimate spatial variation in class identification by analyzing the SSM datasets linked with demographic data from population census in Japan. The SSM is a cross-sectional probability sample survey of adults in Japan conducted every ten years since 1955. The SSM data contain geographic codes that enable us to append data that describe the geographic areas in which respondents reside. Therefore we can analyze individual level data linking to spatial level variables. The SSM survey adopts a multi-stage sampling approach: Voting districts are selected first, and then individuals are selected within each voting district. However, because the information on the voting districts is not open to the public, we use the data of each administrative district of municipality as spatial-level data.

We use the A and B datasets of the 1995 SSM survey and the A dataset of the 1975 SSM survey. Although it is natural to include the 1985 SSM dataset in the analysis, we do not use it because the information on administrative districts of municipalities is not released to the public. Samples used in the analysis are male samples with a job in each datasets.

Next, we show the method to treat spatial-level variables adequately. We use hierarchical linear model (HLM) in this chapter. Almost all social scientific survey data are collected by the method of multi-stage sampling. This means data structure is nested, and nested data may have intra-class correlation, that is, the variance that is explained by group. If data contain intra-class correlation, standard errors that ordinary least squares (OLS) produces are underestimated. This leads to a higher probability of rejection of null hypothesis than if there is no intra-class correlation when using OLS regression. However, HLM can treat micro-level factors and macro-level factors separately, so HLM estimates parameters,[1] taking macro-level variances into account. It means that parameters can be tested more strictly. Therefore if we are interested in the relation between individual and higher level factor, such as school, corporation, country or region, HLM is a better method than OLS. In fact, many articles that treat the relation between the characteristics of regions or neighbors and the attitudes of residents by HLM have been published.[2]

Models

The dependent variable for our analysis is class identification as a five-point scale of respondents' identification of their class. The SSM survey has asked class identification with the same question and choices since the 1955 survey. The question is 'Suppose we were to divide people living in today's Japanese society into the following five strata. To which group do you think you would belong?' The choices are 'Upper,' 'Upper Middle,' 'Lower Middle,' 'Upper Lower' and 'Lower lower,' coded '5' for those who select 'Upper' and coded '1' for those who select 'Lower lower.'

The independent variables consist of two levels, which are individual-level (level-1) and regional-level (level-2). First, individual-level variables[3] are 'Age,' 'Household income,' 'Occupational status,' 'Education' and 'Life satisfaction.' All the individual-level variables are defined in the same way as in Kikkawa's model (1999). That is to say, 'Occupational status' is defined by a measure of occupational prestige. Low scores indicate low prestige and high scores indicate high prestige. The index of 'Education' is years of schooling. 'Life satisfaction' is a five-point scale coded '1' for those who are 'not satisfied' and coded '5' for those who are 'satisfied.'

In addition, we adopt two region-level variables, which are key independent variables in this analysis. These are the rate of Densely Inhabited Districts population (DIDs) and the rate of Population Change (PC). 'DIDs' are the index of the urban–rural classification which has been applied since the 1960 Population Census by the Statistics Bureau. A DID is defined as an area within a shi (city), ku (ward), machi (town) or mura (village) that is composed of a group of contiguous Basic Unit Blocks each of which has a population density of about 4,000 inhabitants or more per square kilometer and whose total population exceeds 5,000, as of October 1st at each Population Census. In this chapter, 'DIDs' represent the percentage of the population who live in 'Densely Inhabited Districts' to the total population who live in each administrative district of a municipality. The rate of Population Change is the value of population change in each administrative district of a municipality, which is compared with 5 years ago based on Population Census.

Our analysis is mainly carried out with the following two models. A random-intercept model is used to evaluate the degree to which the mean value of a given dependent variable varies across level-2 units and to examine whether a level-2 independent variable helps to account for that variation. A random-slope model examines the cross-level interaction effect that is the effect of level-1 independent variable variance across level-2 units. Therefore, we first examine whether the degree of class identification varies across regions by the random-intercept model. Then, we examine whether the effects of region-level variables vary across region by the random-slope model.

The full model that includes all the level-1 variables, level-2 variables and random effects is given by equations below. The level-1 equation looks similar to a typical OLS multiple regression model. However, the coefficients of the level-1 equation are explained by each level-2 equation. Thus, level-2 equations show that different level-1 models are estimated for units at the second level. It means that the model shown by HLM corresponds to the nested structure of the data. All the models presented in this chapter are estimated with HLM 5.04 for Windows, which was written by Raudenbush, Bryk and Congdon (2000).

Equations of the full model

Level-1

- (Class Identification)$_{ij}$ = β_{0j} + β_{1j} (Age)$_{ij}$ + β_{2j} (Income)$_{ij}$ + β_{3j} (Occupation)$_{ij}$ + β_{4j} (Education)$_{ij}$ + β_{5j} (Satisfaction)$_{ij}$ + r$_{ij}$

Level-2

- β_{0j} = γ_{00} + γ_{01}(DIDs)$_j$ + γ_{02}(PC)$_j$ + u$_{0j}$
- β_{1j} = γ_{10} + γ_{11}(DIDs)$_j$ + γ_{12}(PC)$_j$ + u$_{1j}$
- β_{2j} = γ_{20} + γ_{21}(DIDs)$_j$ + γ_{22}(PC)$_j$ + u$_{2j}$
- β_{3j} = γ_{30} + γ_{31}(DIDs)$_j$ + γ_{32}(PC)$_j$ + u$_{3j}$
- β_{4j} = γ_{40} + γ_{41}(DIDs)$_j$ + γ_{42}(PC)$_j$ + u$_{4j}$
- β_{5j} = γ_{50} + γ_{51}(DIDs)$_j$ + γ_{52}(PC)$_j$ + u$_{5j}$

Results

Analysis of the 1995 data

First, we analyze the 1995 dataset. We see two simple models before examining the random-intercept model and the random-slope model. Model 1 of Table 6.1 presents results from a regression equation that includes only an intercept parameter and a variance component. Since the intercept parameter describes the mean of class identification in this model, the significant variation in the parameter indicates that the degree of class identification varies across the regions. It is natural that we have questions as to what factors might account for differences in the degree of class identification across regions. Model 2 includes individual-level variables. All except 'Age' have significant effects. However, the variance components of 'Education' still have significant variation, even after controlling for individual-level variables. This outcome indicates that there is a room for other factors explaining the variance across regions.

Table 6.1: Hierarchical linear regression model with class identification as the dependent variable for the 1995 data

		Model 1				Model 2				Model 3				Model 4				Model 5			
		Coefficient	SE	t-ratio	d.f.	Coefficient	SE	t-ratio	d.f.	Coefficient	SE	t-ratio	d.f.	Coefficient	SE	t-ratio	d.f.	Coefficient	SE	t-ratio	d.f.
Fixed effects:																					
Intercept, B0	Intercept2, G00	3.034808	0.020794	145.947ᵃ	332	3.030982	0.018015	168.247ᵃ	332	3.049055	0.034907	87.349ᵃ	330	3.047492	0.034503	88.325ᵃ	330	3.048019	0.034638	87.996ᵃ	330
	DIDs, G01									-0.044024	0.048463	-0.908	330	-0.057898	0.048825	-1.186	330	-0.048898	0.049003	-0.998	330
	PC, G02									0.006517	0.003641	1.79	330	0.008125	0.003654	2.224ᵃ	330	0.006642	0.00365	1.82	330
Age slope, B1	Intercept2, G10					0.000195	0.001608	0.121	332	0.000378	0.001593	0.237	332	0.003423	0.002895	1.182	330	-0.000042	0.001604	-0.026	1777
	DIDs, G11													-0.00481	0.004197	-1.146	330				
	PC, G12													-0.000282	0.000347	-0.811	330				
Income slope, B2	Intercept2, G20					0.05932	0.006265	9.468ᵃ	332	0.058773	0.006285	9.351ᵃ	332	0.027037	0.012571	2.151ᵃ	330	0.024535	0.011621	2.111ᵃ	331
	DIDs, G21													0.052059	0.016973	3.067ᵇ	330	0.054186	0.015512	3.493ᵇ	331
	PC, G22													0.00003	0.00109	0.028	330				
Education slope, B3	Intercept2, G30					0.037452	0.00824	4.545ᵃ	332	0.038472	0.008332	4.618ᵃ	332	0.030723	0.01908	1.61	330	0.038023	0.008407	4.523ᶜ	332
	DIDs, G31													0.019689	0.023714	0.83	330				
	PC, G32													-0.002374	0.001447	-1.64	330				
Occupation slope, B4	Intercept2, G40					0.007811	0.001632	4.785ᵃ	332	0.007992	0.001638	4.88ᵃ	332	0.007938	0.002959	2.683ᵇ	330	0.007665	0.001624	4.72ᵃ	1777
	DIDs, G41													-0.000596	0.004165	-0.143	330				
	PC, G42													-0.000214	0.000293	-0.729	330				
Life satisfaction slope, B5	Intercept2, G50					0.179281	0.019698	9.102ᵃ	332	0.179548	0.019685	9.121ᵃ	332	0.123251	0.042133	2.925ᵃ	330	0.178825	0.020492	8.72ᵃ	1777
	DIDs, G51													0.093636	0.055946	1.674	330				
	PC, G52													-0.002932	0.003838	-0.764	330				

Table 6.1: continued

	Model 1			Model 2			Model 3			Model 4			Model 5		
	Variance Component	chi square	d.f.	Variance Component	chi square	d.f.	Variance Component	chi square	d.f.	Variance Component	chi square	d.f.	Variance Component	chi square	d.f.
Random effects:															
Intercept1, U0	0.01543	380.98514a	332	0.01317	169.29669	147	0.01187	168.99127	145	0.01111	169.42186	145	0.01055	286.36448	285
Age slope, U1				0.00003	171.01119	147	0.00003	171.23489	147	0.00002	169.6056	145			
Income slope, U2				0.00066	159.36259	147	0.00066	159.53333	147	0.00007	157.88793	145	0.00011	282.20804	286
Education slope, U3				0.00134	184.30684a	147	0.00131	184.58636c	147	0.0012	182.9755a	145	0.00256	329.20843a	287
Occupation slope, U4				0.00002	152.54416	147	0.00002	152.70678	147	0.00001	152.83373	145			
Life Satisfaction slope, U5				0.02349	168.0913	147	0.02376	168.26503	147	0.02512	168.32366	145			
level-1, R	0.49924			0.49868			0.49855			0.52980					
Model Fit Deviance	4413.072			4015.635			4011.785			3988.825			4015.900		
Number of estimated parameters	3			28			30			40			16		

Notes.

The chi-square statistics reported above are based on only units that had sufficient data for computation in each model. Fixed effects and variance components are based on all the data.

a: $p < 0.05$; b: $p < 0.01$; c: $p < 0.001$

Thus, we examine the random-intercept model that contains the region-level variables. Model 3 includes all of the individual-level variables, plus the 'DIDs' and 'PC' as level-2 variables that account for the variance of intercept that shows the mean of degree of class identification. Consequently, there is no significant effect of both 'DIDs' and 'PC' for the variation of intercept. It means that the mean of degree of class identification is not higher or lower in the regions that are higher in 'DIDs' and 'PC,' leading us to conclude that spatial characteristics do not have an effect on class identification. However, there is still the possibility that spatial characteristics have effects on the determinants of class identification. Therefore, the random-slope model needs to be examined. Model 4 is the random-slope model that includes all of the individual-level variables, plus the 'DIDs' and 'PC' as level-2 variables that account for the variance of intercept and the differences of slope of each individual-level variable on the degree of class identification across the regions. Interestingly, the intercept of 'PC' and the cross-level interaction between 'Income' and 'DIDs' have significant effects. The effect of cross-level interaction between 'Income' and 'DIDs' is positive, showing that people have a stronger tendency to identify their class identification by taking their income into consideration in densely populated residential areas. In other words, the slope of 'Income' that depends on 'DIDs' means that spatial characteristics affect determinants of class identification. Model 5 is the best model that was selected by comparing deviance with the full model, taking parsimony[4] into consideration. In model 5, the tendency between 'Income' and 'DIDs' is not changed, although the main effect of 'PC' becomes insignificant and the main effect of 'Education' becomes significant. It reconfirms the results that Kobayashi reported (2004).

Analysis of the 1975 data

As the results of the analysis of the 1975 dataset, five models are presented in the same format as that of Table 6.1. Model 1 of Table 6.2 shows significant variation in the intercept parameter, meaning that the degree of class identification varies across the regions. Model 2 includes individual-level variables, and they have significant effects except 'Age' and 'Occupation.' However, the variance components of some variables still have significant variation. Also for 1975, we need to examine the spatial characteristics that might explain the variance across regions.

Model 3 contains the region-level variables, the 'DIDs' and 'PC.' Intriguingly, 'PC' has significant negative effect in this model. It means that the mean of degree of class identification is lower in the regions where the population increases. The question is then, is there any difference in slope of each individual-level variable across the regions? Model 4 examines this question. While the tendencies of individual level variables are not changed, there are significant effects of cross-level interaction between 'Age' and 'PC,' and 'Income' and 'PC.' The effect of cross-level interaction between 'Age' and 'PC' is negative, showing that younger people tend to identify their class higher in the region where the population increases are larger. The effect of cross-level interaction between 'Income' and 'PC' is positive, showing that people have a stronger tendency to identify their class position by taking their income into consideration in the region where the population increases are larger. Model 5 that is a parsimonious model shows the same tendencies. However, attending to random effects, there are still significant variations in 'Intercept,' 'Age' and 'Income,' suggesting that variation across the region cannot be completely explained yet. In short, although the main effect of 'DIDs' is significant, the cross-level interaction effects of 'DIDs' are not significant at all. In contrast, cross-level interaction effects between 'Age' and 'PC,' and between 'Income' and 'PC' are significant, showing that there are different tendencies between the 1995 data and 1975 data.

Summary and discussion

We summarize the results we obtained above, examining the two hypotheses and discussing them. With regard to H1 hypothesis that the effect of income is stronger and the explanatory power of the model is also higher in the region where the population increases more quickly, the hypothesis is not supported in 1995 data, because 'PC' does not have a significant effect on both the main effect and cross-level interaction effects in the 1995 data. On the other hand, the hypothesis is supported in 1975 data, because the main effect of 'DIDs' is significant and the cross-level interaction effects between 'Age' and 'PC,' and 'Income' and 'PC' are significant, even after controlling for the effect of 'DIDs.' This result demonstrates the effect of population as flow, not the effect of population as stock. Thus H1 hypothesis is partially supported.

Table 6.2: Hierarchical linear regression model with class identification as the dependent variable for the 1975 data

		Model 1				Model 2				Model 3				Model 4				Model 5			
		Coefficient	SE	t-ratio	d.f.	Coefficient	SE	t-ratio	d.f.	Coefficient	SE	t-ratio	d.f.	Coefficient	SE	t-ratio	d.f.	Coefficient	SE	t-ratio	d.f.
Fixed effects:																					
Intercept1, B0	Intercept2, G00	3.00858	0.020356	147.801[c]	302	3.010874	0.01912	157.474[c]	302	3.080763	0.036662	84.031[c]	300	3.081713	0.036574	84.26[a]	300	3.088617	0.038291	80.661[c]	300
	DIDs, G01									−0.001398	0.000537	−2.606[a]	300	−0.001434	0.000541	−2.651[b]	300	−0.001558	0.00056	−2.781[b]	300
	PC, G02									0.000973	0.001311	0.742	300	0.000248	0.001425	0.174	300	−0.000029	0.00137	−0.021	300
Age slope, B1	Intercept2, G10					0.000604	0.001622	0.372	302	0.000758	0.001617	0.468	302	0.0021	0.00282	0.745	300	0.002824	0.001714	1.647	301
	DIDs, G11													0.000014	0.000044	0.312	300				
	PC, G12													−0.000336	0.000113	−2.983[b]	300	−0.000299	0.000106	−2.825[b]	301
Income slope, B2	Intercept2, G20					0.035313	0.00521	6.778[a]	302	0.035017	0.005177	6.764[a]	302	0.030418	0.009389	3.24[a]	300	0.030175	0.005872	5.139[c]	301
	DIDs, G21													−0.000007	0.000131	−0.05	300				
	PC, G22													0.000722	0.000297	2.432[a]	300	0.000626	0.000291	2.148[a]	301
Education slope, B3	Intercept2, G30					0.023312	0.007052	3.306[a]	302	0.02619	0.007116	3.681[c]	302	0.028417	0.014071	2.02[a]	300	0.02871	0.007083	4.053[c]	2366
	DIDs, G31													0.000022	0.000208	0.105	300				
	PC, G32													−0.000451	0.000593	−0.76	300				
Occupation slope, B4	Intercept2, G40					0.002441	0.001638	1.49	302	0.002579	0.001625	1.587	302	−0.000347	0.003194	−0.109	300	0.002846	0.001611	1.767	2366
	DIDs, G41													0.000045	0.000048	0.948	300				
	PC, G42													0.000023	0.000137	0.169	300				
Life satisfaction slope, B5	Intercept2, G50					0.15558	0.01797	8.658[a]	302	0.154591	0.018034	8.572[a]	302	0.179631	0.033257	5.401[a]	300	0.15535	0.018266	8.505[a]	2366
	DIDs, G51													−0.000415	0.0005	−0.829	300				
	PC, G52													−0.000405	0.001051	−0.385	300				

Table 6.2: continued

	Model 1			Model 2			Model 3			Model 4			Model 5		
	Variance Component	chi square	d.f.	Variance Component	chi square	d.f.	Variance Component	chi square	d.f.	Variance Component	chi square	d.f.	Variance Component	chi square	d.f.
Random effects:															
Intercept1, U0	0.05064	517.15997[c]	302	0.04184	328.78393[c]	235	0.03966	325.40901[c]	233	0.03958	327.86861[c]		0.04505	461.01185[c]	294
Age slope, U1				0.00018	288.35524[a]	235	0.00018	287.78825[a]	235	0.00016	286.79234[b]		0.0001	363.04132[b]	295
Income slope, U2				0.00092	285.11264[a]	235	0.0009	284.47697[a]	235	0.00093	280.83032[a]		0.001	359.28306[b]	295
Education slope, U3				0.00202	266.81582	235	0.00006	250.64322	235	0.00188	267.18692				
Occupation slope, U4				0.00007	251.01782	235	0.01865	262.4867	235	0.00006	251.03794				
Life Satisfaction slope, U5				0.01922	263.09932	235	0.00195	265.46936	235	0.01878	263.82913				
level-1, R	0.49924			0.49924			0.44813			0.44658			0.47633		
Model Fit Deviance	5525.485			5237.892			5230.926			5217.958			5250.029		
Number of estimated parameters	3			28			30			40			17		

Notes.

The chi-square statistics reported above are based on only units that had sufficient data for computation in each model. Fixed effects and variance components are based on all the data.

a: $p < 0.05$; b: $p < 0.01$; c: $p < 0.001$

With regard to H2 hypothesis that spatial characteristics consistently affect the determinants of class identification, the hypothesis is supported, because, in the 1995 data, the cross-level interaction effect between 'Income' and 'DIDs' is significant, as I reported in the previous study. Also in the 1975 data, there are the cross-level interaction effects as shown above. Therefore, both in 1975 and in 1995, spatial characteristics have significant effects on determinants of class identification. Thus, H2 hypothesis is supported.

However, there are different tendencies of region level variables between the two datasets. What does this mean? We think that the results reflect the difference in population change between the two time periods. After World War II, the rapid economic growth took place in Japan. It made many people migrate from rural areas to urban areas. As Figure 6.1 shows, the most intensive migration of population occurred in the 1960s and early 1970s. Table 6.3 shows that the mean of 'DIDs' increases and the mean and the standard deviation of 'PC' decrease from 1975 to 1995, meaning that the great migration of population had calmed down in 1995.

From this trend, it appears that the regions where many 'strangers' gather and reside are most represented by the rate of population change as flow in 1975 and by the densely inhabited districts as stock in 1995. In short, the results show that the effect of 'Income' as determinants

Figure 6.1: Intra-prefectural migrants and inter-prefectural migrants (1954–2002)

Figure created by Daisuke Kobayashi from the data of Sōmushō Tōkeikyoku (2004)

Table 6.3: Descriptive statistics of region-level variables at two time points

	1975	1995
DIDs		
Mean	56.3%	64.6%
Standard deviation	36.4%	35.2%
PC		
Mean	6.9%	1.4%
Standard deviation	13.3%	5.3%

of class identification is consistently stronger in the region occupied by immigrants. Why then did these tendencies appear in the region where demographic mobility is large?

Unfortunately, we can, at best, only propose some interpretations to answer this question for the moment. One possibility is that the 'rootless' mind of 'strangers' makes them eager to identify their own positions by some objective status, because of an absence of a clear standard of class among them. As many social theorists have argued, such as Veblen (1899), Whyte (1956), Baudrillard (1970), Bauman (1988), Giddens (1991), Beck (1992) and Warde (1994), the process of modernization freed people from traditional social relations, but ironically it simultaneously caused a problem of self-identity. In modernized countries, political and institutional equality is guaranteed for people in principle. Furthermore economic growth narrowed the economic gap between them. However, just the absence of difference causes the anxiety of identity. The theorists insisted that the anxiety of identity makes people compare themselves with others. In addition, some of them focused on the relation between urbanized space and self-identity (Veblen 1899; Whyte 1956).

From this point of view, the results obtained here could imply that the tendency to compare with others and to search for their identities is greater in the region where demographic mobility is greater.

Another possibility is that people who are freed from traditional social relations can do nothing but identify their position by the principles of achievement. If the immigrants tend to identify their classes by evaluating their own achievements such as income or occupation rather than ascriptions such as lineage, the results are consistent with this interpretation.

In any case, these interpretations are tentative and rough. Furthermore both interpretations imply that whether people immigrate or not can explain the tendencies obtained here. Therefore, we need to study further in order to answer this question and to elaborate these interpretations, taking another possibility[5] into consideration.

Still, it is certain that the study presented here suggests the probability that spatial characteristics would play an important role in identifying their class by a sophisticated method. If class consciousness essentially could not be understood only by the individual-level, this finding would urge us to reconsider the work of scholars who regard class consciousness as a random guess and as meaningless for class researchers. It is important to study spatial characteristics that intervene between objective class situation and subjective identification in order to explore the relation between inequality and various reactions such as political movement, citizens movement and consumption behavior in society.

Acknowledgement

The author would like to thank the SSM Research Committee for its permission to use the SSM datasets for the analysis. This study was, in part, supported by the Grants-in-aid for Scientific Research from the Ministry of Education, Culture, Sports, Science and Technology, Japan (No. 17730296).

7 Deterioration in Employment Practice and Career Images

Yoshimichi Sato

The analysis of career images in Japan

The Japanese employment practice that consists of the long-term employment practice and the seniority-based wage system has been weakening, thanks to a prolonged recession and the increasing exposure of the Japanese economy to globalization. A recent increase in part-time workers reflects this change (see Figure 7.1). As predicted by arguments about the gender-segregating labor market in Japan (Brinton 1993), the percentage of male part-time workers is lower than that of female part-time workers. However, it has been increasing since the mid-90s. The deterioration in the Japanese employment practice has also increased unemployment rates (see Figure 7.2). Although Japan once enjoyed a reputation as a country with low unemployment rates, the rates have steadily been increasing since 1997. In particular, the rate of the youth aged 15–19, most of whom are high school graduates, is very high.

Sato and Arita (2004) also point out an increase in fluidity in the Japanese labor market. Some indices of social mobility patterns, they argue, indicate that social mobility of the Japanese new middle class is getting closer to that of their Korean counterpart.[1] The Japanese new middle class, which comprises white-collar workers, is the major recipient of the Japanese employment practice. In contrast, the Korean new middle class does not enjoy the practice. Thus the convergence of social mobility patterns of the Japanese new middle class to that of their Korean counterpart is a symptom of the deterioration in the Japanese employment practice.

Although the practice has protected a certain portion of workers, that is, male college graduates working for large companies (Brinton 1993; Nomura 1994), being employed under this system has been considered to have achieved a position of desirable status in Japan. Companies with the practice, however, incur opportunity costs

Figure 7.1: Percentage of part-time workers

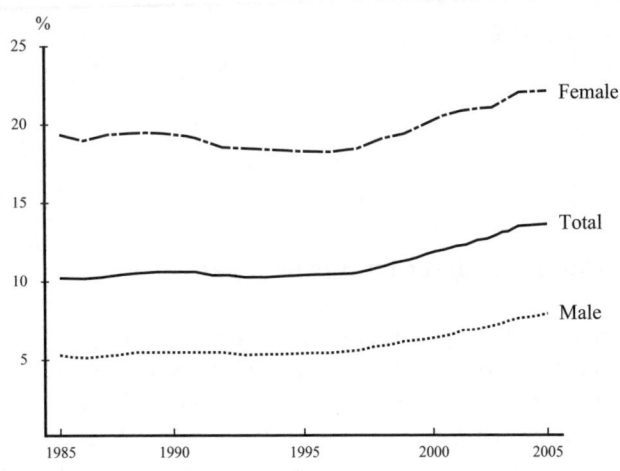

Source: The Labor Force Survey by the Ministry of Health, Labour and Welfare

because they miss opportunities for finding better workers at lower labor costs in the labor market. They were able to compensate for it while they enjoyed fruits of the high economic growth period. The prolonged recession since the burst of the bubble economy has made it prohibitive for the companies to maintain the practice.

Facing this radical change in the employment practice, workers seem to have changed their attitudes toward their career. They have voluntarily or involuntarily begun to think about their future careers. When the Japanese employment practice was strong, workers did not need to think about their careers once they got a job in a company with the practice. The internal career ladder was prepared for them, so what they had to do was simply climb it to the top. Competition with coworkers of the same cohort was severe, but the workers were able to find their positions in their company depending on their performance. In other words they were able to predict their future career in their company without thinking about the possibility of switching companies. Such predictions, however, are not possible under the weakening Japanese employment practice. Thus workers need to imagine their future careers including the possibility of switching companies.

With these changes in the Japanese employment practice and workers' attitudes toward their career as the motif, this chapter

Figure 7.2: Unemployment rates in Japan

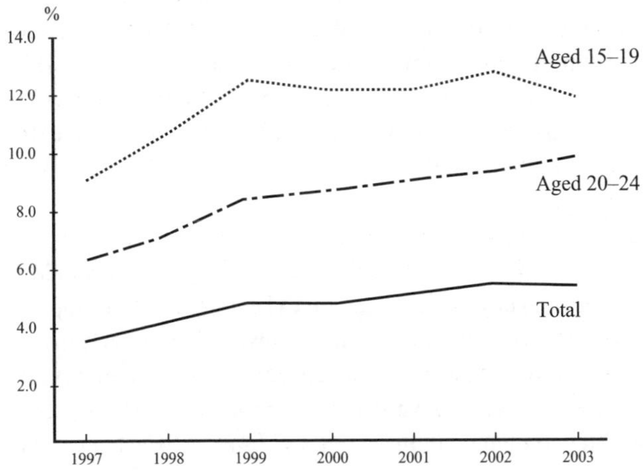

```
%
14.0
                                                          Aged 15–19
12.0
10.0
                                                          Aged 20–24
 8.0
 6.0
                                                          Total
 4.0
 2.0
     1997   1998   1999   2000   2001   2002   2003
```

Source: The Labor Force Survey by the Ministry of Health, Labour and Welfare

explores how Japanese workers develop images of their future career. As will be shown below, the long-term employment practice, which is a major component of the Japanese employment practice, is compared with three other career images. They are 'specialization,' 'income' and 'independence.' 'Specialization' means a work pattern of pursuing specialized skills rather than sticking to one company; 'income' means a work pattern of trying to maximize one's income; and 'independence' means a work pattern of being independent or self-employed. These three work patterns are in sharp contrast with the long-term employment. Thus exploring factors that affect people's choice of the three patterns is an important research question with which to understand their reaction to the weakening of the Japanese employment practice.

Theoretical arguments and hypotheses

The main task of this chapter is to explore the mechanism by which people create their career images and, particularly, to analyze the effect of factors that facilitate the deviation from the long-term employment practice. I would argue that three factors function in the mechanism. The first factor is the actual career that they have developed thus far. This factor must be the primary determinant of career images for two reasons. First, people have invested their time, energy and resources in their human capital to develop their career (Becker 1993). In addition, in the case of self-employed workers, social networks around them are important social capital through which they get know-how and information necessary for their business (Yu 2001). Thus a radical change in career would ruin such an investment in human and social capital. To avoid this waste of their capital, people would have the same career image as their actual career.

The second reason is that people have psychological inertia related to their career. Theories of backward-looking rationality (Macy and Willer 2002) and cognitive dissonance (Festinger 1957) support this. If they have succeeded in the labor market with their career, they will try to keep it and thus have the same career image as their actual career. If they have not, the backward-looking rationality theory predicts that they will try to change their career and have a different career image than their actual career. However, they have invested in their career, as pointed out above. Thus the self-justification mechanism is set off so that people with unsuccessful careers can attribute their failure in the labor market to factors other than their careers. As a result they tend to have the same career image as their actual career.

The above arguments lead us to the following hypothesis:

Hypothesis 1: People tend to have the same career image as their actual career.

The second factor in the creation of career image is people's positions in the labor market. Their positions reflect the possibility of changes in career because the possibility is affected by the structure of the labor market. I consider three variables that are the main characteristics of positions in the Japanese labor market: gender, employment status, and firm size. Female workers are more likely to be pushed toward the periphery of the labor market than their male counterparts. In particular, if a woman quits her full-time job in her mid-career, it is very difficult for her to return to the labor market as a full-time worker. Rather, what she can find is a part-time job with less job security. Thus women are less likely to think that they will be employed under the long-term employment practice. This argument is summarized as follows:

Hypothesis 2-1: Female workers are less likely to choose the long-term employment practice as their career image than their male counterparts.

Employment status is divided into four categories: Full-time workers, managers, part-time workers and self-employed workers. Full-time workers have been the main recipient of the Japanese employment practice, so they are more likely to stick to the long-term employment practice than workers in other categories. Part-time workers do not expect that they will work under the practice because of their unstable position in the labor market. In addition they have not accumulated specialized skills or know-how with which to become independent. Thus they must pursue maximization of their income. Managers and self-employed workers tend to expect independence as their career image because of their current position. Thus the hypotheses about the effect of employment status are as follows:

Hypothesis 2-2a: Part-time workers are more likely to choose income maximization than full-time workers.

Hypothesis 2-2b: Managers and self-employed workers are more likely to choose independence than full-time workers.

The effect of firm size is straightforward. Large firms and the public sector tend to have the long-term employment practice in themselves (Odaka 1984). Thus a hypothesis about the effect is as follows:

Hypothesis 2-3: Workers in large firms and the public sector are more likely to choose the long-term employment as their career image.

The third factor that is supposed to affect career images is education. Human capital theory argues that education is a type of human capital with which workers enhance their returns in the labor market (Becker 1993). Colleges in Japan, however, channel their graduates into large firms with the Japanese employment practice. This leads to the following hypothesis:

Hypothesis 3: College graduates are more likely to stick to the long-term employment than less educated workers.

We have discussed the sole effect of each factor on career images thus far. The factors, however, interact with each other. For example, most of self-employed workers are found in small firms. It is impossible to predict how the sole effect of an explanatory variable will change after controlling for other explanatory variables. However, the actual career, the first factor, must have the strongest explanatory power because of the two mechanisms mentioned above and null the effect of the second and the third factors. Thus the following hypothesis can be proposed:

> *Hypothesis 4*: The actual career nulls the effects of workers' positions in the labor market and their education on career image.

We test the empirical validity of these hypotheses with a data set collected in Japan in the following sections.

Data and methods

I analyze the *2003 National Survey on Work and Daily Life* data.[2] The survey was conducted in December, 2003 in Japan with a national representative sample aged 20–69. The designed sample size is 2,000, and the number of actual respondents is 1,154 (The response rate is 57.7%).

I use one dependent variable and five independent variables for analysis to test the empirical validity of the hypotheses proposed in the previous section. The dependent variable is the career images respondents have for their future. Respondents are shown the four following working patterns and asked to choose one out of the four as their ideal pattern if they continue to work:

A. Working for one company continuously until retirement, and being promoted through the experience of performing many types of work.

B. Not necessarily working for the same company for all of one's work life, but focusing instead on one type of work and becoming a specialist.

C. Not necessarily working for the same company for all of one's work life, but rather building one's career and increasing one's income by changing companies when good conditions present themselves.

D. Being independent and forming one's own company or becoming self-employed.

Henceforth the alternatives A, B, C and D are called 'long-term employment,' 'specialization,' 'income' and 'independence,' respectively. 'Long-term employment' is compared with other alternatives based on the argument in the previous section.

The five independent variables are respondents' recognition of their career, gender, employment status, firm size and education.[3] Respondents' recognition of their career is a substitute for actual careers of respondents because the survey did not ask respondents their actual career or job history. Respondents were asked to choose one of the above work patterns as the work pattern they have followed thus far. Employment status consists of four categories: Full-time workers, managers/owners, part-time workers and self-employed workers.[4] Firm size is divided into four categories: small size with 1–9 workers, mid-size with 10–499 workers, large-size with more than 499 workers and the public sector. Education is divided into four categories: Junior high school, high school, specialized training college and college (four-year colleges and junior colleges). Specialized training colleges are different from four-year colleges and junior colleges, and high school graduates who want to master specialized skills enroll in them.

The basic statistics of the variables are shown in Table 7.1.[5] There are two interesting findings in the table. First, as dual labor market theorists argue (Brinton 1993; Nomura 1994), the share of workers in the long-term employment is not very high – around 32% based on the distribution of respondents' recognition of their career. It is the case that some of the respondents who chose 'specialization' and 'income' are actually under the practice, but they subjectively identify themselves as workers not under the practice. Second, comparison between respondents' recognition of their career and their future career image shows that the share of the long-term employment practice decreases slightly, while those of specialization and independence increase. These changes reflect change in respondents' attitude toward their career caused by their increasing exposure to news about the deterioration in the Japanese employment practice, such as massive lay-offs of middle-aged white-collar workers. They think that they have to be more independent of their company, which does not offer job security, by acquiring market-competitive specialized skills and/or preparing for being independent.

Multinomial logit regression analysis is conducted to test the empirical validity of the hypotheses. The dependent variable is career image with 'long-term employment' as the baseline category. Independent variables are the five variables mentioned above. This modeling will reveal the mechanism that creates respondents' career images.

Results of the analysis

The first step of the analysis is to conduct single multinomial logit regression analyses with each independent variable to see their sole

Table 7.1: Basic statistics

Variable	Category	N	Percentage
Career image	Long-term employment	179	27.4
	Specialization	209	32.0
	Income	117	17.9
	Independence	149	22.8
Recognition of career	Long-term employment	202	31.9
	Specialization	183	28.9
	Income	135	21.3
	Independence	114	18.0
Gender	Male	391	56.1
	Female	306	43.9
Employment status	Managers	53	7.7
	Full-time workers	316	45.9
	Part-time workers	193	28.1
	Self-employed workers	126	18.3
Firm size	1–9	237	36.7
	10–499	266	41.2
	500–	107	16.6
	Public sector	36	5.6
Education	Junior high school	90	13.0
	High School	331	48.0
	Specialized training college	62	9.0
	College	207	30.0

Note. Respondents in the agricultural sector are excluded from calculation.

effect on career image. The results are summarized in Table 7.2. Recognition of career has perfectly predicted effects. Each category of it has a large, positive coefficient in the same category of career image. The explanatory power of the model, in addition, is very high, compared with other models in the table. These results support Hypothesis 1 in the second section.

Female workers are more likely to choose 'income' than male workers. This does not mean they are materialistic, of course. Forty-five percent of female workers are part-time workers, while only twelve percent of male workers are in the same category. They do not expect career development in the future, so it is expected that they will be interested in increasing income. The negative coefficient of female in the column of 'independence' reflects a similar mechanism. Female workers who are placed in the periphery of the labor market do

Table 7.2: Results of simple multinomial logit regression analysis

	Specialization	Income	Independence
Recognition of career			
Long-term employment	–	–	–
Specialization	3.02[a]	1.67[a]	2.78[a]
Income	1.38[a]	3.04[a]	2.55[a]
Independence	1.32[b]	2.06[a]	5.21[a]
Constant	−1.16[a]	−1.91[a]	−2.55[a]

$N = 616$; Log likelihood = -608.76736; Prob > chi2 = 0.0000; Pseudo R^2 = 0.2742

	Specialization	Income	Independence
Gender			
Male	–	–	–
Female	0.17	0.67[a]	−0.46[b]
Constant	0.08	−0.75[a]	−0.02

$N = 654$; Log likelihood = -881.80834; Prob > chi2 = 0.0001; Pseudo R^2 = 0.0115

	Specialization	Income	Independence
Employment status			
Full-time workers	–	–	–
Managers	0.92[c]	0.52	3.02[a]
Part-time workers	0.19	0.97[a]	0.56[c]
Self-employed workers	1.01[a]	−0.72	2.94[a]
Constant	−0.04	−0.75[a]	−1.30[a]

$N = 645$; Log likelihood = -792.4969; Prob > chi2 = 0.0000; Pseudo R^2 = 0.0995

	Specialization	Income	Independence
Firm size			
1-9	–	–	–
10-499	−0.42	−0.08	−1.66[a]
500-	−0.79[b]	−0.18	−2.10[a]
Public sector	−1.14[a]	−1.93[b]	−3.89[a]
Constant	0.59[a]	−0.33	0.95[a]

$N = 608$; Log likelihood = -782.47407; Prob > chi2 = 0.0000; Pseudo R^2 = 0.0530

	Specialization	Income	Independence
Education			
College	–	–	–
Junior high school	−0.14	0.74[c]	0.10
High School	−0.18	0.33	−0.24
Specialized training college	0.76[c]	−0.22	0.85[c]
Constant	0.19	−0.69[a]	−0.15

$N = 648$; Log likelihood = -872.82351; Prob > chi2 = 0.0077; Pseudo R^2 = 0.0127

Notes.
Respondents in the agricultural sector are excluded from calculation.
a: $p < 0.01$; b: $p < 0.05$; c: $p < 0.10$

not have enough human, financial and social capital with which to set up their own business. No effect of female workers on 'specialization' implies the same mechanism. Thus Hypothesis 2-1 is supported when 'income' is compared with 'long-term employment,' but their limited capital caused by their location in the labor market does not lead female workers to 'specialization' or 'independence.'

On the third panel of the table part-time workers show a predicted pattern: their coefficient is positive and statistically significant when 'income' is compared with 'long-term employment.' This is a result of the same reason as identified for female workers, and Hypothesis 2-2a is supported. The positive coefficients of managers and self-employed workers in the 'independence' column support Hypothesis 2-2b. The positive coefficient of self-employed workers in the 'specialization' column was not stated as a hypothesis but understandable. Becoming self-employed needs specialized skills for business unless self-employed workers inherited their business from their parents. Thus they choose 'specialization' as well as 'independence' when these alternatives are compared with 'long-term employment.'

The fourth panel shows that firm size has an effect predicted by Hypothesis 2-3. The larger their firm size becomes, the more firmly workers stick to the long-term employment. In addition workers in the public sector are more likely to prefer 'long-term employment' to 'income' than workers in the private sector. This is because the public sector in Japan is the stronghold of the Japanese employment practice.

Education does not have a clear effect on career image. However, graduates of specialized training colleges show different patterns than college graduates do. Although they are not statistically significant at the 5% significance level, their coefficients in the 'specialization' and the 'independence' columns are very high. This means that graduates of specialized training colleges are more conscious about using their specialized skills or becoming independent with those skills than college graduates. There are two possible explanations for this. The first possibility is that those who plan to succeed in the labor market with specialized skills are more likely to go to specialized training colleges. The second possibility is that graduating from specialized training colleges makes their graduates conscious about skills they acquired in school. Junior high school graduates, on the other hand, are more likely to choose 'income' than college graduates are at the 10% significance level. This stems from the same mechanism as for female workers. Junior high school graduates are located in the periphery of the labor market and do not have high human capital such as specialized skills and financial capital. Therefore they tend to choose 'income' when compared with 'long-term employment.' Thus I would argue that these results weakly support Hypothesis 3.

The results of the single multinomial logit regression analyses basically support the hypotheses. Some independent variables, however, are correlated as suggested in the discussion about the effect of gender and employment status. Thus I included all the independent variables in multinomial logit regression analysis to see the effect of each independent variable after controlling for effects of other independent variables. I conducted the analysis with two models. The first model has all the independent variables except for recognition of career, and the second one adds this variable to the first model to see the empirical validity of Hypothesis 4.

The results are shown in Table 7.3. As is obvious in the table, when recognition of career is added to model 1, effects of other independent variables disappear in the 'specialization' and 'income' columns. This supports Hypothesis 4. In the 'independence' column, however, gender, employment status and education have effects on career image. The coefficient of female is negative and statistically significant at the 10% significance level. The strong effects of managers and self-employed workers, which are found in the single multinomial logit regression model, remain after controlling for the effect of recognition of career. Effect of education is unpredicted and interesting. The coefficients of junior high school and high school are negative and statistically significant at the 10% significance level, but the positive coefficient of specialized training college is not significant. This means that lower educated workers are less likely to choose 'independence.'

This configuration of the coefficients in the 'independence' column is worth exploring, because it implies the importance of human and social capital when people become independent or self-employed. It is clear why managers and self-employed workers are more likely to choose 'independence' as their career image. They have skills and knowledge with which to do independent business. Education also increases the human capital necessary for independence. Graduates of specialized training colleges have specialized skills, while college graduates have general cognitive skills. College degrees are not a good certificate when one runs his/her own business, but college education enhances general cognitive skills, which is also necessary for independence. Then why are female workers less likely to choose

Table 7.3: Results of multinomial logit regression analysis

	Specialization		Income		Independence	
	Model 1	Model 2	Model 1	Model 2	Model 1	Model 2
Gender						
Male	–	–	–	–	–	–
Female	0.03	−0.14	0.50[c]	0.14	−0.65[b]	−0.71[c]
Employment status						
Full-time workers	–	–	–	–	–	–
Managers	0.68	0.84	0.25	0.44	2.64[a]	2.10[a]
Part-time workers	0.12	0.07	0.52	0.25	0.66[c]	0.52
Self-employed workers	0.77[c]	0.87	−1.25[c]	−0.98	2.50[a]	1.70[a]
Firm Size						
1-9	–	–	–	–	–	–
10-499	−0.10	0.48	−0.39	−0.11	−0.36	−0.01
500-	−0.40	−0.01	−0.18	0.26	−0.66	0.04
Public sector	−0.70	0.50	−1.89[b]	−1.16	−2.29[b]	−0.85
Education						
College	–	–	–	–	–	–
Junior high school	−0.18	−0.50	0.53	0.10	−0.47	−1.15[c]
High school	−0.16	−0.30	0.16	−0.20	−0.47	−0.75[c]
Specialized training college	0.83[c]	0.53	−0.37	−0.66	0.90[c]	0.64
Recognition of career						
Long-term employment		–		–		–
Specialization		2.92[a]		1.51[a]		2.51[a]
Income		1.27[a]		2.84[a]		2.61[a]
Independence		1.40[b]		2.32[a]		4.95[a]
Constant	0.20	−1.30[a]	−0.65	−1.79[a]	−0.42	−2.31[a]

Notes.
Respondents in the agricultural sector are excluded from calculation.

a: $p < 0.01$; b: $p < 0.05$; c: $p < 0.10$

Model 1: $N = 594$; Log likelihood = −706.31808; Prob > chi2 = 0.0000; Pseudo R^2 = 0.1251

Model 2: $N = 560$; Log likelihood = −517.51163; Prob > chi2 = 0.0000; Pseudo R^2 = 0.3183

'independence'? This is because the mechanism mentioned above functions. That is, female workers are pushed to the periphery of the labor market, so they do not have opportunities to accumulate the skills, knowledge and social capital necessary for independence.

Conclusion

Although it has been reported by mass media almost everyday, the weakening of the Japanese employment practice, based on the above analysis, has different effects on workers with different human capital and in different positions in the labor market. This finding rejects a rough argument that the deterioration in the Japanese employment practice would throw all the Japanese workers into severe competition for scarce job security. Rather the results of the analysis encourage us to study subtle differences among the various types of worker.

In addition, the 'independence' column in Table 7.3 has an important implication for social policy. Facing the weakening of the Japanese employment practice, many Japanese commentators and writers have been publishing books that encourage readers to become independent. It would be wonderful to become independent and succeed in business. The analysis of this chapter, however, points out that becoming independent depends on one's position in the labor market and human capital. Changing one's position in the market would be very difficult, but enhancing one's human capital via education would be feasible. Thus establishing educational programs that offer specialized skills and know-how necessary for becoming independent is a critical policy target of the Japanese government and local governments.

8 Long-term Trends in Status Homogamy
Satoshi Miwa

Introduction

Status homogamy has been studied as an indicator of the 'openness' or 'closedness' of social stratification (e.g. Glass 1954; Blau and Duncan 1967). Apart from those classic studies in the area, Wright (1997) also analyzes homogamy from the Neo-Marxist point of view, calling it 'class permeability.' If members of similar status groups in a society marry among themselves, it reflects a tendency towards the self-perpetuation of those status groups, and the society can be seen to have strict status divisions. The resulting implications vary according to which status-related factors are used and how they are combined. The often-used factors are occupation and education. When marriages are analyzed using the husband's and wife's fathers' occupations, it is called homogamy of social origin. Likewise, when the couple's current status is used, such as the husband's and wife's occupations or their educational levels, it is known as attainment-oriented homogamy (Watanabe and Kondo 1990).

Among those categories of homogamy, educational homogamy, a form of attainment-oriented homogamy, has been studied most extensively. There are a number of reasons for this. From a theoretical point of view, an individual's educational level is closely related to his/her social status and sense of values. We know that the level of education tends to determine one's job and future income, and that it influences one's range of knowledge and cultural preference. This makes it a key indicator of the social status of an individual. Empirically, too, a tighter tendency of homogamy is often observed with the educational factor than other factors such as social background or current occupation (Kalmijn 1998).

On the other hand, social background is perhaps the most relevant indicator of the openness of a society. The study of social mobility focuses on the generational procreation of social classes because the social background is predetermined and thus beyond the control of the individual; therefore one may argue that homogamy of social origin most closely reflects the closedness of social stratification system. Educational homogamy, in contrast, indicates that the status of the spouses is similar: it is understandable that educational level plays a stronger role in choosing a spouse than social origin. However, for the purpose of measuring status boundaries that are beyond the control of the individual, educational homogamy is not always suitable. Thus one needs to consider the spouses' educational level, which indicates the individual achievement, as well as their family background, which is a predetermined factor that reflects the closedness of status groups (Kalmijn 1991).

Based on these arguments, this chapter examines the patterns and the trends of homogamy of social origin and educational homogamy in Japan in order to understand the openness/closedness of its social stratification. It thus intends to show the degree of openness of present Japanese society through the study of homogamy.

Previous research and problems

Patterns of status homogamy

Previous studies have found that the spouses' own status plays a more important role than family background in selecting marriage partners (Kalmijn 1991; Uunk *et al.* 1996). Furthermore, it has been observed that similarity in educational attainment is usually a stronger factor for the choice of a spouse than occupation. Empirical results in Japan also supported these findings (Watanabe and Kondo 1990; Shida *et al.* 2000). The importance of educational attainment in partner selection implies that barriers in marriage tend to be socio-cultural rather than economic. One study of occupational homogamy shows that the cultural status of occupation, rather than the income associated with it, is a prevailing factor in marriage (Kalmijn 1994). This supports the view, if indirectly, that status homogamy can be seen as cultural barrier in society.

In-marriage (or endogamy) is usually more common among the highest and the lowest in social stratification. This is observed in terms of not only the social background and educational level of the spouses but also the association between the spouses' occupations (Hout 1982). The most prominent feature of homogamy of social origin is that the in-marriage rate is particularly high within the agricultural sector. Japanese empirical data also support this (Watanabe 1998; Shida *et al.* 2000). Kalmijn (1998) considers that this is because the agricultural communities are often geographically and socially isolated from the rest of society. Another prominent feature is that graduates of higher education are most likely to marry among themselves (Mare 1991): one may surmise, then, that the marriage market is divided by educational achievement.

Another feature of social barriers is that, with both the family background and achieved status of the spouses, a gap exists between the 'blue-collar' and 'white-collar' groups (Hout 1982; Kalmijn 1991). As often pointed out in the study of social mobility, there are similarities between some different social strata, which form a 'bloc.' This is also the case in homogamy. That is, the 'white-collar bloc' and 'blue-collar bloc' seem to exist in homogamy, too.

One would notice that covariation exists between educational homogamy and homogamy of social origin. Spouses with similarly high (low) educational achievements usually have both come from high (low) socio-economic backgrounds. It is also a well-known fact that the family origin and educational achievement are strongly related (e.g. Shavit and Blossfeld 1993). These facts mean that homogamy of social origin has elements that are dependent on educational homogamy, while part of educational homogamy is influenced by the strength of homogamy of social origin. Due to this covariation, one needs to consider the two forms of homogamy simultaneously to analyze them accurately.

A model that incorporates plural positions is called the by-product hypothesis. The origin of this model can be traced to a study by Kennedy (1944), in which he showed that homogamy among ethnic groups partly overlaps with religious homogamy. Warren (1966) applied this model to the study of educational and social background homogamy. In so doing, Warren showed that a significant part of the homogamy of social origin originates in educational homogamy. His finding has since been supported by a number of scholars (Kalmijn 1991; Uunk *et al.* 1996). Japanese scholars, however, have repeatedly claimed that in Japan the extent that homogamy of social background is mediated by educational homogamy is not as substantial as that found by Kalmijn and Uunk *et al.* (Watanabe and Kondo 1990; Shida *et al.* 2000).

Trends in status homogamy

Empirical studies of status homogamy show that homogamy of social origin and educational homogamy have different trends. Many have observed that homogamy of social origin has declined over time. For example, Kalmijn (1991) showed using OCG data that homogamy of social origin has weakened. Also, studies by Uunk *et al.* (1996) for Hungary, Forse and Chauvel (1995) for France, Bihagen and Hallerod (2000) for Sweden and Shida *et al.* (2000) for Japan support this view. An exception is a study by Watanabe and Kondo (1990), which claims that homogamy of social origin in Japan has not shown a marked decline. Thus in Japan the trend is not conclusive.

In regards to trends in educational homogamy, on the other hand, it seems that no consensus has been formed. The current mainstream argument is that educational homogamy has strengthened over time. In Europe, systematic comparative studies largely conform to this trend (Blossfeld and Timm 2003). Other studies that support this position include studies in the U.S. by Mare (1991) and Kalmijn (1991), a study in Ireland (Halpin and Chan 2003) and another in Hungary (Uunk *et al.* 1996). Other scholars, however, claim that the strength of educational homogamy has not changed over time (Forse and Chauvel 1995; Jones 1987). The confusion is reflected in the comparative study of national trends by Ultee and Luijkx (1990). According to Ultee and Luijkx, some countries have seen a strengthening trend in educational homogamy while others have remained unchanged. Some countries even show declining trends. In other words, one cannot determine a trend in any general direction. Studies of Japanese trends are also inconclusive: While Shida *et al.* (2000) stress that no change has been observed in educational homogamy, Raymo and Xie (2000) claim it declined from the 1970s to the 1980s.

With this background, recent years have seen an increase in comparative international trend studies (Smits *et al.* 1998; Raymo and Xie 2000; Smits *et al.* 2000; Prandy and Jones 2001; Smits 2003; Blossfeld and Timm 2003). These studies attempt to explain the diversity in the degree of and trends in educational homogamy in different countries by introducing variables such as religion and the degree of technological development. Among them, the study of the correlation between industrial/economic development and homogamy needs attention. Some conflicting hypotheses have been formulated in this area (Smits 2003).

First, the status attainment hypothesis claims that as industrialization progresses, educational homogamy strengthens. Second, the general openness hypothesis holds that industrialization weakens all status-related factors, including education, in marriages. It thus predicts that educational homogamy also declines. Third, another hypothesis proposes that educational homogamy strengthens itself in the early stage of industrialization but weakens with its further growth. Finally, the saturation hypothesis holds that educational homogamy declines until the openness of a society reaches a certain level, when the decline ceases and remains constant. These hypotheses all provide a valuable basis for the present study, which attempts to probe the association between openness of a society and the degree of industrialization.

Research questions

As seen above, in Japan, studies on status homogamy have been accumulating, but there are several problems which are to be re-examined.

Firstly, the pattern of homogamy in terms of off-diagonal cell frequencies has not been adequately addressed. This problem concerns the analysis methods used, such as coefficient of openness and odds ratio. This is because, fundamentally, they are just a means of capturing association on diagonal cells. Secondly, the previous studies do not deal directly with the by-product hypothesis. As covariation exists between homogamy of social origin and educational homogamy, we need to control for the effect of one form of homogamy to extract the net effect of the other form of homogamy. Thus some analytical problems must be solved to study the patterns of homogamy properly.

There are some other issues related to the re-examination of homogamy trends. The third problem is that the size of the sample data is not large enough to present reliable results; subtle differences may have been overlooked due to lack of statistical power. Fourth, past examinations have been limited to short periods, thus a long-term trend has not been obtained. Fifth, previous studies have not arrived at a consensus in terms of trends in homogamy of social origin: Watanabe and Kondo (1990) concluded as 'unchanged' while Shida et al. (2000) claimed 'declined.' The validity of either position has been inconclusive. And lastly, in regards to the correlation between industrialization and homogamy trends, no serious efforts have been made to check the empirical validity of the theoretical hypotheses. We must precisely examine their theoretical implications because the purpose of this chapter is to explore the openness of society from the aspect of homogamy.

To this end, I will deal with methodological issues and then pursue more reliable findings. The questions posed for this purpose are:

1. To describe the patterns of homogamy of social origin and educational homogamy
2. To extract pure effects of homogamy of social origin and educational homogamy
3. To re-evaluate the two conflicting results of previous studies on trends in homogamy of social origin and educational homogamy and determine which is more representative of the reality
4. To compare and examine which hypothesis best explains the homogamy trend in Japan

Data and methods

Data

The data used in this chapter are taken from the Social Stratification and Social Mobility Survey (SSM Survey).[1] This survey is known to provide the most reliable information for research on social stratification in Japan. As the survey has been conducted every ten years since 1955, it is suitable for analysis of various trends and cohort comparisons.

In the following, I will use the SSM data of the years of 1965, 1985 and 1995 because they can supply the following five variables: the year of marriage, occupation of the husband's father, occupation of the wife's father, the husband's education and the wife's education.[2] After merging all the data of the three research years and dividing it by marriage cohort, I will analyze trends in homogamy. Table 8.1 shows the sample sizes for each cohort.

Variables

For father's occupation, I have used the five categories shown in Table 8.2.[3] A previous study has established that the pattern of homogamy of social origin within the 'self-employed' group is not different from those within other occupational categories in Japan (Watanabe and Kondo 1990). Therefore I did not use it as an independent category. I also divided the educational qualification into three categories according to the highest-attained educational level: 'Low' indicates the modern compulsory education (junior high school [*chūgakkō*]) and its equivalent in the pre-war system (common primary [*jinjō shōgakkō*] and high primary schools [*kōtō shōgakkō*]); 'Middle' indicates high school [*kōtōgakkō*] and its old equivalent (old junior high [*kyūsei*

Table 8.1: Sample size by cohort

Marriage cohort	N
1920–39	383
1940–49	692
1950–59	1223
1960–69	1332
1970–79	986
1980–95	684

Table 8.2: Categories of father's occupation and educational level

Categories	Examples
Father's occupation	
Upper Non-manual	Professionals, Managers
Lower Non-manual	Clerical workers, Salespersons
Upper Manual	Craftsmen, Foremen
Lower Manual	Operatives, Laborers
Farm	Farmers, Agricultural laborers
Education	
High	University, Junior College
Middle	High school
Low	Junior High school

chūgaku] and girls' high schools [kōtō jogakkō], vocational school [jitsugyō gakkō] and teachers' school [shihan gakkō]); and 'High' indicates higher education.

Model

In order to examine the by-product hypothesis, I will use the multivariate model shown in Figure 8.1. We are interested in patterns and trends of homogamy of social origin (arrow A) and educational homogamy (arrow B). The vertical arrows C_1 and C_2 indicate the influence of the couples' father's occupation on their educational level. All the arrows are expected to have positive association. Therefore, in order to accurately measure the strength of and changes in homogamy of social origin, it is necessary to consider educational homogamy and vice versa.

Figure 8.1: Multivariate model of status homogamy

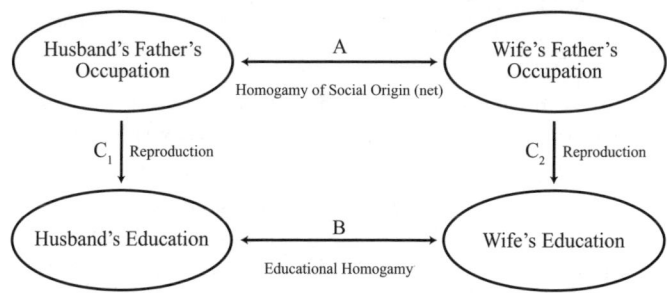

Methods of analysis

Loglinear model is used for analysis: this method explains logarithmic values of expected frequencies of each cell by various interaction effects in a linear form. This enables us to decompose total amount of effects to the influence of marginal frequencies and net relationship between variables involved.[4] I will consider multiple patterns of two-variable association using design matrices and examine both homogamy of social origin and educational homogamy.[5]

To capture trends in homogamy, I used the Uniform Difference Model developed by Xie (1992) to compare the degree of association between multiple cross tabulations. For example, to analyze the difference in association between the husband's social position (H) and that of the wife (W) between the marriage cohorts (C), the following model is used:

$$\log_e F_{ijk} = \lambda + \lambda_i^H + \lambda_j^W + \lambda_k^C + \lambda_{ik}^{HC} + \lambda_{jk}^{WC} + \lambda_{ij}^{HW} \times \Phi_k^C$$

This model only differs from the normal loglinear model in that λ^{HW} (the parameter representing the association between the couple's status) is multiplied by the Unidiff parameter Φ^C: the Uniform Difference Model supposes that the relative pattern of association between the spouses' status is the same in all cohorts, but the strength of association differs among cohorts. The larger the value of Φ^C, the stronger the association between the spouses' status; that is, the stronger the homogamy tendency.

In recent years this model has been applied to trend studies (e.g. Breen 2004). To examine a linear trend, one can add the following condition to the Unidiff parameter. Note that X represents the actual figure of marriage cohort:

$$\Phi_k^C = 1 + \beta X$$

If we make a linear adjustment so that the base year of the marriage cohort is 0, the Unidiff parameter at the base year is fixed as 1, and then the model shows that the Unidiff parameter makes a straight line. Where X changes by one unit, the parameter changes by β. For example, let us assume that X changes in the unit of 10 years, and the estimated value of β is 0.05. This means that the strength of association indicated by the Unidiff parameter increases by 5% as the cohort becomes younger by 10 years.

Furthermore, this model can also accommodate a quadratic curve by expanding the conditions as follows. This model is well suited to testing the hypothesis that educational homogamy is strengthened in the early stage of industrialization but weakens in the later stage:

$$\Phi_k^C = 1 + \beta_1 X + \beta_2 X^2$$

Analysis

It is important to distinguish absolute homogamy and relative homogamy conceptually before conducting the actual analysis. Absolute homogamy denotes observable practice that can be measured as, say, in-marriage rate: it is indicative of what is really happening. Relative homogamy, on the other hand, is a latent homogamy tendency, which can be captured by means of loglinear model, in which the influence of marginal frequencies has been controlled for: it is suitable for comparing the degree of homogamy relatively because net association between two variables can be extracted. They both represent different aspects of a social phenomenon, so I will show results for both.

Absolute homogamy

Let us begin with computing two in-marriage rates for Japan.[6] They are calculated as follows:

Total in-marriage rate = $\Sigma n_{ii} / N$

Origin-specific in-marriage rate = $n_{ii} / (\Sigma n_{i.} + \Sigma n_{.i} - n_{ii})$

Figure 8.2: Absolute in-marriage rates in Japan

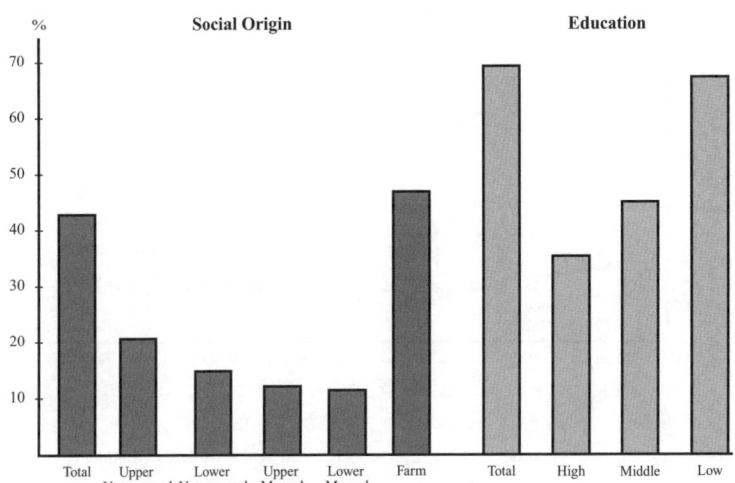

The left side of Figure 8.2 shows the in-marriage rate by social origin in Japan. The figure indicates that the overall in-marriage rate is about 40%, and that the farming sector has a far higher rate of endogamy than any other social groups. The overall rate is pushed to the high level because the in-marriage rate in the farming sector, as mentioned, is high and the share of the sector was large in parents' generation.

Education shows a higher in-marriage rate than the status origin (see the right side of Figure 8.2).[7] Almost two thirds of all marriages are between those at similar educational levels, and the in-marriage rate is higher among those with lower levels of education. These absolute homogamy rates do not show a high rate of in-marriage between those at higher educational level.

Let us look at the trends in in-marriages by analyzing in-marriage rates by cohort. Figure 8.3 shows the temporal changes in the in-marriage rate by father's occupation. They indicate that the overall rate has declined. The decline is not common to all the social status groups, but most prominently in the farming sector. Thus the sharp decline in in-marriage rate in the farming sector seems to have pushed down the overall rate.

Figure 8.4 shows the temporal changes in in-marriage rates by educational level. It is clear that the rate at the low educational level has shown a significant decline, while the rate at the higher educational

Figure 8.3: In-marriage trend by father's occupation

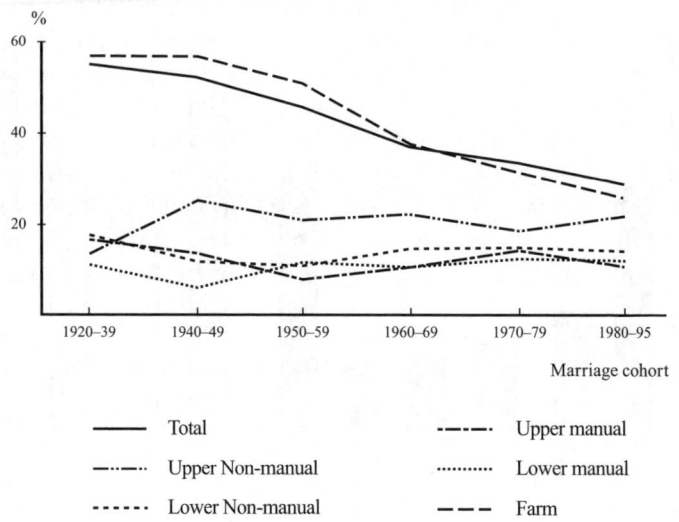

Figure 8.4: In-marriage trend by educational level

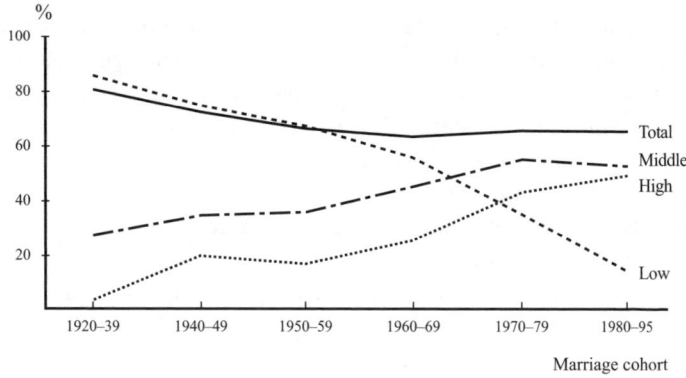

level has slowly increased. It is likely that changes in the marginal distribution of educational levels have played a significant part in these results. The overall in-marriage rate was at almost 80% in the pre-war period and has been flat at about 60% since 1950. This is because the decreasing trend in educational homogamy of the low educational level has been offset by the increasing trend in those of the middle or high educational level.

Patterns of relative homogamy

I analyze relative homogamy using loglinear models in this subsection. Table 8.3 shows the fit indices for various models of homogamy pattern[8]. Let us begin with homogamy of social origin. Starting with model 1, the so-called 'independence' model, I have added/extracted effects to find a model with good fit. In models 2, 3 and 4 the diagonal cells (the husband's father's status is identical to that of the wife's father) are specified. Clearly, model 2 is a better fit than 1, and model 3 better than 2. This means that the paternal statuses of the husband and wife are not independent, and that the diagonal effect varies according to different social origins. In other words, the extent of homogamy is stronger in some social status groups than others. However, it is not different in all groups: rather, it is different only in the upper white-collar and farming sectors. This pattern is assumed in model 4. This model implies that the degree of homogamy of the three groups except for the upper white-collar and farming have similar strength. Furthermore, statistically, this model is preferable to model 3 because the former is simpler than the latter, although both of them have the same goodness of fit.

In the goodness-of-fit test of the likelihood ratio, however, model 4 is significant at a level of 10%, which is not necessarily a good fit. This indicates that off-diagonal cells have some effects. Thus, based on model 4, I have attempted to specify patterns on off-diagonal cells in models 5, 6 and 7. Model 5 is called the 'corner model': it assumes different effects of four off-diagonal cells – upper non-manual/lower non-manual, lower non-manual/ upper non-manual, lower manual/ farming and farming/ lower manual. (A/B means that A is the husband's father's occupation and B is the wife's father's occupation.) Although this model has a better fitness than model 4, there is no difference in the goodness of fit between models 5, 6 and 7. As a result, model 7 was selected as the most favourable in the test of difference in the likelihood ratio as well as BIC.[9]

Model 7 sets only one effect in the off-diagonal section: the symmetrical effect between upper non-manual and lower non-manual groups. This parameter suggests that within the white-collar category there is a certain closed range of family relationships through marriage. In other words, the 'white-collar bloc' exists in marriages as well as in other aspects of society.

Table 8.3 also shows three models for educational homogamy. As this is a 3 by 3 table, the number of effects to be specified is limited.

Table 8.3: Fitting statistics for the homogamy pattern

		df	G^2	p-value	BIC
Origin					
1	Independence	16	358.9	.000	235.0
2	1 + D	15	84.0	.000	−32.1
3	1 + D_i	11	20.0	.045	−65.1
4	2 + D_1, D_5	13	21.6	.061	−79.0
5	4 + Corner	9	3.7	.932	−66.0
6	4 + C_{12}, C_{21}	11	4.5	.955	−80.7
7	4 + C_{12} ($C_{12} = C_{21}$)	12	4.5	.973	−88.4
Education					
1	Independence	4	1277.5	.000	1246.5
2	1 + D	3	311.1	.000	287.9
3	1 + D_1, D_3, C_{13} ($C_{13} = C_{31}$)	1	0.2	.693	−7.6

Model 3 provides independent diagonal effects on the groups of higher education group and lower educated group: it also assumes that a large educational gap between spouses (i.e., where the husband is highly educated while wife is not, and where the wife is highly educated while the husband is not) has a negative effect in marriages. I consider this as the final model for educational homogamy.

Now let us examine the empirical validity of the by-product hypothesis. Table 8.4 shows parameter estimates for bivariate and multivariate models. Design matrices are applied to model 7 for the social origins and model 3 for educational attainment of the spouses, the two models found to be the best fit for our purpose. The results show that, within the social status groups, when the education factor is excluded, in-marriage is strongest among the upper non-manual sector, followed by the farming sector. Surprisingly, intermarriage between the high and low non-manual sectors is slightly stronger than in-marriage within the middle sectors. This clearly indicates that one needs to look into off-diagonal cells.

When the influence of educational level is introduced, the order of in-marriage strength changes: it becomes strongest in the farming sector, followed by the upper non-manual sector, then other sectors, and lastly the effect of the off-diagonal corners. In other words, the coefficients of the corner effect and upper non-manual in-marriage effect decreased due to taking educational homogamy into account. In these, approximately 40–50% of association in the bivariate model disappears when educational homogamy is introduced. This suggests

Table 8.4: Parameter estimates in bivariate and multivariate models

	Bivariate model		Multivariate model		
	B	s.e.	B	s.e.	B_{multi}/B_{bi}
Origin					
Upper Non-manual	1.400	(0.159)	0.874	(0.165)	62%
Lower Non-manual	0.308	(0.086)	0.312	(0.087)	101%
Upper Manual	0.308	(0.086)	0.312	(0.087)	101%
Lower Manual	0.308	(0.086)	0.312	(0.087)	101%
Farm	1.182	(0.096)	0.960	(0.099)	81%
Corner (C_{12})	0.494	(0.117)	0.270	(0.119)	55%
Education					
High	1.786	(0.157)	1.721	(0.158)	96%
Low	2.525	(0.116)	2.434	(0.117)	96%
Distance (C_{13})	−1.214	(0.197)	−1.156	(0.198)	95%

that part of the homogamy of social origin can be explained in terms of educational homogamy. Furthermore, it proves, if only partly, that the by-product hypothesis can be applied to Japan. Having said that, no other effects show significant decrease. Also, the coefficients of the corner effect and the upper non-manual in-marriage effect are still statistically significant, although they become smaller. One can conclude, therefore, that homogamy of social origin has latent patterns that are independent of educational homogamy.

The parameter estimates for educational homogamy, on the other hand, remain almost unchanged in both bivariate and multivariate models. This is probably because educational homogamy has stronger association than homogamy of social origin has. The degree of homogamy of social origin is not very high, and the association between social origin and educational attainment is far from perfect. Therefore, their indirect effects on educational homogamy are very weak.

Trend in relative homogamy

Table 8.5 compares four models on trends in homogamy of social origin and educational homogamy. No constraints such as design matrices have been imposed upon the association of homogamy. As for the homogamy of social origin, model 1, which is a good fit, indicates that in all marriages between the 1920s and 1990s the strength of homogamy remains the same. When checked using

Table 8.5: Fitting statistics for the homogamy trends

	df	G²	p-value
Origin			
1 Constant	80	84.3	.348
2 Unidiff	75	73.9	.514
3 Linear	79	77.7	.520
4 Curvilinear	78	77.2	.503
1 vs 2	5	10.4	.064
1 vs 3	1	6.6	.010
2 vs 3	4	3.8	.431
3 vs 4	1	0.5	.496
Education			
1 Constant	20	29.1	.085
2 Unidiff	15	22.5	.097
3 Linear	19	24.5	.177
4 Curvilinear	18	23.9	.157
1 vs 2	5	6.7	.247
1 vs 3	1	4.6	.032
2 vs 3	4	2.1	.724
3 vs 4	1	0.6	.448

BIC, models 1 and 3 are relatively good. When the likelihood ratio difference is tested, it becomes clear that model 3, by estimating a new parameter, greatly improves the fit of model 1. Furthermore, even when compared to more complex models 4 (in which a quadratic curve in trend is assumed) and 2 (in which an independent parameter is assigned to each marriage cohort), model 3 does not show a significant difference in fitness. It can be assumed, therefore, that the trend in homogamy of social origin has formed a straight line.

A similar result is obtained for the educational homogamy trend. Here, too, model 3 is selected. This means that, contrary to the previous studies on the trends in the strength of educational homogamy in Japan, which has tended to stress its steadiness (Shida et al. 2000), this study has recognized a linear change.[10]

Figures 8.5 and 8.6 give graphic representations of the changes. They show the Unidiff parameters for the homogamy of social origin and educational homogamy in Japan respectively. The plots indicate the estimated values derived from models 2, 3 and 4 in Table 8.5; that is, the Unidiff parameter estimates for each cohort and the estimates when linear and curvilinear changes are imposed. Of the two forms

Figure 8.5: Bivariate trends in UNIDIFF parameter for homogamy of social origin

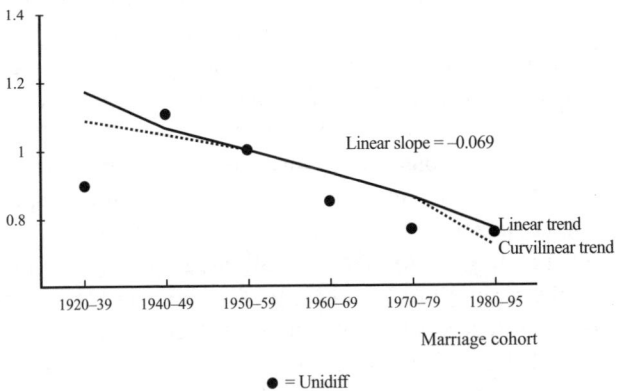

Figure 8.6: Bivariate trends in UNIDIFF parameter for educational homogamy

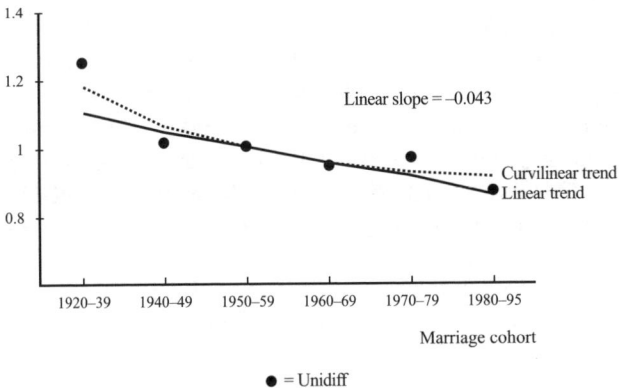

of homogamy, homogamy of social origin shows a clearer decreasing trend: except for the earliest marriage cohort,[11] the declining trend forms an almost straight line. Since the 1950s, the Unidiff parameter (strength of homogamy of social origin) has constantly decreased by about 7% per decade. The trend slope in educational homogamy is a little less steep at about 4% per decade. In sum, both forms of homogamy show slow, linear decreasing trends.

I have also verified the trends using multivariate models as shown in Table 8.6.[12] Model 1 assumes that the strength of both forms of homogamy has been steady over time; model 2 assumes a linear slope only in educational homogamy; and model 3 assumes a linear slope in both. When the goodness-of-fit test among the three models is conducted, significant differences can be observed between models 1 and 2, and models 1 and 3. It is reasonable to think, therefore, that some changes have occurred in the strength of homogamy. As there is no difference in the goodness of fit between models 2 and 3, one can claim that only educational homogamy saw changes during the period concerned.[13] More concretely, we have discovered a slow, linear trend in educational homogamy.

The test result using the multivariate model did not support the view that the strength of homogamy of social origin has changed (See Table 8.6). It seems that, although the degree of change itself is greater than that of educational homogamy, its strength of association is not strong originally, and, as a result, inclusion of linear trend in the model did not improve the fit of the model as a whole. Therefore, whether the net effect regarding homogamy of social origin has in fact decreased or not is difficult to judge.

Table 8.6 also shows the best-fit slopes for the trend lines in the multivariate model. Because the declining trends in the two forms of homogamy overlap to a certain degree, the absolute values of the slopes in this model are smaller than those in the bivariate model. The decreasing trend of homogamy of social origin was about 7% per decade in the bivariate model, but in model 3 with multivariable it is 5%. This implies that the decline in homogamy of social origin has partly been affected by the decrease in educational homogamy.

Table 8.6: Fitting and slopes for multivariate trend models

	df	G^2	*p*-value
1 Constant	1236	1193.5	.803
2 Linear trend for educational homogamy	1235	1189.6	.819
3 Linear trend for both types of homogamy	1234	1187.4	.825
1 vs 2	1	3.9	.048
2 vs 3	1	2.1	.145
1 vs 3	2	6.0	.049

		Multivariate	
Linear Slope	**Bivariate**	Model 2	Model 3
Origin	−0.069	0.000	−0.050
Education	−0.043	−0.041	−0.039

On the other hand, the decline in educational homogamy remained constant at about 4% even after the trend in homogamy of social origin is controlled for. This is probably because the effect of homogamy of social origin is not large enough to substantially influence educational homogamy. Consequently, it has become clear that the two forms of homogamy have both declined at similar rates.

Conclusion

This study set itself four tasks: 1) to explore patterns in homogamy; 2) to examine the by-product hypothesis; 3) to re-examine homogamy trends; and 4) to evaluate the hypotheses on the relationship between homogamy and industrialization. For each task I have either added new knowledge to the previous findings or overturned previous study results. I will now summarize my findings.

In regards to the patterns in homogamy, I have shown that intermarriage between high and low non-manual sectors tends to occur. This implies that, as with intergenerational social mobility, a 'white-collar bloc' exists in homogamy of social origin. Furthermore, a large part of this intermarriage between the two white-collar sectors and the in-marriage in the upper non-manual sector has been influenced by educational homogamy. The by-product hypothesis was only supported for marriages in the non-manual sector.

Homogamy of social origin has shown a slow, linear declining trend. However, when the influence of educational homogamy is controlled for, the decline is not statistically significant. Educational homogamy, on the other hand, has a more gradual but definite declining trend. While both forms of homogamy showed decline, the extent of the changes was not substantial. Thus, this chapter concludes that the status homogamy in Japan has shown a trend of very slow decline.

Among the hypotheses presented by Smits (2003), the 'general openness hypothesis' seems to be closest for the Japanese trend. As far as verified by marriages between the 1920s and the first half of the 1990s, educational homogamy neither strengthened nor formed an inverted 'U' shape. This leaves two of his hypotheses: the 'general openness hypothesis' and the 'saturation hypothesis.' Since absolute homogamy has definitely declined and relative homogamy has also shown a decline, however small, the former seems to apply better than the latter.

It is clear that during the period of over seventy years considered, Japanese society has undergone great changes. Marriage itself has also changed: earlier in the period, marriages were arranged by others, while now individuals find their own partners; forms of meeting future spouses also changed; and more people are now marrying much later in their lives. Considering these radical transformations of the marriage environment, the changes discovered in this chapter may seem very small.

Perhaps that is the nature of changes in latent structures. Breen (2004) says that the difference in the absolute mobility rates across European nations has been brought about almost entirely by the difference in marginal frequencies. The same can be said of homogamy. The large drop in the absolute homogamy and small decline in the relative homogamy are not mutually exclusive.

What is important here is that even a small decline in the two forms of homogamy reflects a small increase in the openness of society. Intermarriages between individuals from different social groups lead to weakening of ascriptive principles of society, which in turn suggests eroding of an aspect of the social stratification. In addition, educational homogamy has also declined. That is, the spouses are less likely to maintain a specific social status group and therefore the barriers in the choice of a marriage partner have gone down. Thus, industrialization has not replaced social background with educational attainment in the marriage market. Both social background and educational achievement have become less influential in selection of marriage partners. I would like to derive a conclusion from this study that, during the period of dramatic economic changes, if any, the openness of Japanese society measured by marriage pattern has increased although only slightly.

However, this does not mean that the trends mentioned above will continue in the future. As Smits (2003) shows in his saturation hypothesis, the openness may have reached its peak. If so, the strength of status homogamy will remain unchanged. Another point is that the increase in female employment in Japan can result in stronger educational homogamy: when highly educated women use their abilities in the labour market, this may alter men's preference over spouses. Blossfeld and Timm (2003) analyzed thirteen European countries and claim that educational homogamy has become stronger due to an increase in couples both working.

Lastly, I would like to add that this study has suffered some theoretical and technical limitations. Firstly, it has not discussed theoretically why status homogamy occurs, and why it has weakened. This was largely due to the limits in the data. That is, we were unable to use variables necessary for more detailed analysis and to use data in other countries for comparative studies. To solve the first problem, we will have to use data on the spouse selection processes. As for the second problem, two research strategies are critical. First, we need to conduct secondary data analysis of other countries that focuses on their comparable institutional settings. Second, multi-level data files for many countries are to be created. There also remain some doubts as to whether the models proposed in this chapter could apply to new trends such as marrying later in life or not marrying at all, and increase in divorce and cohabitation.[14] Further constraints include that the samples are not limited to first marriages. Also, as the analysis relied on synthetic cohort analysis for current couples, irregularities such as the impact of divorce have not been removed. These problems cannot be corrected after the data have been collected: they should be addressed through designing new data collection methods.

Appendix

See Figure 8.A: Design Matrices for Homogamy.

Figure 8.A: Design matrices for homogamy

					Origin					
		Model 2					Model 5			
2	1	1	1	1		2	5	1	1	1
1	2	1	1	1		6	3	1	1	1
1	1	2	1	1		1	1	3	1	1
1	1	1	2	1		1	1	1	3	7
1	1	1	1	2		1	1	1	8	4
		Model 3						Model 6		
2	1	1	1	1		2	5	1	1	1
1	3	1	1	1		6	3	1	1	1
1	1	4	1	1		1	1	3	1	1
1	1	1	5	1		1	1	1	3	1
1	1	1	1	6		1	1	1	1	4
		Model 4						Model 7		
2	1	1	1	1		2	5	1	1	1
1	3	1	1	1		5	3	1	1	1
1	1	3	1	1		1	1	3	1	1
1	1	1	3	1		1	1	1	3	1
1	1	1	1	4		1	1	1	1	4

	Education	
Model 2		Model 3
2 1 1		2 1 4
1 2 1		1 1 1
1 1 2		4 1 3

**Part III:
Inquiring beyond Japan**

9 Educational Reform and Inequality in Japan and Korea[1]

Ki Hun Kim and Satoshi Miwa

Introduction

Most researchers recognize that the state plays an important role in education. It may shape the provision of educational opportunities and determine the structure of the educational system through its educational policies (Buchman and Hannum 2001: 80). There has been only a small body of literature on educational policies and their effect on inequality in education. This is because, according to Post (1994: 121), state actions are difficult to measure and are often as much the consequence as the cause of broader societal change.

Our main interest is to investigate the effects of educational reform[2] on social class gaps in transitions between schools, across age cohorts. A national comparative study of thirteen countries did not find any systematic differences between socialist East European countries and capitalist Western countries regarding the role social origins played in educational achievement over time (Blossfeld and Shavit 1993). This study concluded that reforms in education have not led to a reduction in inequality in education. Previous studies also reached similar conclusions (Dronkers 1993; Smith and Cheung 1986). On the other hand, in case studies about states where education is strongly controlled or closely regulated by government authority, some authors insisted that strong states such as China (Deng and Treiman 1997; Zhou, Moen and Tuma 1998), Hong Kong (Post 1994) and France (Garnier *et al.* 1989) increased or decreased the effect of class on education.

Based on these contradictory results, we try to answer the following question in this study by analyzing survey data in Japan and Korea: Can educational reforms change the association between social class and educational continuation? Both Japan and Korea are interesting cases, which can provide evidence of the effect that policy has on inequality in education. This is due partly to the fact that their states have strongly controlled education, and partly because both experienced similar great transformations in their educational policies and systems between the pre and post-war periods.

In the following section we review previous research and describe the Japanese and Korean educational systems. We then elaborate on this topic by exploring historical trends and patterns of education in both Japan and Korea.

Educational reform and inequality

Researchers of educational inequality have paid close attention to the relationships between social origins and whether or not students continue on to higher levels of education. Many researchers have mainly focused on how the relationships vary over time at each level of transition between schools (Mare 1993: 351). Previous research has found that social origin differentials have not decreased across age cohorts, despite a rapid expansion of education (Blossfeld and Shavit 1993).

Why have social class differentials persisted over time despite the expansion of education? Several hypotheses have been proposed to explicate this. Raftery and Hout (1993) suggest that inequality in educational opportunity is maximally maintained (the MMI, the *Maximally Maintained Inequality hypothesis*). They argue that the effects of social origins do not change, unless the attendance rates of the upper classes to a given level of education are saturated. These results may emerge from rational choices of parents and students. Parents and students in advantaged backgrounds are more interested in furthering their own goals and aspirations than in blocking the advance of lower-class students (Hout, Raftery and Bell 1993:26). Another hypothesis proposed is the *Relative Risk Aversion hypothesis* (Breen and Goldthorpe 1997). This is similar to the MMI hypothesis and suggests that parents of all classes want their children to progress or to at least avoid downward mobility. Although the efforts to avoid downward mobility are the same among all classes, the results of such efforts are substantially different between classes. Working class children might be satisfied with belonging to either the middle or working class, while middle class children expect to be at least in the middle class.

These hypotheses imply that educational inequality can be explained by the decision making of parents and students with regard to educational achievement. They share the assumption that educational expansion is a response to growing educational demands from the general population. However, states have regulated educational demands for political needs in many countries and their educational policies tend to change over time. Some countries have shown trends of deregulation and privatization facilitating rapid expansion, while other countries have undergone the opposite trends reinforcing the government's intervention. According to Gamoran, Shavit and Arum (2004), educational systems can be divided into two regimes with regard to the government's educational policies: Demand-driven systems for the population and supply-driven ones for the government authority. They suggest that demand-driven systems are more likely to undergo a more rapid, differentiated expansion, compared to supply-driven systems. In supply-driven systems where expansion is closely regulated, upper classes are likely to be best positioned to take advantage of new opportunities, while in demand-driven systems there could be lower educational inequality than in supply-driven systems because lower class people have some opportunity to advance to higher education in demand-driven systems.

Case studies of developing countries focused in particular on discovering the effect educational reform has had on social classes. However, results have been inconsistent. According to Dronkers (1993), the educational reform in the Netherlands merely promoted equal educational opportunities by the increase in educational participation, while the selection and allocation of students did not change, despite the reforms. Smith and Cheung (1986) also propose that the association between social origins and transition between schools in the Philippines shows a remarkable stability over time despite fast educational expansion.

Post (1994) showed results which contradict the previous findings with a Hong Kong case study. When Governor Murray MacLehose mandated free and universal lower secondary education in 1978 and the government provided substantial spending for secondary schools during the 1970s, this educational reform eliminated the role of family backgrounds as a determining factor in school transition from elementary school to lower secondary school. Lillard and Willis (1994) also put forward that government policy can play a role in eliminating social class distinction in educational progress. They highlighted that the New Economic policy (NEP) in Malaysia, which was adopted in 1970 as a result of race riots, is one of the most radical affirmative action programs and found evidence to suggest that this policy has reduced or even reversed the traditional pattern of higher levels of educational attainment among Chinese and Indian people, compared to the Malay majority (Lillard and Willis 1994: 1164). The Cultural Revolution in China is one of the most exceptional cases regarding the change in government policies, and research on its impact shows that the advantage of family background was dramatically reduced after the Cultural Revolution (Deng and Treiman 1997; Zhou, Moen and Tuma 1998).

The case of Japan and Korea

Historically, both Japan and Korea experienced great transformations in their educational systems and policies between the pre and post-war periods. Following World War II, the Allied Forces reformed the old educational system of the two countries into a new one. It was in this historical context that Korea and Japan adopted the single-track '6-3-3-4' school grade system. The compulsory education of the two countries was also expanded during this period. In Japan in 1947, compulsory education was required up to the 9th grade, and lower secondary education was the minimum official standard for educational participation during the 1950s. In 1946, compulsory elementary education in Korea was also introduced by the Allied Forces (Lee 1991; Lee 2003).

Figure 9.1 shows the Japanese trends of enrollment rates for both primary and secondary school education.[3] Although Japan began to modernize its educational systems much later than Western societies, we can see that as of 1900, the rate for elementary school enrollment had already reached as much as 80%. After ten years, the rate of 98% had been attained, with almost all children now attending elementary schools. As for secondary education, the striking expansion in enrollments after the mid-1940s is also shown in Figure 9.1. The percentage of school attendance has constantly increased with a rapid rise caused by the educational reform after World War II that made the lower secondary education compulsory.

Figure 9.2 shows the change in the enrollment rate in elementary school and the change in the advancement rate to lower secondary school from elementary school in Korea. When Korea was liberated from the Japanese colonial government in 1945, the rate of those enrolled in elementary school was only 48% of the relevant aged children, and the illiteracy rate for those over 13 years old was as large as 78% (Kimura 1997: 49). Although primary education expanded rapidly from the mid-1930s,[4] the rate of Korean children advancing

Figure 9.1: Change in the enrollment rates between the old and new systems in Japan

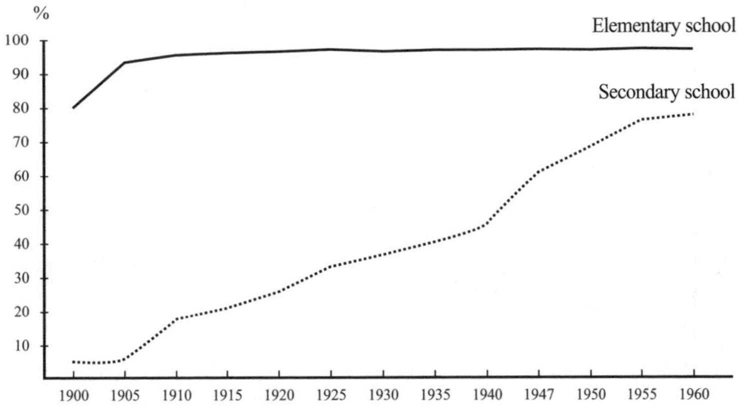

Source: The Japanese Ministry of Education (1962)

to secondary schools did not increase during the colonial period. According to Joo (1998: 102), this even decreased from 15% in 1925 to 11% in 1942. A few Korean children enrolled in middle schools, while many Japanese residents in Korea enrolled. This may be a result of discriminatory policies by the Japanese colonial government.

When the Allied Forces reformed the old educational system, Korean educational opportunities increased rapidly in elementary and secondary education. The enrollment rate for elementary school increased from 48% in 1945 to 75% in 1948, and the rate for students advancing to junior high school expanded to over 20% (Mungyobu 1958). The illiteracy rate of Koreans also decreased from 78% in 1945 to 41% in 1948.

In addition to this, other great transformations in both Japan and Korea include the reforms of higher education after the mid-1970s. Figure 9.3 shows changes in the rates of advancement to higher education in both countries. Although the higher education of both countries has been expanded rapidly since World War II, the increasing pattern has not been the same. In Japan, this rate did not increase between 1975 (39%) and 1990 (37%); its reverse trend resulted from the change in educational policies. The Japanese Ministry of Education has exercised tight control over the number of admissions to private institutes in 1975, and rejected any proposals to increase admissions in major cities until 1980 (Ishida 2003: 10).

Figure 9.2: Change in the enrollment (advancement) rates between the old and new systems in Korea

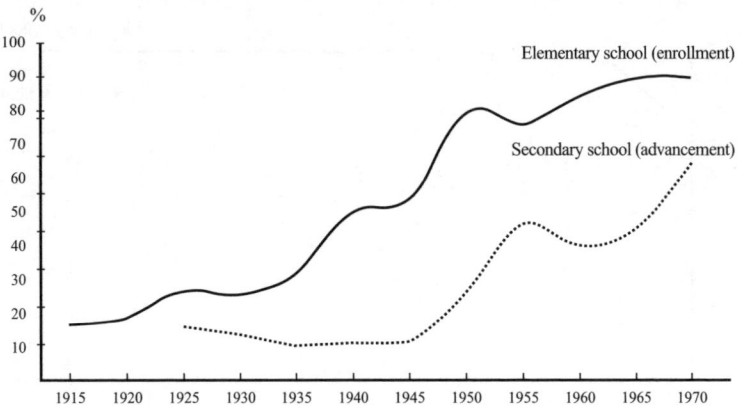

Source: The Korean enrollment rates in elementary school before 1940 are from Oh (1999), but we recalculated this to include the number of students attending traditional elementary schools (Seodong). The enrollment rates between 1945 and 1970 are from Hankook Gyoyuk 10nyeonsa Pyeonchanwiwonhoe (1960), Mungyobu (1959), and the Korean Ministry of Education & Human Resources Development and Korean Educational Development Institute (2003). The advancement rates from elementary school to junior high school attendance before 1940 are from Joo (1998), and other data are from Mungyobu (1958, 1965) and the Korean Ministry of Education & Human Resources Development and the Korean Educational Development Institute (2003). Because the advancement rate for 1945 is not available, we replace it with that for 1946.

The diverse needs of specialized technical education in Japan have also been solved through special training schools (*Senmon-gakko no Senshu-katei*), which play a unique role in post-secondary education in Japan. Although they are not considered to be a formal pathway into the Japanese school system, they have developed steadily as lifelong learning institutes since 1975.

The Korean government also constrained further expansion of their higher education through control policies until 1979, while it has tried to accelerate the expansion of higher education since 1980. These situations were reinforced after the advent of the democratic government. In particular, the increasing pattern of advanced rates between 1981 and 1986 was related directly to the introduction of the graduation quota system. The Korean Ministry of Education introduced the graduation quota system instead of the admission

Figure 9.3: Change in the rate of advancing to higher education, 1965–1990

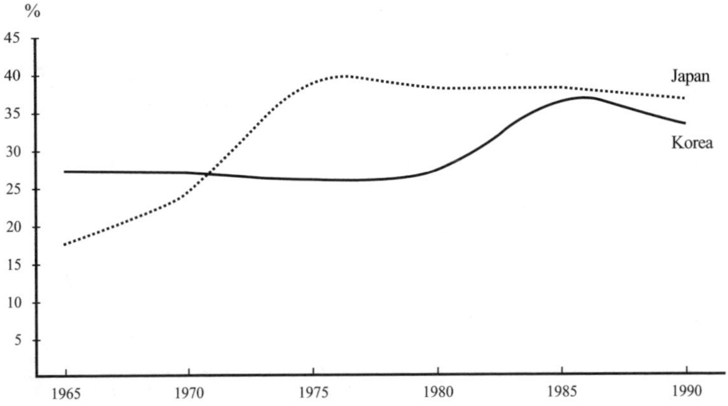

```
%
45
40                              ............Japan
35                       ......
30                 .....                    Korea
25  _____
20       ......
15   ....
10
 5
    1965   1970   1975   1980   1985   1990
```

Source: The Korean Ministry of Education & Human Resources Development and the Korean Educational Development Institute (2003) and the Japanese Ministry of Education, Culture, Sports, Science and Technology (2004)

quota system in 1981, which saw increased freshman enrollments. However, each four-year university was required to fail the lowest 30 % of its students. Consequently, the number of graduates would be lower than the number of entrants. The new quota system was proposed in the expectation of increasing competitiveness among college students and improving their achievement (Park 2003). Although college students added excess numbers to their admission quotas, most have graduated, contrary to the intention behind the policies. The Korean Ministry of Education therefore abolished this policy in 1987 due to this problem.

In both Japan and Korea, there exists a clear difference in the proportion of female students enrolled in higher education (See Figures 9.4 and 9.5). Although Korea and Japan show similar trends in the proportion of female university students during the post war period, the number of women in junior colleges displays a remarkable difference. Enrollment numbers at Korean junior colleges show that male students constitute almost 60% of all students, while Japanese junior colleges are highly gender-segregated. Over 80% of junior college students were female during the post war period.

Previous research in both countries did not consider educational reforms and these great transformations for educational opportunities.

Figure 9.4: Percentage of female students enrolled in universities, 1970–2003

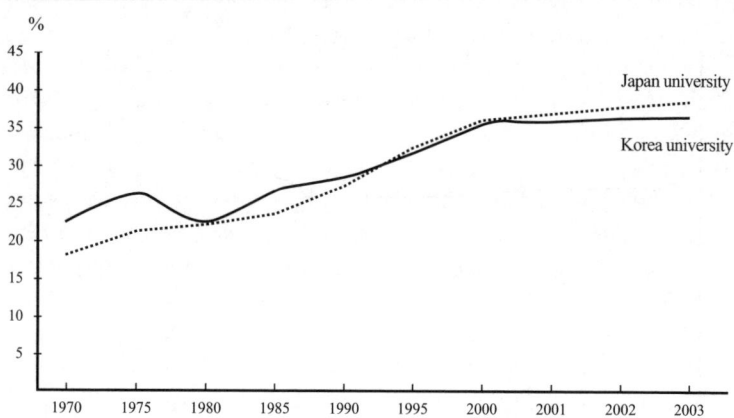

Source: The Korean Ministry of Education & Human Resources Development and the Korean Educational Development Institute (2003) and the Japanese Ministry of Education, Culture, Sports, Science and Technology (2004).

Figure 9.5: Percentage of female students enrolled in junior colleges, 1970–2003

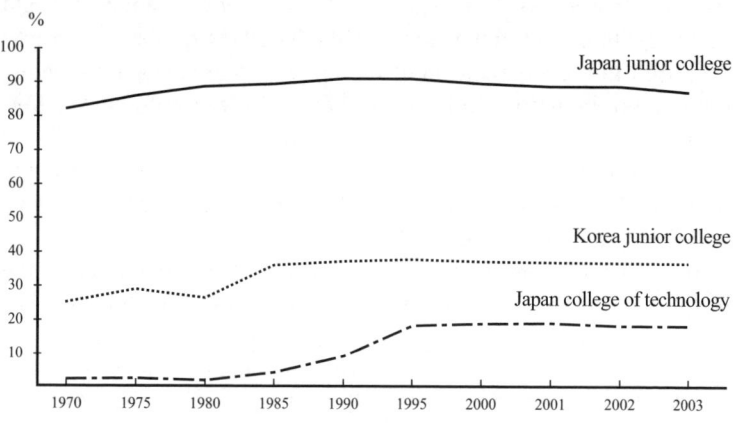

Source: See Figure 9.4

Although many researchers analyzed trends in educational inequality over time (Chang 2003, 2004; Kim 2005; Ishida 2003; Phang and Kim 2003; Park 2003; Treiman and Yamaguchi 1993), we do not yet know if the reforms have a substantial effect on educational continuation in Korea or Japan. It has merely been concluded that the effects of social origins have not decreased across age cohorts, despite a rapid expansion of education in both Japan and Korea.[5]

This study addresses the following two questions. *First, we analyze whether or not the change from the old system to a new one affected social class differentials in both Japan and Korea.* We focus in particular on the introduction of compulsory education in this period. *Second, we are interested in whether or not these different policies produced different results.* More concretely, the Japanese government constrained further expansion of higher education through control policies during the mid-1970s, while the Korean government tried to accelerate the expansion of higher education in the beginning of 1980s. This difference, therefore, would create opposite trends in educational inequality in Japan and Korea.

Data and methods

In order to overcome the limitation of sample size, we will use several data sets including family background variables of students. Japanese surveys used for the analysis are the 1955 to 1995 Social Stratification and Social Mobility Surveys (SSM)[6] and the 2000, 2001 and 2002 Japanese General Social Surveys (JGSS).[7] These surveys were combined into one data set. Korean surveys are the 1990 and 1995 Social Inequality and Justice Surveys (SIJ)[8] and the 2002 Korean Labor and Income Panel Study (KLIPS). These surveys were also combined into one data set.

The dependent variables in this analysis were the transitions from lower to higher stages in the furthering of one's education. We tested social origin differentials based on educational continuation in two time points, by focusing on policy effects. The first point (Point A) is the year that compulsory education was introduced. Point A in the Japanese case is 1947, and the dependent variable is the transition from junior high school to high school.[9] Point A in the Korean case is 1946, and the dependent variable is the transition from elementary school to junior high school.

The second point (Point B) is the year when new educational policies were implemented in higher education. The Japanese government introduced stricter regulation over the number of admissions by private institutes from 1975 to 1980, while the Korean government introduced the graduation quotas system, which resulted in the rapid expansion of higher education from 1981 to 1986. Point B in the Japanese case is 1975, and the dependent variable is the transition from high school to (junior) college. Point B in the Korean case is 1981, and the dependent variable is the same transition to (junior) college.

Independent variables are respondents' family background (their father's education and occupation), gender and the change in the educational system. Father's education ($FEDUC$) is measured by the highest grade and level of school completed, which is converted into the unit of year. If the father dropped out or was not officially registered, we use half-completed years. For example, if he dropped out of high school in Japan, $FEDUC$ is 10.5 (= 6 + 3 + 1.5).

Father's occupation is measured by social class categories using the four-class version of the EGP schema (Erikson and Goldthorpe 1992).

1. I + II + III White-collar Workers (WC): I + II: Service Class (professionals, administrators and managers; higher-grade technicians, supervisors of non-manual workers) and III: Routine non-manual workers (routine non-manual employees of administration and commerce areas; sales personnel; other rank-and-file service workers)
2. IVab Petty bourgeoisie (PB): proprietors and artisans, etc., with and without employees
3. V + VI + VIIa Manual Workers (WO): V + VI: Skilled (lower-grade technicians; supervisors of manual workers; skilled manual workers) and VIIa: Non-skilled (semi-and unskilled manual workers)
4. IVc + VIIb Farmers (FA): farmers, smallholders and self-employed workers involved in primary production; agricultural and other workers involved in primary production.

This study could not consider the mothers' educational background or family income as some data sets do not offer these variables. Academic ability is also an important variable in the analysis of continuing on to higher levels of education, and is known as a factor mitigating the disparity between family background and educational attainment (Mare 1980: 296). However, the KLIPS provides information about the academic ability of only young people under 30 years old in the 5th (2002) wave. In regards to gender variable ($Female$), we could not consider it in the case of Point A due to sampling bias of female respondents in the SSM and the SIJ data sets.

To estimate the effect of one's family background on his/her progression between schools in Point A, we used the Mare model (Mare 1980, 1981), which employs binary logistic regression to estimate the effects of family background on each transition between schools. As for Point B, we utilized the multinomial logit model in which the dependent variable is constituted as a 3-state transition: (1) entrance to 2–3 year junior colleges, (2) entrance to 4–6 year universities, and (3) leaving school.

We also use a dummy variable (*SYSTEM*) that indicates change in the educational system to check the impact of the change in policy. This variable has the value of 0 if respondents advanced to schools of higher grades before the change and the value of 1 if they did after the change. After we control for the trend effect (*TREND* [= the year of advancement – the year of the change in the system]) in the model, the coefficient of *SYSTEM* indicates an increase in the probability of advancement that is not affected by the trend. We assume that the increase measures the impact of the change in policy (See Appendix).

We focus on the five-year period before as well as the five-year period after the year when the new educational policy was implemented to minimize the influence of long-term trends. This research strategy makes it possible to analyze the 'pure' effect of the change in the educational system. In Point A, Japanese analytic cases were male junior high school graduates born from 1928 to 1937, and Korean analytic cases were male elementary school graduates born from 1930 to 1939. In Point B, Japanese ones were high school graduates born from 1953 to 1962, and Korean ones were high school graduates born from 1958 to 1967.

Results

Table 9.1 shows the results of binary logistic analysis of the chance for compulsory schooling graduates born from 1928 to 1937 to enroll in the secondary education in Point A. In the baseline model of Model 1, the trend variable is included, along with one's father's education and class. As is clear in the table, father's education and class affect students' opportunities to attend high school, and the probability of attending high school increased during the ten years.

Models 2 and 3 focus on the interactions between father's class and *TREND* and between father's class and *SYSTEM*. With regard

Table 9.1: Binary logit models of high school attendance conditional on junior high school male graduates born from 1928 to 1937 in Japan in Point A (N = 3,017)

	Model 1 B	Model 2 B	Model 3 B	Model 4 B	Model 5 B
Constant	−1.08^c	−1.07^c	−1.07^c	−1.15^c	−1.13^c
FEDUC	0.28^c	0.28^c	0.28^c	0.29^c	0.32^c
PB	−0.62^c	−0.63^c	−0.49^a	−0.61^c	−0.63^c
FA	−1.41^c	−1.43^c	−1.07^c	−1.40^c	−1.42^c
WO	−1.08^c	−1.10^c	−1.19^c	−1.07^c	−1.09^c
TREND	0.04^b	0.01	0.01	0.16^b	0.17^b
TREND × PB		0.00	0.04		
TREND × FA		0.05	0.15^b		
TREND × WO		0.03	0.01		
SYSTEM × PB			−0.26		
SYSTEM × FA			−0.66^b		
SYSTEM × WO			0.19		
TREND × FEDUC				−0.02^a	−0.01
SYSTEM × FEDUC					−0.05^b
model chi-square	577.3	579.8	590.1	582.1	589.3
df	5	8	11	6	7
Deviance	3599.5	3596.9	3586.7	3594.7	3587.5

Notes.
Reference group of father's class is white-collar workers (WC).
a: $p < .05$; b: $p < .01$; c: $p < .001$.

to differentials between persons' social origins, we understand that simple, linear trends cannot be seen. Model 3 shows an important result. The interaction between the system variable and the farming background has a negative coefficient. After controlling for the trend variable, we see that the new educational system widened the gap in educational opportunities between farmers and white-collar workers. This may be caused by a structural change at a particular period rather than by the new educational system. Hara and Seiyama (1999) argue that many servicemen and expatriates returned to Japan without jobs right after the post-war period and ended up in the agricultural sector, which temporarily increased the number of poor farmers. Their children seem to have been at a disadvantage in educational attainment because of their limited economic resources. We would argue that this temporal social change, rather than the change in the educational system, produces the above-mentioned result.

Next let us take a look at Models 4 and 5. The negative coefficient of *TREND* × *FEDUC* in Model 4 means that the effect of father's education on the opportunity to enroll in the secondary education weakened between the pre- and post-war periods. Model 5, however, shows that the interaction between *SYSTEM* and *FEDUC* is statistically significant, while that between *TREND* and *FEDUC* is not. Thus we argue that the change in the system in this period was the major factor in decreasing educational inequality.

Why then did the change in the system weaken the effect of father's education and reduce educational inequality? Our answer is as follows. In this period an important change occurred in the educational system: The transition from the double-track system to the single-track American system. This change in turn caused two other crucial changes. First, students began to delay their decision making on their career – academic and occupational – because the period of compulsory education became longer. Second, almost every child studied the standardized contents because children were educated in the same compulsory educational system up to a minimum age of fifteen. These two changes, we would argue, weakened the effect of the father's education and eventually reduced educational inequality.

Table 9.2 shows the coefficients of the independent variables for the binary logistic models of junior high school attendance conditional on elementary school male graduates born between 1930 and 1939 in Korea. Model 1 describes the coefficients of the baseline model, considering only the main effects. In this model, we tested whether or not the trend variable shows a significantly positive (+) effect. A positive effect means that the conditional possibility for transiting to junior high school increased during the 10 years of changing from the old to the new education system. According to Model 1, the coefficient of the trend variable is positive and significant. It can be interpreted that the secondary education expanded during this period in Korea.

Models 2 and 4 show the coefficients of the models with interaction terms between family backgrounds and the trend variable to see whether or not the effects of family backgrounds changed over time. The primary interest of this study is to question whether or not parental effects declined over time in Korea during the change period of the educational policy. These results show that the impact of one's father's class and educational background has not changed over time in Korea.

Models 3 and 5 give an answer to our main question: whether or not educational policies affected disparities between social classes. The

Table 9.2. Binary logit models of junior high school attendance conditional on elementary school male graduates born from 1930 to 1939 in Korea in Point A (N = 740)

	Model 1 B	Model 2 B	Model 3 B	Model 4 B	Model 5 B
Constant	1.19^a	1.18^a	1.18^a	1.21^b	1.19^a
FEDUC	0.17^c	0.17^c	0.17^c	0.16^c	0.09
PB	0.02	0.10	0.31	0.02	0.05
FA	−1.35^b	−1.32^b	−1.39^b	−1.36^b	−1.35^b
WO	−1.54^b	−1.80^b	−1.49	−1.55^b	−1.50^a
TREND	0.12^c	0.27	0.27	0.11^b	0.11^b
TREND × PB		−0.22	−0.17		
TREND × FA		−0.16	−0.18		
TREND × WO		0.001	0.08		
SYSTEM × PB			−0.38		
SYSTEM × FA			0.12		
SYSTEM × WO			−0.60		
TREND × FEDUC				0.01	−0.02
SYSTEM × FEDUC					0.14
model chi-square	109.7	112.0	112.3	109.9	112.3
df	5	8	11	6	7
Deviance	869.9	867.6	867.3	869.7	867.3

Notes.
Reference group of father's class is white-collar workers (WC).
a: $p < .05$; b: $p < .01$; c: $p < .001$.

results of Models 3 and 5 with the system variable and the interaction terms between it and family backgrounds show that the interaction effect is statistically significant only in Japan. Then why is it that the impacts of one's family backgrounds did not decrease after the change in the educational system in Korea, even though it experienced the same reforms as Japan? Although compulsory education in Korea was promulgated in 1946, it was not fully realized until 1959 thanks to a lack of public expenditures on education and the Korean War. Moreover, primary education in Korea was not free until 1979. In contrast, the Japanese government provided substantial spending for junior high schools as compulsory and free education during the 1950s.

Results of the multinomial logit model are summarized in Table 9.3. As for the continuation to universities (*Daigaku*), neither the trend variable nor the system variable has any effect. Their interaction terms do not have effects, either. These results imply that inequality

Table 9.3. *Multinomial logit models of attending university or junior college conditional on high school graduates born from 1953 to 1962 in Japan in Point B (N = 2,418)*

	Model 1 B	Model 2 B	Model 3 B	Model 4 B	Model 5 B	Model 6 B	Model 7 B
University/leave							
Constant	−2.02[c]	−2.02[c]	−2.02[c]	−2.01[c]	−2.01[c]	−2.02[c]	−2.02[c]
FEDUC	0.25[c]	0.25[c]	0.25[c]	0.25[c]	0.25[c]	0.25[c]	0.25[c]
PB	−0.43[b]	−0.44[b]	−0.28	−0.43[b]	−0.43[b]	−0.43[b]	−0.43[b]
FA	−1.19[c]	−1.20[c]	−1.03[c]	−1.20[c]	−1.20[c]	−1.20[c]	−1.20[c]
WO	−0.95[c]	−0.95[c]	−0.94[c]	−0.95[c]	−0.95[c]	−0.95[c]	−0.95[c]
Female	−1.38[c]	−1.38[c]	−1.38[c]	−1.38[c]	−1.38[c]	−1.39[c]	−1.49[c]
TREND	−0.01	−0.02	−0.02	0.05	0.05	−0.03	−0.03
TREND × PB		0.02	0.06				
TREND × FA		0.00	0.05				
TREND × WO		0.02	0.03				
SYSTEM × PB			−0.29				
SYSTEM × FA			−0.34				
SYSTEM × WO			−0.02				
TREND × FEDUC				−0.01	−0.01		
SYSTEM × FEDUC					0.00		
TREND × Female						0.05	0.02
SYSTEM × Female							0.19
Junior College/leave							
Constant	−3.22[c]	−3.22[c]	−3.21[c]	−3.23[c]	−3.23[c]	−3.22[c]	−3.21[c]
FEDUC	0.13[c]	0.14[c]	0.14[c]	0.14[c]	0.13[c]	0.13[c]	0.13[c]
PB	−0.33	−0.34	−0.95[a]	−0.34	−0.34	−0.33	−0.34
FA	−0.47[b]	−0.48[b]	−0.84[a]	−0.48[b]	−0.48[b]	−0.47[b]	−0.48[b]
WO	−0.51[b]	−0.57[b]	−0.77[a]	−0.55[b]	−0.55[b]	−0.52[b]	−0.52[b]
Female	1.37[c]	1.36[c]	1.37[c]	1.37[c]	1.37[c]	1.37[c]	1.17[c]
TREND	0.02	−0.02	−0.02	0.21[b]	0.21[b]	0.01	0.01
TREND × PB		0.02	−0.14				
TREND × FA		0.03	−0.07				
TREND × WO		0.11	0.05				
SYSTEM × PB			1.07				
SYSTEM × FA			0.65				
SYSTEM × WO			0.37				
TREND × FEDUC				−0.02[b]	−0.02[a]		
SYSTEM × FEDUC					0.01		
TREND × Female						0.01	−0.04
SYSTEM × Female							0.38
model chi-square	802.9	806.7	813.6	810.2	810.3	804.5	806.3
df	12	18	24	14	16	14	18
Deviance	1878.7	1874.9	1868.0	1871.4	1871.3	1877.1	1875.3

Notes.

Reference group of father's class is white-collar workers (WC).

a: $p < .05$; b: $p < .01$; c: $p < .001$.

in educational opportunities has been stable for the period of our analysis.

Now let us move on to the results of those who continue on to junior college (*Tanki-daigaku*). In Models 2 and 3, factors significant at the 5% level are few, and therefore we do not have definitive results as we did not in the case of the continuation to university. The only clear result is that the relationship between the trend variable and one's father's education exists in Models 4 and 5. Certainly, in this period, we can see that the effect of father's education on whether or not one advances to junior college reduces.The Japanese government had restricted the supply of higher education during this period by strictly controlling the establishment of new universities in urban areas. Special training schools, which enrolled some of the high school graduates, were institutionalized in 1975 in order to compensate for the proscriptive policy. It was then argued that the schools would not be an alternative to universities and junior colleges and that, therefore, inequality in educational opportunities would increase. The argument, however, is not the case. Compared to the overall opportunities for higher education, the influence of the proscriptive policy and the institutionalization of special training schools was not substantial. For this reason, results from the analysis of samples taken from all over Japan might not support the hypothesis that the proscriptive policy increases inequality in educational opportunities. Metropolitan areas such as Tokyo and their vicinities were under a strong influence of the policy. Thus we may get different results if we reanalyze the data with information on respondents' residential areas.

Table 9.4 shows results of the multinomial logit models of those attending university (*Daehakgyo*) or junior college (*Jeonmundaehak*) conditional on high school graduates born 1958 to 1967 in Korea in Point B. Model 1 shows that the trend variable has a significantly positive (+) effect only in the case of transition from high school to university. This means that the expansion of higher education can be explained by the rapid expansion of the number of university students during this period. This result is particularly related to the graduation quota system. An additional 30% of the quota was accepted in universities under this system, while junior colleges were only permitted to add a quota of about 15 %.

Models 2 and 4 show the coefficients of the models with the interaction terms between the trend variable and family backgrounds to see whether or not the effects of family backgrounds changed over time. These results show that the impact of one's father's class and

Table 9.4. Multinomial logit models of attending university or junior college conditional on high school graduates born from 1958 to 1967 in Korea in Point B (N = 1,998)

	Model 1 B	Model 2 B	Model 3 B	Model 4 B	Model 5 B	Model 6 B	Model 7 B
University/leave							
Constant	−0.61[b]	−0.60[b]	−0.63	−0.65[b]	−0.64[b]	−0.61[b]	−0.75[b]
FEDUC	0.13[c]	0.13[c]	0.13[c]	0.13[c]	0.12[c]	0.13[c]	0.13[c]
PB	−0.58[b]	−0.59[b]	−0.60	−0.58[b]	−0.60[b]	−0.58[b]	−0.59[b]
FA	−1.24[c]	−1.27[c]	−1.37[b]	−1.25[c]	−1.26[c]	−1.24[c]	−1.25[c]
WO	−1.19[c]	−1.21[c]	−1.61[b]	−1.19[c]	−1.19[c]	−1.19[c]	−1.20[c]
Female	−1.18[c]	−1.18[c]	−1.19[c]	−1.19[c]	−1.19[c]	−1.18[c]	−1.12[b]
TREND	0.06[b]	0.09[a]	0.09	−0.02	−0.02	0.06[a]	0.02
TREND × PB		−0.03	−0.04				
TREND × FA		−0.08	−0.10				
TREND × WO		−0.02	−0.12				
SYSTEM × PB			0.05				
SYSTEM × FA			0.17				
SYSTEM × WO			0.68				
TREND × FEDUC				0.01	0.01		
SYSTEM × FEDUC					0.03		
TREND × Female						0.002	0.02
SYSTEM × Female							0.24
Junior College/leave							
Constant	−0.88[b]	−0.88[b]	−0.62	−0.88[b]	−0.89[b]	−0.88[b]	−0.71[a]
FEDUC	0.06[b]	0.06[b]	0.06[b]	0.06[b]	0.07[b]	0.06[b]	0.06[b]
PB	−0.45[a]	−0.45[a]	−0.01	−0.45[a]	−0.44[a]	−0.45[a]	−0.44[a]
FA	−1.26[c]	−1.26[c]	−1.89[c]	−1.26[c]	−1.26[c]	−1.26[c]	−1.23[c]
WO	−0.85[c]	−0.86[b]	−1.66[a]	−0.85[c]	−0.85[c]	−0.85[b]	−0.85[b]
Female	−0.69[c]	−0.69[c]	−0.71[c]	−0.69[c]	−0.69[c]	−0.70[c]	−1.12[b]
TREND	0.03	0.03	0.10	0.03	0.03	0.03	0.07
TREND × PB		−0.002	0.12				
TREND × FA		0.01	−0.16				
TREND × WO		−0.004	−0.21				
SYSTEM × PB			−1.26[a]				
SYSTEM × FA			1.09				
SYSTEM × WO			1.38				
TREND × FEDUC				0.001	0.004		
SYSTEM × FEDUC					−0.02		
TREND × Female						−0.01	−0.12
SYSTEM × Female							0.43
model chi-square	364.2	366.7	376.9	367.6	369.8	364.2	367.1
df	12	18	24	14	16	14	18
Deviance	1566.7	1564.2	1554.0	1563.3	1561.1	1566.7	1563.8

Notes.
Reference group of father's class is white-collar workers (WC).
a: $p < .05$; b: $p < .01$; c: $p < .001$.

education did not change over time in Korea. In other words, the class composition of the students attending higher education was stable over time, despite the expansion of education in Korea. Models 3 and 5 give an answer to our main question: whether or not educational policies affect the gaps between the social classes. As a result, we did not find that the impacts of educational policies on social class were different between Korea and Japan.

Lastly, Models 6 and 7 in Tables 9.3 and 9.4 do not indicate changes in gender differences. Because we focused on a relatively short period of time for the analysis, we may have missed a decreasing trend of gender differences, which has often been reported in long-term trend analyses.

Conclusions

This study has analyzed the effects of educational reforms on social class differentials in school transitions over time in Japan and Korea. Previous research has found that social class differentials have not decreased over time despite a rapid expansion of education, and that the reforms have not led to a reduction in educational inequalities. However, in case studies about states where education is strongly controlled or closely regulated by government authority, some authors have insisted that strong states may increase or decrease the effect of class on education. Japan and Korea are interesting cases, which can provide evidence of the influence that policy has on inequality in education. This is due partly to the fact that both countries belong to strong states with regard to education, and partly because both countries experienced similar great transformations of their educational policies and systems between the pre and post-war periods.

In this analysis, we examined whether the change in the educational systems affected the difference in the probability of educational continuation between classes. Firstly, we analyzed whether or not the change from the old educational system to a new one affected social class differentials during a ten-year period. We focused in particular on the introduction of compulsory education in this period. Free and compulsory education up to junior high school was materialized in Japan in 1947, and compulsory elementary education was also introduced in Koreas in 1946 by the Allied Forces. As a result, we found that only Japan's case shows significant results for reducing the gaps between social classes due to the change in educational policies.

Although Korea has experienced fast expansion of education since the introduction of compulsory education, the Korean government could not provide substantial funding for compulsory education due to a lack of public expenditures and the Korean War, while the Japanese government realized this during the 1950s. If the state does not play a leading role in the realization of educational reforms, we cannot expect that its reforms will have substantial effects on associations between one's social class and one's continuation of education. Furthermore, although the promotion policies on educational opportunity themselves may have some effect on reducing gaps between social classes, this does not necessarily mean that such policies reduce overall class disparities in educational opportunity.

Secondly, we tested whether or not different patterns of educational reforms led to different results for school transitions between the two countries. The Japanese government policies constrained further expansion of higher education through control policies during the mid-1970s, while the Korean government tried to accelerate the expansion of higher education in the beginning of 1980s. As a result, we found that social class differentials had persisted for the ten-year period before and after the introduction of the new educational system. We also conclude that the proscriptive policy of educational opportunities did not necessarily increase educational inequality.

Appendix

See Figure 9.A: Methodological notes for the system effect model.

Figure 9.A: Methodological notes for the system effect model

Notation. T: time trend, S: system effect (dummy variable: $S = 1$ if $T > T_0$), X: explanatory variable

The trend of inequality model can be extended to the "system effect model" as follows.

$$Log_e \frac{p}{1-p} = \alpha + \beta_1 T + \beta_2 X + \beta_3 TX \qquad \text{equation 1}$$

$$Log_e \frac{p}{1-p} = \alpha + \beta_1 T + \beta_2 X + \beta_3 TX + \beta_4 SX \qquad \text{equation 2}$$

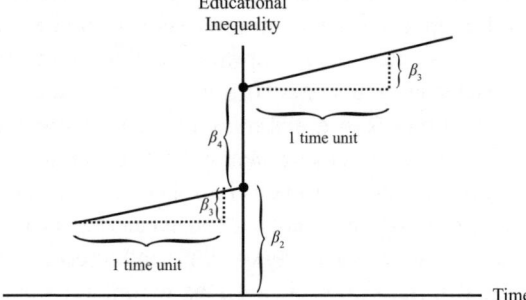

T_0 = time point of system change

	β_3	β_4	Interpretation
Pattern 1	Insignificant	Insignificant	Persistent inequality
Pattern 2	Significant	Insignificant	Trend change, but no system effect
Pattern 3	Insignificant	Significant	System effect, but no trend change
Pattern 4	Significant	Significant	Trend change, and system effect

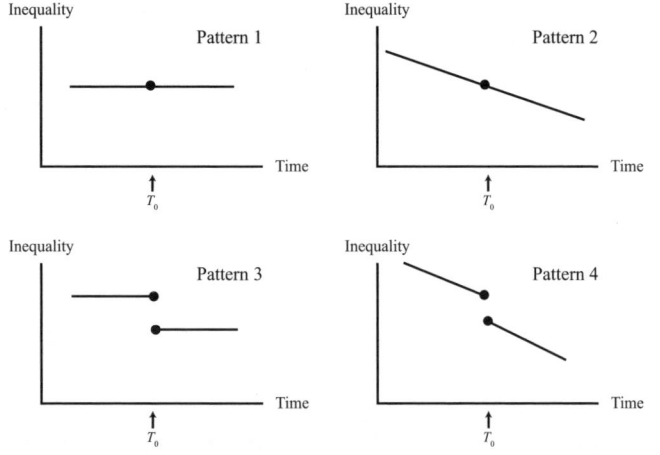

10 Market Transition of Laid-off Workers in Urban China[1]

Guihua Xie

As economic reform proceeded in China, a large number of redundant workers had to be removed from the state-owned enterprises (herein SOEs),[2] which was termed '*xiagang* (layoff)' by the Chinese government. Laid-off workers are allowed to keep their employment relationship with the enterprises for a maximum of three years. The enterprises are still responsible for contributing to their social security funds and offering a basic livelihood allowance during the periods (Wang and Chen 1998; Zhang 1998; MOLSS 1998; Lee 1999).[3] Laid-off workers are required to sign agreements with the reemployment service center of the enterprises on basic livelihood allowance and reemployment. Enterprises have the right to terminate an employment relationship with workers who refuse to sign the agreements. Once workers find new jobs, their employment relationship with the original enterprises ends.[4]

In practice, there are many workers who are either unable to get the benefits because their enterprises cannot afford, or refuse to sign the agreement because they are unwilling to cut off the employment relationship with the enterprises after three years (CCER 1999; Solinger 2002). These workers may not be counted as 'laid-off' in official statistics, but they are regarded as laid-off workers by local government, enterprises and themselves. Therefore the category of laid-off workers is very flexible and extensive in practice. It is difficult to estimate the exact number of laid-off workers. Solinger (2001) discussed the confusion in the layoff and unemployment statistics in China and concluded that, 'it is impossible to come to any kind of statistical judgment about China's current unemployment, particularly one drawing upon official statistics (p. 671).'

Layoff merits extensive attention because of the huge number of laid-off workers and its impact on the current market transformation.[5] Laid-off workers are becoming an important component of the urban poor (Wang 2000; Solinger 2002). Moreover, laid-off workers were also regarded as one of the potential sources of social unrest (Cai 2002). Demonstrations by laid-off workers have occurred in many cities in China, and have sometimes resulted in conflict with police.[6]

This study examines the interaction between market transition and the old labor allocation system in influencing laid-off workers' social mobility. Drawing on the market transition theory and the segmented labor market theory, I have developed an integrated theoretical framework and derived testable hypotheses. The specific aims of the study are: (1) to examine the determinants of layoff by the old labor allocation system at enterprises level, and workers' human capital and political capital; (2) to examine the interaction between market transition and the old labor allocation system in determining laid-off workers' reemployment status and their income from post-layoff jobs.

Market transition and segmented labor market

Market transition theory emphasizes the role of market forces in shaping institutional change and new stratification order. One basic institution of socialism is the redistributive system in which the vast majority of resources and the benefits from these resources were centered in the hands of the state, and redistributed to individuals according to their positions in the system. But under the market economy individuals obtain social resources according to their positions in the market because the market is the main force organizing the production and distribution of social resources (Nee 1996). So the transition from planned economy to market economy leads to changes in the distribution system and interest structure. Since the producers are rewarded according to their human capital under a market economy, an important result of the market transition is the declining role of political capital relative to human capital in the reward system (Nee 1989, 1991, 1996)

Market transition theory was challenged on its optimism about the strength of the market transition and its conceptualization and predictions about the outcomes of the market transition. It was criticized for ignoring the role of the state and the continuity of the old orders in shaping the current transformation – 'institutional persistence' as Zhou termed it, and variations within the market economy and market transition (Zhou 2000; Parish and Michelson 1996; Walder 1996, 2002; Stark 1996). Bian and Logan (1996) and Zhou (2000) argued that the dual transformation of economic and political institutions could lead to the coexistence of the impacts of human capital and political capital on income distribution. The research based on the transformation of Eastern European countries also finds the continuing advantages of political capital through power conversion, social capital, structural inertia and unobserved personal characteristics (Parish and Michelson 1996; Stark 1996; Rona-Tas 1994; Gerber 2000, 2001).

Market transition theory has been extensively applied to examine the transition of post-socialist countries, focusing on changes in the returns to human capital and political capital. The research offers mixed findings and provides supplemental perspectives for studies on transitional societies. Xie and Hannum (1996), using Chinese urban household income data collected in 1988, found that market development (measured by the growth rate of industrial output value) has not affected returns to human capital and political capital – which they attributed to the lack of a true labor market in urban China at that time. While most of the studies showed increasing returns to human capital during market transition in China, there was no sign of a decline of distributive power at the individual level (political capital) or in social structure, for example ownership and bureaucratic ranks of institutions (Bian and Logan 1996; Zhou, Tuma and Moen 1997; Zhou 2000).

The segmented labor market theory was developed based on market economy. Instead of treating labor markets as a single, homogeneous and competitive setting, the segmented labor market theory emphasizes that the specific institutional settings, like dual economy or systematic discrimination, can segment the labor markets. It hypothesizes that income distribution, unemployment and discrimination are results of segmentation (Taubman and Wachter 1986). In addition, segmentation may also result from discrimination based on gender, race or other factors (Kalleberg and Sørensen 1979).

Segmented labor market theory can also be used to analyze socialist economies where the development and distribution of the labor force are managed by a planning system instead of a free market (Kalleberg and Sørensen 1979; Stark 1986; Lin and Bian 1991). Social organizations under planned systems in China were conceived 'to maximize the centralized process relative to allocation, production, and distribution of labor, material, and financial resources (Lin and Bian 1991: 659).' Therefore organizations were segmented according to the degree of the direct control exercised by the central government, which was reflected by the ownership of the organizations and levels of government the organizations belonged to (Bian 1994).[7] Workers in different sectors had 'their own publicly defined rights to income, job tenure, social security, labor insurance and housing and residence (Walder 1986, p.40).' Workers in the SOEs or higher-ranked enterprises had higher wages, better job security and more extensive fringe benefits than workers in the non-SOEs (collective-owned enterprises) or lower-ranked enterprises (Bian 1994; Whyte and Parish 1984; Walder 1986; Croll 1999).

Since labor market segmentation is mainly caused by the institutional settings in the labor market (Kalleberg and Sørensen 1979), it will also change with institutional changes. As economic reform proceeds in China, the state is quitting the role as the patron of SOEs. SOEs have to compete with enterprises of other types of ownership in the market. Failing SOEs are allowed to go bankrupt, or be merged, closed or sold, and workers from these enterprises face layoff (Wang and Chen 1998; Zhang 1998; Lee 1999). Therefore, the old forms of labor market segmentation based on enterprises' ownership may diminish with the market transition.

However, empirical research found that the old segmentation continues in the reform era. The state-owned sector is still placed in a privileged position, and the life chances of workers are still shaped by the different positions of their work organizations (Bian and Logan 1996; Zhou, Tuma and Moen 1997). But all sectors are influenced by market transition. Zhao and Zhou (2002) found that market transition also affects the state sector and induces a change in the allocation system in the state-owned sector. Wu and Xie's research (2003) found that human capital has higher returns in the market sector than in the state sector. But the effect of human capital varies according to workers' market participation time.

Following the new development of China's market reform in recent years, this study will analyze whether further reform has brought about the convergence of the two segmented labor groups defined previously by the ownership of enterprises. In other words, we will examine whether workers' life chances such as employment status and income are still affected by the old segmented structure.

Hypotheses

Integrating market transition theory and segmented labor market theory, this research focuses on the impact of market transformation and labor market segmentation on employment and job returns of workers in the state-owned sector.

> *Hypothesis 1*: With the development of marketization, human capital becomes more important relative to political capital in determining workers' layoff status.

Human capital is measured by education, working experience and job training (Fine 1998). This hypothesis is derived from market transition theory, which posits that one of the institutional mechanisms causing changes in urban stratification is that 'as economic organizations become more dependent on market exchange for key resources, reward distribution within organizations tends to be modified in favor of human capital and productivity (Cao and Nee 2000: 1183).' Therefore, with the marketization of the SOEs, the enterprises tend to keep workers with higher human capital and productivity when they make decisions about who should be laid off.

In addition, marketization may not be homogenous across enterprises. The state-owned, high-ranked or large enterprises used to obtain more protection from the government (Bian 1994; Walder 1992; Lardy 1998). Wu (2002) proposed that, after the reform, the profitability of enterprises might reflect the degree of their involvement into the market economy. Successful market competitors were closer to the market economy and were able to transfer their products into profit.

I argue that as the market transition has proceeded, the effect of ownership, rank and size of enterprises on the well-being of workers has declined in significance. Instead, the market performance of enterprises has become the most important factor affecting workers' employment status.

> *Hypothesis 1A*: The ownership, rank and size of enterprises have no effects on workers' layoff status. Workers in enterprises with better market performance are less likely to be laid off.

Market transition theory expects that marketization brings about an increasing return to human capital, which then provides the incentive for direct producers to participate in the labor market. But a market economy has different human capital requirements from the redistributive economy (Nee 1989). The change in industrial structure may lead to a mismatch of laid-off workers' skills and labor market requirements (Xiao 1998; Sheng 1998). This means the training and experience the workers received in the state-owned sector may not be useful for their job searches in the labor market. Moreover, the former elite could convert their political capital into economic interest through their social networks or through their own personal characteristics (Parish and Michelson 1996; Stark 1996; Rona-Tas 1994; Gerber 2000, 2001). Based on these arguments, I predict that human capital and political capital holders have advantages in reemployment:

> *Hypothesis 2*: Laid-off workers with more education and political capital are more likely to be reemployed than workers with less education and political capital. But working experience and job training workers received before layoff have no effect on workers' reemployment.

As I mentioned above, as the segmentation based on enterprises' ownership types declines, workers in the SOEs may not have privileges over workers in collective-owned enterprises in their reemployment. Meanwhile, workers' probability of reemployment may not vary by the rank and size of their enterprises either. Therefore,

> *Hypothesis 2A*: The ownership, rank and size of enterprises have no effects on their laid-off workers' reemployment probability.

Extending the hypothesis on reemployment to earnings from reemployment, my next hypothesis is:

> *Hypothesis 3*: For reemployed workers, the rewards to their education increase and the rewards to their previous working experience decrease in their post-layoff jobs.

Data and methods

Data used in the research draw from the surveys and in-depth interviews from the Urban Labor Market Integration Project funded by the Ford Foundation, Beijing office.[8] Data were collected in six large cities in China, Beijing, Tianjin, Nanjing, Changchun, Xi'an and Wuhan, from August 1999 to August 2000 (see Figure 10.1).

Figure 10.1: Six surveyed cities in China

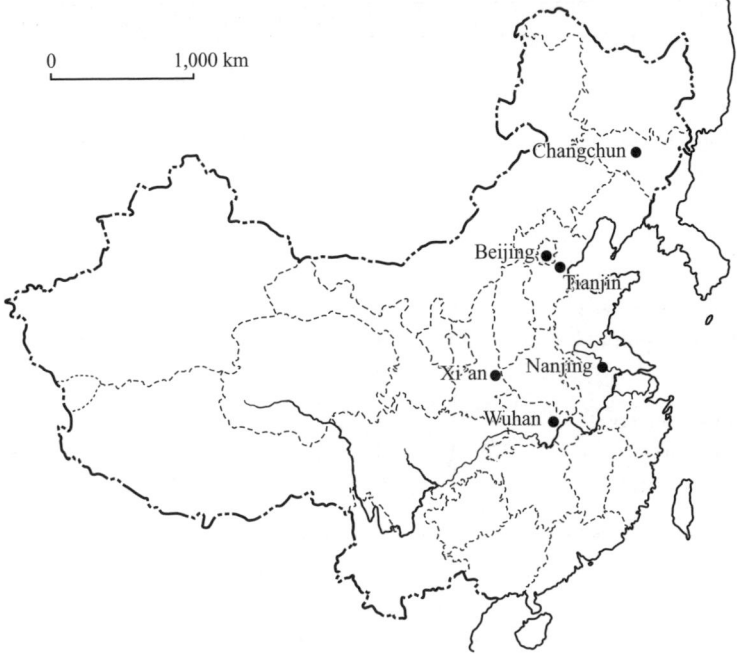

The data were collected at three levels: city, enterprise and individual. In each city, about 15 to 20 enterprises were selected and managers of enterprises were interviewed on the enterprises' history, their current economic situation, labor force components and so on. In each enterprise, approximately 40 workers on average (the number varied by enterprises), including employed workers and laid-off workers, were selected to answer the questionnaire. Employed workers refer to the formal employees with urban *hukou* who had never been laid off before. Laid-off workers refer to workers who had been laid off at some point in their working life. They may or may not have been employed at the time of interview. Some of the surveyed workers were also recruited for in-depth interviews. Altogether 1,841 urban employed workers and 1,560 laid-off workers were selected from 120 enterprises in the six cities (Tables 10.1 and 10.2).[9]

Most of the enterprises were state-owned. A few collective owned enterprises were also selected because, according to local policies, laid-off workers from some collective-owned enterprises were also qualified to receive layoff subsidies. The enterprises were mainly

Table 10.1: Characteristics of surveyed enterprises by city

	Beijing	Tianjin	Nanjing	Xi'an	Changchun	Wuhan	Total
Total	22	21	21	13	23	20	120
Ownership							
State-owned	15	16	13	13	22	18	97
Collective-owned	6	1	3	0	1	2	13
Joint venture	0	1	3	0	0	0	4
Private/foreign invested	1	3	2	0	0	0	6
Rank							
Central/provincial	3	3	3	8	9	6	32
Local enterprises	19	18	18	5	14	14	88
Size							
Small enterprises	14	7	3	0	3	11	38
Medium enterprises	4	8	12	3	10	8	45
Large enterprises	4	6	6	10	10	1	37
Market performance							
Unprofitable	9	10	12	10	17	12	70
Profitable	8	11	9	3	6	8	45
Missing profit information	5	0	0	0	0	0	5

drawn from the city's main industries with an emphasis on the industries with massive layoffs such as manufacturing and textile.

Measurements

Dependent Variables

There are three dependent variables. Layoff status is self-defined by workers or by their enterprises. Laid-off workers include those who involuntarily lose their permanent and contract jobs in the SOEs or collective-owned enterprises. Note that the sample of laid-off workers includes not only workers who registered at reemployment service centers, but also workers who did not register for various reasons, young workers who joined the enterprises as contract workers and lost jobs before their terms were due, and workers who are in involuntary early retirement, also known as inner retirement.

Reemployment is defined as current employment of laid-off workers.

Rewards are constructed in two ways. (1) Monthly income, including wages, bonuses and other income from enterprises.

Table 10.2: Descriptive statistics on workers in survey sample

Variables	Total	Employed workers	Laid-off workers
Layoff status	.46 (.50)		
Male	.48 (.50)	.52 (.50)	.44 (.50)
Age	38.88 (8.65)	38.55 (8.83)	39.26 (8.42)
High school	.49 (.50)	.48 (.50)	.50 (.50)
College and above	.20 (.40)	.28 (.45)	.11 (.31)
On-the-job training	.46 (.50)	.51 (.50)	.41 (.49)
On-the-job training missing	.09 (.29)	.09 (.29)	.09 (.28)
Full-time job training	.15 (.36)	.22 (.36)	.07 (.26)
Full-time job training missing	.09 (.29)	.09 (.29)	.09 (.28)
Party member	.24 (.43)	.32 (.47)	.14 (.35)
Party membership missing	.02 (.13)	.02 (.16)	.01 (.10)
Cadre	.09 (.29)	.14 (.35)	.04 (.19)
Cadre status missing	.01 (.08)	.00 (.06)	.01 (.09)
State-owned/shared	.89 (.31)	.90 (.29)	.88 (.32)
Profitable	.31 (.46)	.37 (.48)	.24 (.43)
Profitable missing	.05 (.21)	.03 (.18)	.06 (.24)
Local enterprises	.72 (.45)	.72 (.45)	.72 (.45)
Medium enterprises	.43 (.49)	.39 (.49)	.46 (.50)
Large enterprises	.32 (.47)	.32 (.47)	.32 (.47)
Tianjin	.17 (.38)	.16 (.37)	.19 (.39)
Nanjing	.17 (.38)	.16 (.36)	.19 (.39)
Xi'an	.13 (.34)	.12 (.33)	.14 (.35)
Changchun	.19 (.39)	.19 (.39)	.18 (.39)
Wuhan	.17 (.38)	.17 (.38)	.18 (.38)
N	3,365	1,805	1,560

Note. Standard errors in parentheses

This definition is widely used in research on income in China. (2) Monthly income plus benefits, including wages, bonuses, other income and benefits. Benefits consist of medical insurance, pension fund and unemployment insurance that enterprise provides.[10] Both measurements of income have been adjusted for inflation by using the local commodity price index (CPI) with base year 1999.

Independent Variables

Variables at the individual level
Human capital includes education, job training and working experience. Education is measured using three categories: (1) junior

middle school or below, including junior middle school, elementary school and illiterate; (2) high school, including vocational high school and technical school; (3) colleges (including three-year college) and above.

Two variables measure working experience: total working experience and current job tenure. Total working experience was used by enterprises as part of the criteria for wages. It is the total number of working years, from workers' first jobs in the state/collective-owned units to the time of the survey, or to the time of layoff. Current job tenure refers to the number of years that workers worked in the current enterprises under any type of ownership system.

Age is an important index for layoff because inner retirement is partly decided by age. It is also important for employers to determine how many years a worker can remain employed when laid-off workers enter the labor market. However, age is highly correlated with workers' total work experience. I will use age or working experience alternatively to test different hypotheses.

Job training variables include two dummy variables: on-the-job training and full-time job training. The value '1' refers to workers that had received on-the-job/full-time job training in the current enterprise or the enterprise before layoff.

Political capital is measured using two variables: the cadre status and communist party membership. Both are dummy variables. Cadre status refers to holding at least a middle-level administrative position in the state/collective-owned enterprises. This was self-reported. Party membership refers to whether the respondent was a member of the Communist Party or not.

Variables at the enterprise level
There are four sets of firm-level variables: the ownership, rank, size and market performance (profitable or not) of the enterprise.

The ownership of the workplace is of four types: state-owned, collective-owned, joint ventures and the private enterprises. State-owned enterprises include shareholding companies (listed or not) where the state holds a controlling number of shares. Collective-owned enterprises include shareholding enterprises where the collective has a controlling number of shares. Foreign-funded/owned enterprises and small household business are included in private enterprises. Joint ventures can be state-shared or collective-shared according to their ownership before the joining of foreign investment.

Enterprises are divided into two ranks. Central enterprises (non-local) include those which are under the administration of central/provincial governments, and therefore, are beyond the control of city government. Local enterprises refer to enterprises under the administration of city or district governments, and therefore, are under the control of city government. All private enterprises are local.

Enterprises are characterized as small, medium and large scale according to the number of workers.[11] An enterprise is small if it employs less than 500 workers, medium if it employs more than 500 and less than 2000 workers, and large if it employs more than 2000 workers.

Enterprises are also classified as profitable or unprofitable during the period of 1995-1998 when the information was collected. A firm is defined as profitable if it never lost money during the period or if it made a profit at end of the period. Otherwise it is defined as unprofitable.

Control variables

I control for gender, year of layoff, weekly working hours, number of years being laid off, layoff allowance, workers' expectations on new jobs and their salary expectations on some low-skilled jobs. Male is a dummy variable. Year is constructed as a dummy variable to measure the timing of layoff with '1' denoting being laid off before 1999 (including 1999) and '0' denoting being laid off after 1999. It is used as a supplement for CPI to adjust income variations by different layoff years.

Workers' expectation about benefits and work conditions from new jobs is constructed as a continuous standardized variable, a composite of six items using Cronbach's alpha (Cronbach 1951; Nunnally and Bernstein 1994; Allen and Yen 1979). Laid-off workers were asked whether they would accept a job if the job could not offer pension/medical insurance/formal employment/long-term contract/two days off per week, or if the workplace was far away from home – '2' denotes a 'no,' '1' denotes a 'not sure' and '0' denotes a 'yes.' These items were standardized with mean 0 and variance 1. The estimated correlation between the newly constructed variable and the underlying factor is 0.94. The larger the value, the higher the expectations are.

Salary expectation is also a composite, constructed using Cronbach's alpha. The workers were asked to identify their salary expectations on a series of low-skilled jobs such as babysitter, janitor and manual worker. Some workers answered that they would never accept the jobs no matter how high the salary is. I first transformed the salary requirement to a 1-7 scale with '1' denoting 'very much willing to accept the job' and '7' denoting 'will never accept the job' and then standardized them. The estimated correlation between the constructed variable and the underlying factor it measures is 0.96. Large value means that workers have higher expectations from new jobs.

Weekly working hours is a continuous variable. It is the average number of hours that workers worked weekly the last month before the survey was conducted. Number of years being laid off is a continuous variable. It counts from the year that workers were laid off to the year the survey was conducted. Layoff allowance refers to the amount of basic livelihood allowance that laid-off workers received after layoff. It is a continuous variable.

Models

For Hypothesis 1

I use logit models to analyze the probability of workers being laid off. The sample includes laid-off workers and employed workers at the time of survey. The probability of being laid off is a function of human capital, political capital, characteristics of the enterprises (the current one for employed workers, and the last one for laid-off workers) and cities.

In addition, controlling for the unobserved heterogeneity across enterprises is important because it is the enterprise that makes decisions about who will be laid off. The criteria for layoff may vary by enterprises and be affected by some unobserved characteristics of enterprises, such as the decision processes in the enterprises and reactions of workers. Therefore workers from the same enterprises may correlate with each other after taking into account the right-hand-side variables, which violates the basic assumption of regression models and yields biased estimates.

I construct a logit model with random effect by assuming that the heterogeneity across enterprises is independent of the right-hand-side variables and normally distributed. Let Y_{ijk} ($i = 1,...,I_{jk}$; $j = 1,...,J_k$; $k = 1,...,K$) denote whether worker i in enterprise j of city k was laid off. The distribution of Y_{ijk} follows a binomial distribution where p_{ijk} denotes the probability of being laid off, $p_{ijk} = P(Y_{ijk} = 1)$, and $(1 - p_{ijk})$ is the probability of not being laid off, $(1 - p_{ijk}) = P(Y_{ijk} = 0)$.

$$\ln(\frac{p_{ijk}}{1-p_{ijk}}) = \beta_0 + \beta_1 H_{ijk} + \beta_2 G_{ijk} + \beta_3 M_{ijk} + \beta_4 E_{jk} + \beta_5 C_k + \mu_{jk} \quad (1\text{-}1)$$

where

$\mu_{jk} \sim N(0,v^2)$.

The left hand side is the log odds of layoff status. H_{ijk} is a vector of human capital variables, including age (representing total working experience), education and job training. G_{ijk} is a vector of political capital variables, referring to cadre status and party member. M_{ijk} denotes gender (male = 1). E_{jk} denotes the observed characteristics of the enterprise, including ownership, profitability, size and rank. C_k denotes a set of dummy variables for cities. Comparison of β_1 and β_2 will explicate the relative effect of human capital and political capital on log odds of layoff status.

Since both human capital and political capital include a set of variables, it is hard to compare the relative effect of β_1 and β_2 in the full model. I employ a group of nested models to test the relative effects of human capital and political capital. The following expresses the nested models (to simplify the presentations, I use the logistic regression model):

$$\ln(\frac{p_{ijk}}{1-p_{ijk}}) = \beta_0 + \beta_3 M_{ijk} + \beta_4 E_{jk} + \beta_5 C_k \quad (1\text{-}2)$$

$$\ln(\frac{p_{ijk}}{1-p_{ijk}}) = \beta_0 + \beta_1 H_{ijk} + \beta_3 M_{ijk} + \beta_4 E_{jk} + \beta_5 C_k \quad (1\text{-}3)$$

$$\ln(\frac{p_{ijk}}{1-p_{ijk}}) = \beta_0 + \beta_2 G_{ijk} + \beta_3 M_{ijk} + \beta_4 E_{jk} + \beta_5 C_k \quad (1\text{-}4)$$

By comparing the likelihood ratio of model 1-2 (the simplest model that excludes both human capital and political capital) to equations 1-3 and 1-4 respectively, I can get the approximate percentage of variations explained by including human capital or political capital.

For Hypothesis 2

Because reemployment is only experienced by workers who were laid off, there is a potential selectivity bias if only laid-off workers are included in the model predicting the probability of reemployment. Since there are no efficient instrumental variables available in the data, I will ignore the selection of layoff for reemployment. The probit equation for reemployment is:

$$\text{probit}(Z_{2i}=1) = \beta_{10} + \beta_{11}H_i + \beta_{12}G_i + \beta_{13}X_i + \beta_{14}E_i + \beta_{15}C_i + \mu_{2i} \quad (2\text{-}1)$$

where

$$\mu_{2i} \sim N(0,1)$$

X_i in model (2-1) denotes predictors for reemployment other than human and political capital such as workers' expectation of benefits, working conditions, and salary from the new job, the subsidy they obtained for layoff, the number of years they have been laid off and control variables, such as workers' personal characteristics.

For Hypothesis 3
Potential double sample selection biases exist in examining the return to workers' human capital at their post-layoff jobs because both the non-laid-off workers and laid-off workers not reemployed are excluded. Since there is no method to solve the double selectivity problem, I will ignore the selection of layoff and only consider the selection of reemployment. By modeling the selection into the sample, we can create λ_{2i} through calculating the ratio of standard normal distribution (ϕ) and cumulative standard normal distribution (Φ) of the probability of reemployment. Using model (2-1) as the selection equation:

$$\Pr(z_{2i} = 1 | W_{2i}) = \Phi(W_{2i}\gamma_2) \quad (3\text{-}1)$$

$$\Pr(z_{2i} = 0 | W_{2i}) = 1 - \Phi(W_{2i}\gamma_2) \quad (3\text{-}2)$$

Z_{2i} denotes whether laid-off worker i found a job after layoff (1 = yes, 0 = no). W_{2i} are the right-hand-side variables of model (2-1). Φ is the cumulative standard normal distribution. I estimate λ_{2i} by

$$\hat{\lambda}_{2i} = \frac{\phi(W_{2i}\hat{\gamma}_2)}{\Phi(W_{2i}\hat{\gamma}_2)}$$

λ_{2i} decreases as the probability of finding a job increases. The estimated λ_{2i} will be included in the linear regression model of laid-off workers' job rewards for hypothesis 3.

$$\ln(y_{2i}) = \beta_{20} + \beta_{21}H_{2i} + \beta_{22}G_{2i} + \beta_{23}X_{2i} + \sigma_2\lambda_{2i} + \varepsilon_{2i} \quad (3\text{-}3)$$

where y_{2i} denotes worker i's income (with and without benefit) after layoff. H_{2i} denotes worker's human capital and G_{2i} represents worker's political capital. X_{2i} is a set of control variables including gender, the ownership of current enterprises and residential cities. Therefore, β_{21} and β_{22} capture the returns to human capital and political capital after layoff. A significant σ_2 indicates there is selectivity and the potential bias is corrected by including λ_{2i} in the model.

In order to understand the change in the returns to human/political capital before and after layoff, I construct a model for returns to human/political capital at the job before layoff. Because of the complexity of two-step selectivity – first selecting on laid-off status and second selection on reemployment, I do not address the selectivity issue in the models for returns to human/political capital:

$$\ln(y_{3i}) = \beta_{30} + \beta_{31}H_{3i} + \beta_{32}G_{3i} + \beta_{33}X_{3i} + \varepsilon_{3i} \qquad (3\text{-}4)$$

y_{3i} is laid-off worker i's total income (with and without benefit) from the last job before layoff. H_{3i} denotes human capital of worker i and G_{3i} represents political capital. β_{31} and β_{32} reflect the returns to human capital and political capital before layoff. Since the sample in models (3-3) and (3-4) are not the same, I will compare the pre- and post-layoff returns in the magnitude and significance level rather than a formal test.

Determinants of layoff status

A few modifications of the measurement are in order. First, age was used as a proxy for working experience in the layoff status model because total working experience is measured differently for employed workers and laid-off workers in this model. Laid-off workers' total working experience counts the number of years from their first job to the time they were laid off. But employed workers' total working experience counts to the time of survey. Therefore, for workers who got their first job in the same year, employed workers always have more total working experience than workers who were laid off before the year of survey. This may lead to an overestimation of the effect of total working experience on layoff. In addition, since few respondents were from joint ventures, and the national layoff policy was designed for workers under state ownership (both solely owned and shared), I reclassified the joint ventures into state-owned or collective owned enterprises according to the ownership of their domestic shares. Table 10.3 presents the estimations from the logit model with random effects.

Table 10.3: Logit estimates on layoff status

Variables	Logit with RE	Model 2	Model 3	Model 4
Male	−.34c (.09)	−.36c (.07)	−.41c (.08)	−.23c (.07)
Age	.02c (.01)		.00 (.00)	
High school	−.45c (.10)		−.49c (.09)	
College and above	−1.36c (.14)		−1.44c (.12)	
Received on-the-job training	−.24c (.09)		−.36c (.08)	
Received full time training	−1.05c (.13)		−1.18c (.12)	
Job training missing	−.52c (.15)		−.49c (.14)	
Party member	−1.00c (.12)			−.81c (.10)
Party member missing	−1.28c (.33)			−1.05c (.30)
Cadre	−1.00c (.19)			−1.06c (.16)
Cadre missing	.75 (.57)			.71 (.50)
Collective-owned or shared	−1.33c (.22)	−.19 (.13)	−.29b (.14)	−.27b (.14)
Profitable enterprises	−1.61c (.18)	−.57c (.08)	−.49c (.09)	−.57c (.09)
Missing success	.68b (.33)	.82c (.19)	.83c (.20)	.79c (.19)
Local enterprises	.07 (.21)	−.14 (.10)	−.19a (.11)	−.18a (.10)
Medium enterprises	.66c (.18)	.26b (.11)	.35c (.11)	.24b (.11)
Large enterprises	1.14 (.26)	.10c (.13)	.24 (.14)	.07a (.13)
Tianjin	.07 (.25)	.65c (.13)	.47c (.14)	.56c (.14)
Nanjing	1.17c (.24)	.73c (.14)	.76c (.14)	.78c (.14)
Xi'an	1.09c (.24)	.59c (.16)	.77c (.16)	.55c (.16)
Changchun	.24 (.23)	.44c (.14)	.69c (.15)	.44c (.14)
Wuhan	.61c (.21)	.57c (.14)	.65c (.14)	.55c (.14)
Constant	−.70a (.37)	−.36b (.16)	.44 (.27)	−.08 (.16)
LR		−2241	−2074	−2144

Notes.
Standard errors in parentheses.
a: $p < 0.1$; b: $p < 0.05$; c: $p < 0.01$

Both human capital and political capital are significant determinants for workers' layoff status. In general, the more human capital and political capital workers have, the less likely they are to be laid off. However, older workers are more likely to be laid off (Age Square is dropped from the model because it is not significant). Holding all other variables constant, increasing age by one year increases the odds of being laid off by about 2%. This is different from what some local officials claimed in interviews that workers above a certain age were not allowed to be laid off by enterprises. It is also different from Appleton and his co-authors' conclusion (2001) that both younger workers and older workers are less likely to be laid off. Since age and total working experience are highly correlated at coefficiency of 0.9, it can be concluded that the accumulated working experience as part of human capital does not have an effect on workers' layoff status. In other words, the workers are laid off regardless of their working experience.

Both education and job training have effects in the expected direction: workers with higher education or more job training are less likely to be laid off. Compared to workers who received junior high school education and below, the odds of being laid off decrease by 36% for workers who received high school education,[12] and 74% for workers who received college education. When compared to workers who did not receive any kind of job training, the odds of being laid off decrease by 21% for workers who received on-the-job training and by 65% for workers who received full-time job training. The chi-square test shows that workers who received full-time job training are significantly less likely to be laid off than workers who only received on-the-job training. It is reasonable because job training can be regarded as enterprises' investment in workers. Full-time job training needs more investment than on-the-job training since enterprises need to give workers paid-leave, and often have to pay for the training. Therefore the enterprises are reluctant to lay off trained workers, especially workers who have received full-time training.

As for political capital, both party members and cadres are less likely to be laid off than non-party members or non-cadres controlling for other variables. Party membership can decrease the odds of being laid off by 63% while cadre status also can decrease the odds of being laid off by 63%. Since 72% of cadres are party members at the same time, in general cadres have a much higher chance to stay in the enterprises than non-cadres.

Model comparison (Table 10.3, models 2–4) shows that human capital plays a more important role than political capital in deciding who will be laid off, but the difference between the effects of the two kinds of capital is very small. The percentage of explained variation in workers' layoff status (likelihood ratio) increases by about 7.5% after adding human capital (model 2 vs. 3), compared to 4.3% by adding political capital (model 2 vs. 4).

However, since age as representative of working experience fails to decrease workers' chances of being laid off, it is hard to conclude that human capital plays a more important role than political capital in determining workers' layoff status as I stated in hypothesis 1. Instead, the estimations support the viewpoint of 'power persistence' in income studies which argues that both human capital and political capital are important factors in affecting income inequality in transitional economies (Bian and Logan 1996; Zhou 2000). In addition, human capital and political capital are not totally independent of each other. Workers with more human capital are more likely to be recruited as party members or be promoted to be cadres (Gerber 2000, Walder, Li and Treiman 2000). The statistics show that by the middle of 2002, about 52.5% of party members received high school and above education, and 23.2% of them received college education. In comparison, national statistics show that in 2001, about 16% of labor force received high school and above education.[13]

The estimates on the observed characteristics of enterprises show that almost all of the observed characteristics of enterprises in general strongly affect workers' layoff status (Table 10.3). The privilege structure is reversed in the estimations on layoff status where workers in the SOEs are more likely to be laid off than workers in the collective-owned enterprises, and workers in larger enterprises are more likely to be laid off than workers in the smaller enterprises. Ranks of enterprises do not have a significant effect on workers' layoff status.

The odds of being laid off are 74% higher for workers in the SOEs. It is different from the tendency reflected by national statistics, which show that in 1999, 13.5% of workers in collective-owned enterprises were laid off, compared to 7.3% in the SOEs.[14] One possible explanation for the effects of ownership on layoff is that fewer laid-off workers were drawn from the collective-owned enterprises than from the SOEs. In the sample, 47% of workers from the SOEs and 41% of workers from the collective-owned enterprises were laid-off workers. Another possible explanation is that, according to state policy, layoff only covers workers in the SOEs. Whether workers in the collective-owned enterprises can be treated as layoff and obtain related benefits depends on local policies. Even if they can get the benefit, what they receive may be worse than what workers in the SOEs get.[15] Therefore, the collective-owned enterprises are more cautious about laying off workers. On the other hand, unlike SOEs, the collective-owned enterprises may not be under pressure from the government to lay off their surplus workers.[16] The cost to keep a worker in the collective-owned enterprise is much lower than that in the SOEs: the average wage per worker in the collective-owned enterprises was only 67.6% of that in the SOEs in 1999.[17]

The probability of being laid off is not significantly different by the ranks of enterprises. Workers from higher ranked enterprises do not get more protection from being laid off than workers from lower ranked enterprises. It is consistent with Zang's (2002) finding in his research in Zhongshan that the enterprises' bureaucratic rank no longer affects workers' income.

In general, the more workers the enterprise has, the higher the probability that the workers will be laid off after controlling for all other variables. Compared to workers in small enterprises, the odds of layoff increase 94% for workers in medium enterprises, and 213% for workers in large enterprises. National statistics also show that 39% of laid-off workers in SOEs came from medium and large enterprises in 1999.[18] This may be because (1) there is a different reform strategy for small and medium/large scaled enterprises, which was called 'grasp the big, release the small (Lardy 1998).' Medium and large enterprises play the main roles in the government's plan of 'reducing the number of workers and improving the efficiency.' (2) Some successful medium and large enterprises were forced by the government to merge or purchase other SOEs that were almost bankrupt, and take over their workers (Lardy 1998). Lots of workers from the merged/purchased enterprises were laid off. Some of the buyers in the survey fell into difficulties because of the merger and had to lay off their own workers. (3) Medium and large enterprises have more resources for laying off workers, that is, they can get more attention from the government and therefore give better deals to their laid-off workers than smaller enterprises. On the other hand, small enterprises have fewer resources, but their cost of keeping a worker is also lower than medium or large enterprises.

Therefore, the old hierarchy system that ranked enterprises by their ownership, bureaucratic rank and size has lost its significance in deciding workers' welfare, at least the welfare of not being laid off. On the contrary, the enterprises' market success becomes a key factor for protecting workers from being laid off. The odds of being laid off are 80% less for workers in the profitable enterprises than for workers in unprofitable enterprises.

The estimations here are different from Appleton and his coauthors' predictions (2001) that workers in central SOEs are less likely to be laid off than workers in the local SOEs, and workers in collective owned enterprises are more likely to be laid off than local SOEs. Since the data for both studies are not collected from national surveys, and have different sampling structures, the effects of characteristics of enterprises such as ownership and rank on layoff need to be tested further by national representative data.

One more thing I would like to discuss here is the effect of gender and age on layoff. Female workers are in a disadvantaged position facing layoff. The odds of male workers being laid off are 29% lower than that of female workers. The difference between the two genders is significant. National data also show that the proportion of female laid-off workers is much higher than the proportion of urban female employment. In 1999, 46.7% of laid-off workers who had registered in reemployment service centers were female – 8.7% higher than the proportion of female employment in urban units.[19]

However, only one out of 93 enterprises acknowledged that gender is the main determinant for layoff. In addition, only 2% of all laid-off workers and 3.2% of female laid-off workers agreed that workers were laid off based on gender. Instead, many workers and managers of enterprises mentioned the important effects of age on layoff. In the data, 23% of the enterprises (21 out of 93) responded that age is the main criterion for layoff. For many other enterprises, age may be not the most important factor, but it is at least one of the main factors in their decisions about who is to be laid off. For example, 11 out of 18 surveyed state/collective-owned enterprises in Tianjin, and 9 out of 15 in Nanjing mentioned that age is either the only, or one of the criteria for layoff: younger workers might also be laid off, but all workers above certain ages have to be laid off in the form of inner/ earlier retirement. Only a few enterprises emphasized that this kind of a criterion was not suitable for technicians. The age requirements are different between male and female workers in most of the cases (usually 42–53 for female and 45–55 for male, varied by enterprises), and different between cadres and non-cadres in some cases: male workers are laid off at an older age than female workers; and cadres are laid off at an older age than non-cadres.[20] Therefore, part of the gender effect may come from the different age criterion that is used for layoff by some enterprises.

Age was chosen by policy makers in the enterprises as the criterion for layoff because it is clear-cut, less disputable and easier to manage. Generally older workers can be laid off in the form of inner retirement. After being laid off, they are still considered as formal workers of the enterprise although they lose their jobs; and they are still paid (with living subsidy) by the enterprise although what they get might be less than their original salary. However, once the younger workers were laid off, they would not be paid as well as inner retired workers. Moreover they had to cut off the employment relationship with the enterprise after three years. Therefore, if layoff based on age is not the best choice, it is at least a choice that can be accepted by both managers and workers. First, it is very easy to manage. The enterprises are able to avoid confusion and then disputes that might be caused by other criteria, and avoid resistance from younger workers. Second, it is consistent with the egalitarian tradition within the SOEs. It looks fair and is easy for workers to accept. Although older workers may complain, at least they can keep the employment relationship with the enterprises and they are promised their pension once they reach the retirement age. Also they have the chance to find jobs elsewhere and get the second income.

Older workers can get more protection than younger workers if they can obtain a good deal for inner retirement. Since the policies on layoff keep changing and get tighter and tighter, workers who were laid off earlier may get better deals than those being laid off later.[21] Therefore, workers in enterprises that were able to provide a relatively good deal applied for inner retirement as soon as they reached the age requirement, and few people dared to wait for the next chance.[22] In addition, usually female workers can be inner retired at earlier ages than male workers. Therefore, female and older workers are not necessarily disadvantaged groups in layoff. On the one hand, older workers and female workers are disadvantaged because they are more likely to be laid off. One the other hand, older laid-off workers and female laid-off workers may belong to advantaged groups if they can get relatively good packages for inner retirement. However, this kind of advantage is limited, constrained by the economic ability of enterprises and/or local government.

Reemployment of laid-off workers

Results from the probit estimation for reemployment status are presented in Table 10.5 (see Table 10.4 for descriptive statistics). In order to make it easier to interpret, I transfer the results to the change in the probability for an infinitesimal change in contiguous variables (dF/dx) and the discrete change in the probability for dummy variables.

Whether laid-off workers can be reemployed depends on such considerations as their personal characteristics and their expectations about new jobs. Estimations on the effects of human capital only partly support the hypothesis that workers with more education have a higher probability of being reemployed, and workers' working experience and skills obtained before layoff would not help with getting reemployed.

Table 10.4: Descriptive statistics of laid-off workers' reemployment and earnings

Variables	Employment			Earnings	
	All	Reemployed	Unreemployed	Before layoff	After layoff
Returns from jobs (without benefit)				432.70 (182.46)	566.61 (470.90)
Log returns from jobs (without benefit)				5.98 (.44)	6.17 (.50)
Returns from jobs (with benefit)				508.55 (215.43)	604.36 (477.26)
Log returns from jobs (with benefit)				6.14 (.45)	6.24 (.50)
Male	.43 (.50)	.42 (.49)	.45 (.50)	.44 (.50)	.40 (.49)
Age	39.31 (8.42)	38.54 (8.31)	40.29 (8.45)		
Total working experience				18.49 (8.60)	20.01 (8.28)
Square of total working experience				415.91 (341.69)	469.09 (342.08)
Current job tenure				16.47 (8.92)	2.72 (1.62)
Square of current job tenure				350.91 (331.09)	10.00 (12.85)
High school	.50 (.50)	.54 (.50)	.46 (.50)	.50 (.50)	.54 (.50)
College and above	.11 (.31)	.12 (.32)	.10 (.30)	.11 (.32)	.11 (.31)
Received on-the-job training	.40 (.49)	.43 (.50)	.37 (.48)	.41 (.49)	.41 (.49)
Received full time training	.07 (.26)	.08 (.27)	.07 (.25)	.07 (.26)	.07 (.26)
Missing job training	.09 (.28)	.09 (.28)	.08 (.28)	.09 (.28)	.09 (.28)
Working hours/week				43.47 (6.85)	46.77 (12.56)
Working hours missing				.03 (.18)	.17 (.38)
Party member	.14 (.35)	.14 (.35)	.14 (.35)	.15 (.35)	.14 (.35)
Party member missing	.01 (.10)	.01 (.11)	.01 (.08)	.01 (.10)	.01 (.09)
Cadre	.04 (.19)	.04 (.19)	.04 (.19)	.04 (.19)	.10 (.31)
Cadre missing	.01 (.10)	.01 (.10)	.01 (.09)	.01 (.09)	.20 (.40)
Expectation about benefit (for new jobs)	−.01 (.76)	−.02 (.75)	.01 (.78)		
Missing benefit expectation	.08 (.27)	.07 (.25)	.10 (.30)		
Expectation on salary	−.08 (.79)	−.10 (.76)	−.07 (.83)		
Missing salary expectation	.05 (.22)	.06 (.23)	.04 (.20)		
Subsidy for layoff /100	1.98 (1.16)	1.92 (1.13)	2.05 (1.19)		
Missing subsidy for layoff	.10 (.29)	.10 (.30)	.09 (.28)		
# of years from being laid off	2.93 (1.41)	3.14 (1.39)	2.65 (1.39)		
Collective-state-owned/shared	.10 (.30)	.12 (.32)	.07 (.26)		
Collective owned				.08 (.28)	.07 (.26)
Joint venture				.02 (.14)	.04 (.20)
Private/foreign-owned					.39 (.49)
Others ownership/Don't know					.23 (.42)
Cadre, state/collective-owned enterprises or joint venture				.04 (.19)	.05 (.23)
Non-managers, private or ownership missing enterprises					.57 (.50)
Manager, private or ownership missing enterprises					.05 (.22)
Profitable	.24 (.43)	.23 (.42)	.26 (.44)		
Missing profitable	.06 (.24)	.09 (.29)	.03 (.17)		
City/district firms	.72 (.45)	.72 (.45)	.72 (.45)		
Medium size	.47 (.50)	.45 (.50)	.49 (.50)		
Large size	.32 (.46)	.28 (.45)	.36 (.48)		

Table 10.4: continued

	Employment			Earnings	
Variables	All	Reemployed	Unreemployed	Before layoff	After layoff
Tianjin	.19 (.39)	.20 (.40)	.19 (.39)	.18 (.39)	.24 (.43)
Nanjing	.19 (.39)	.20 (.40)	.17 (.38)	.19 (.39)	.23 (.42)
Xi'an	.14 (.35)	.12 (.33)	.16 (.37)	.14 (.35)	.10 (.30)
Changchun	.18 (.38)	.19 (.39)	.17 (.38)	.19 (.39)	.14 (.35)
Wuhan	.18 (.38)	.14 (.34)	.23 (.42)	.18 (.38)	.13 (.34)
Lamda					.61 (.28)
Before 1999				.74 (.44)	
N	1,504	841	663	1,551	601

Note. Standard errors in parentheses

On the one hand, workers with middle-level education (high school), not high-level education, have a higher probability of being reemployed. Having received high school education significantly increases the expected probability of reemployment by 8%. But having received college education does not significantly increase the probability of reemployment. On the other hand, total working experience and full-time job training workers received before layoff do not significantly affect the probability of being reemployed. But on-the-job training as a kind of basic job training can increase the probability of finding a job after layoff by 9%. Representing total working experience the workers obtained before layoff, age has a negative effect on the predicted probability of reemployment.[23] Older workers are in an inferior position in the job market: for each additional year of age, the expected probability of reemployment decreases by 1%. These findings suggest that the jobs laid-off workers obtained were relatively low-skilled requiring only basic skill and education, and therefore workers' accumulated working experience, professional job training and extra education were not valued.

In contrast to other research (RG1 2001; RG2 2002; Appleton et al. 2001), estimations from the probit model show that there is no significant difference between male and female workers on the probability of reemployment. This may result from urban characteristics – all cities in the survey have a relatively more developed tertiary industry in which male workers may not have much advantage over female workers.

Political capital does not affect the probability of reemployment either. Neither party members nor ex-cadres have any advantages over non-party members or non-cadres in the probability of reemployment.

Table 10.5: Probit estimates for reemployment

Variables	Coefficients	dF/dx
Male	.02 (.07)	.01 (.03)
Age	−.01c (.00)	−.01 (.00)
High school	.22c (.08)	.08 (.03)
College and above	.18 (.13)	.07 (.05)
Received on-the-job training	.24c (.08)	.09 (.03)
Received full time training	.06 (.13)	.02 (.05)
Missing job training	.11 (.13)	.04 (.05)
Party member	.17 (.11)	.07 (.04)
Party member missing	.17 (.37)	.06 (.14)
Cadre	.01 (.19)	.01 (.08)
Cadre missing	.32 (.38)	.12 (.14)
Expectation on benefit	−.08a (.05)	−.03 (.02)
Missing benefit expectation	−.44c (.13)	−.17 (.05)
Expectation on salary	−.09a (.05)	−.04 (.02)
Missing salary expectation	.18 (.17)	.07 (.06)
# of subsidy for layoff	−.01 (.04)	.00 (.01)
Missing # of subsidy for layoff	.04 (.12)	.02 (.05)
# of years from being laid off	.17c (.03)	.07 (.01)
Collective-owned/shared	−.02 (.14)	−.01 (.06)
Profitable	.10 (.09)	.04 (.03)
Missing profitable	.49c (.18)	.18 (.06)
Local enterprises	−.45c (.10)	−.17 (.04)
Medium size	−.39c (.11)	−.15 (.04)
Large size	−.81c (.13)	−.31 (.05)
Tianjin	−.31b (.14)	−.12 (.06)
Nanjing	−.21 (.14)	−.08 (.06)
Xi'an	−.59c (.16)	−.23 (.06)
Changchun	−.39b (.16)	−.16 (.06)
Wuhan	−1.04c (.15)	−.39 (.05)
Constant	1.14c (.28)	

Notes.
Standard errors in parentheses.
a: $p < 0.1$; b: $p < 0.05$; c: $p < 0.01$

Consistent with what was observed by other researchers (CCER 1999), laid-off workers with higher expectations on job benefits and salary are less likely to be reemployed. Workers who have been laid off for a longer time are more likely to be reemployed. The predicted probability of reemployment increases by 7% with one more year of being laid off. But there is no significant relationship between the amount of basic living allowance and the probability of reemployment – maybe the amount of layoff allowance is not high enough, or the variations in layoff allowance are not big enough, to discourage some workers from looking for jobs.

The test on the effects of enterprises' ownership, rank and size on workers' reemployment probability obtains mixed findings. The characteristics of the original enterprises do affect the probability of workers' reemployment. After controlling for all other variables, the ownership and the market performance of the enterprises do not have significant effects on workers' job search outcomes. However, the rank and the size of the enterprises affect significantly the probability of their laid-off workers' reemployment. Workers from local enterprises are 17% less likely than workers from central enterprises to be reemployed. Workers from small enterprises have the highest probability of reemployment: their expected probability of reemployment is 15% higher than workers from medium enterprises and 31% higher than workers from large enterprises. It seems a little puzzling: central enterprises may have more resources and are able to take better care of their workers, and medium and large enterprises also have relatively more resources than small enterprises. Recalling from the previous estimations that workers in medium and large enterprises are more likely to be laid off, a possible explanation is that the medium and large enterprises may have too many laid-off workers to take care of. Also since workers in the larger enterprises might have better incomes and benefits than workers in smaller enterprises before layoff, they may have higher expectations for new jobs, such as stable jobs in the state ownership. Another possible explanation is that the reform of small enterprises started earlier than the reform of medium and large enterprises. The reform policy on small enterprises is clear and laid-off workers from small enterprises know that they would not get jobs by watching and waiting. But some workers from larger enterprises believe that the governments would not let the enterprises down and leave workers alone, and they still hope to be called back by the enterprises or wait for the enterprises and governments to arrange their reemployment (CCER 1999).

Rewards from post-layoff jobs

Using the probit model for reemployment status as a selectivity model and laid-off workers' expectation of job benefits, work conditions and salary and the number of years being laid off as instrumental variables, a Heckman probit model with selection was constructed to examine the returns to human capital at post-layoff jobs. A linear regression model was used to examine rewards to human capital before layoff.

Tables 10.6 and 10.7 present the estimations of rewards from post-layoff and pre-layoff jobs (see Table 10.4 for descriptive statistics). Since the dependent variables are logarithm income, the coefficiencies can be interpreted as percentage change in income due to one unit change in the regressors. Two kinds of income are used as dependent variables: one includes benefits and the other does not. There are two sub-models again for each kind of income: one uses total working experience (models 1 and 3, Tables 10.6 and 10.7) and the other uses current job tenure (models 2 and 4, Tables 10.6 and 10.7).

Comparing the estimates from various models for rewards (with and without benefits) from post-layoff jobs, the models using current job tenure (models 2 and 4, Table 10.6) are better than those using total working experience (models 1 and 3, Table 10.6) because more variations are explained by using current job tenure. In addition, the coefficients for the total working experience are not only negative, but also smaller in magnitude than the coefficients for current job tenure. This means that the post-layoff employers do not value laid-off workers' accumulated working experience as assumed in hypothesis 3. In addition, younger workers are better paid than older workers from post-layoff jobs because of the strong correlation between age and total working experience. So current job tenures, instead of total working experience, will be used to analyze the rewards from post-layoff jobs.

When current job tenure instead of total working experience is introduced into the income models, the selectivity bias, lamda (λ), loses its significance. It could be that there is no significant difference between the earnings of laid-off workers who have found jobs and the potential earnings of workers who have not, or the instrumental variables are not powerful for the reward equation.

Comparing the estimates for income with and without benefits (models 2 and 4, Table 10.6), the effect of weekly working hours decreases if benefits are included. However, since including or excluding benefits does not make a big difference in estimations of other variables, I am going to use the model estimated for income with benefits as my final model for analysis (model 4).

Contrary to my hypothesis, workers' income after layoff is not significantly affected by their human capital, except current job

Table 10.6: OLS regressions for rewards from post-layoff jobs (with sample selection for reemployment)

Variables	Income without benefit		Income with benefit		
	(1)	(2)	(3)	(4)	(5)
Male	.14ᶜ (.04)	.13ᶜ (.04)	.11ᶜ (.04)	.11ᶜ (.04)	.10ᵇ (.04)
Total working experience	-.02ᵇ (.01)		-.02ᵇ (.01)		
Square of total working experience	.00ᶜ (.00)		.00ᵇ (.00)		
Current job tenure		.11ᶜ (.04)		.13ᶜ (.04)	.14ᶜ (.04)
Square of current job tenure		-.01ᵃ (.00)		-.01ᵇ (.00)	-.01ᵇ (.00)
High school	-.07 (.04)	-.05 (.04)	-.07 (.04)	-.05 (.04)	-.05 (.04)
College and above	.03 (.07)	.06 (.07)	.03 (.07)	.06 (.07)	.06 (.07)
Received on-the-job training	.03 (.04)	.05 (.04)	.04 (.04)	.07 (.04)	.06 (.04)
Received full time training	.07 (.07)	.08 (.07)	.07 (.07)	.08 (.07)	.08 (.07)
Missing job training	.02 (.07)	.03 (.07)	.01 (.07)	.02 (.07)	.03 (.07)
Weekly working hours/100	.43ᵇ (.17)	.44ᵇ (.17)	.31ᵃ (.17)	.32ᵃ (.17)	.36ᵇ (.17)
Working hours missing	-.02 (.05)	-.02 (.05)	-.08 (.06)	-.08 (.05)	-.07 (.05)
Party member	-.13ᵇ (.06)	-.11ᵇ (.05)	-.13ᵇ (.06)	-.11ᵇ (.06)	-.10ᵃ (.06)
Party membership missing	-.13 (.21)	-.13 (.21)	-.17 (.21)	-.16 (.21)	-.21 (.21)
Cadre/manager	.32ᶜ (.07)	.32ᶜ (.06)	.33ᶜ (.07)	.32ᶜ (.06)	
Cadre/manager status missing	.06 (.07)	.01 (.07)	.12ᵃ (.07)	.07 (.07)	-.05 (.06)
Collective owned	-.24ᶜ (.08)	-.21ᵇ (.08)	-.23ᶜ (.08)	-.19ᵇ (.08)	–
Joint venture	-.18ᵃ (.10)	-.11 (.10)	-.18ᵃ (.10)	-.10 (.10)	–
Private	-.04 (.05)	-.02 (.05)	-.07 (.05)	-.05 (.05)	–
Other ownership/refusal	-.23ᶜ (.07)	-.22ᶜ (.07)	-.27ᶜ (.07)	-.25ᶜ (.07)	–
Cadre, state/collective-owned enterprises or joint venture	–	–	–	–	.18ᵇ (.09)
Non-managers, private or ownership missing enterprises	–	–	–	–	-.09ᵃ (.05)
Manager, private or ownership missing enterprises	–	–	–	–	.34ᶜ (.09)
Tianjin	.14ᵇ (.07)	.15ᵇ (.07)	.04 (.07)	.05 (.07)	.12ᵃ (.07)
Nanjing	-.02 (.07)	-.03 (.07)	-.08 (.07)	-.09 (.07)	-.02 (.07)
Xi'an	.15ᵃ (.09)	.13 (.09)	.03 (.09)	.00 (.09)	.03 (.09)
Changchun	-.20ᵇ (.08)	-.16ᵇ (.08)	-.28ᶜ (.08)	-.25 (.08)	-.19ᵇ (.08)
Wuhan	-.11 (.08)	-.13ᵃ (.08)	-.21ᵇ (.08)	-.24 (.08)	-.20ᵇ (.08)
Lamda	-.28ᶜ (.09)	-.11 (.09)	-.22ᵇ (.09)	-.04 (.09)	-.06 (.09)
Constant	6.33ᶜ (.14)	5.81ᶜ (.14)	6.51ᶜ (.14)	5.96ᶜ (.14)	5.87ᶜ (.13)
R^2	.21	.22	.20	.21	.20

Notes.
Standard errors in parentheses.
a: $p < 0.1$; b: $p < 0.05$; c: $p < 0.01$

tenure. The effect of current job tenure is not linear. Workers with one year experience in their current jobs earn 13% more than workers who just entered the enterprises. Both education and job training

Table 10.7: OLS regressions for rewards from laid-off workers' pre-layoff job

Variables	Income without benefit		Income with benefit	
	(1)	(2)	(3)	(4)
Male	.04ᵃ (.02)	.03 (.02)	.04ᵇ (.02)	.04ᵃ (.02)
Total working experience	.01ᵃ (.00)		.01ᵇ (.00)	
Square of total working experience	.00 (.00)		.00 (.00)	
Current job tenure	−.00 (.00)		−.00 (.00)	
Square of current job tenure	.00ᵇ (.00)		.00ᵇ (.00)	
High school	.05ᵇ (.02)	.04ᵃ (.02)	.06ᵇ (.02)	.04ᵃ (.02)
College and above	.16ᶜ (.04)	.14ᶜ (.04)	.17ᶜ (.04)	.14ᶜ (.04)
Received on-the-job training	.05ᵇ (.02)	.04ᵃ (.02)	.05ᵇ (.02)	.04ᵃ (.02)
Received full time training	−.02 (.04)	−.02 (.04)	−.02 (.04)	−.02 (.04)
Missing job training	−.09ᵇ (.04)	−.09ᵇ (.04)	−.08ᵇ (.04)	−.09ᵇ (.04)
Weekly working hours/100	−.00ᵃ (.00)	−.00ᵇ (.00)	−.00ᵇ (.00)	−.00ᵇ (.00)
Working hours missing	.02 (.06)	.02 (.06)	.05 (.06)	.05 (.06)
Party member	.05ᵃ (.03)	.07ᵇ (.03)	.06ᵃ (.03)	.07ᵇ (.03)
Party membership missing	−.14 (.10)	−.16 (.10)	−.14 (.10)	−.16 (.10)
Cadre	.15ᶜ (.06)	.18ᶜ (.06)	.14ᵇ (.06)	.17ᶜ (.06)
Cadre status missing	−.03 (.11)	−.03 (.11)	−.03 (.11)	−.02 (.11)
Collective owned	−.15ᶜ (.04)	−.15ᶜ (.04)	−.16ᶜ (.04)	−.16ᶜ (.04)
Joint venture	.10 (.08)	.13ᵃ (.08)	.09 (.08)	.12ᵃ (.08)
Tianjin	−.10ᵇ (.04)	−.12ᶜ (.04)	−.16ᶜ (.04)	−.18ᶜ (.04)
Nanjing	−.08ᵃ (.04)	−.09ᵇ (.04)	−.07ᵃ (.04)	−.08ᵇ (.04)
Xi'an	−.30ᶜ (.04)	−.32ᶜ (.04)	−.32ᶜ (.04)	−.34ᶜ (.04)
Changchun	−.30ᶜ (.04)	−.33ᶜ (.04)	−.34ᶜ (.04)	−.37ᶜ (.04)
Wuhan	−.38ᶜ (.04)	−.40ᶜ (.04)	−.41ᶜ (.04)	−.43ᶜ (.04)
Before 1999	−.11ᶜ (.02)	−.11ᶜ (.02)	−.11ᶜ (.02)	−.11ᶜ (.02)
Constant	6.11ᶜ (.09)	6.27ᶜ (.08)	6.31ᶜ (.09)	6.47ᶜ (.08)
R^2	.20	.19	.21	.20

Notes.
Standard errors in parentheses.
a: $p < 0.1$; b: $p < 0.05$; c: $p < 0.01$

that workers received before layoff do not significantly affect their income from the current jobs. Party membership has no positive effect on job reward either. But cadres in public-owned enterprises and managers in private enterprises are much better rewarded than non-cadres or non-managers. Differentiating the effects of cadres and managers by the ownership of enterprises (model 5, Table 10.6), the income difference between cadres and non-cadres still exist within the non-private enterprises. Cadres in general earn 18% more than non-cadres. But the income gap between managers and non-managers in private enterprises is much larger: managers earn 43% more than non-managers.

Male workers earn much more than female workers from their post-layoff jobs. After controlling for all other variables, male workers are paid 11% more than female workers (model 4, Table 10.6). Earnings also depend on weekly working hours: one more hour working means 0.3% higher returns in total income. Ownership still plays a part in explaining income differences. Workers in collective-owned enterprises earn about 19% less than workers in SOEs.

In contrast to post layoff jobs, total working experience is more powerful than current job tenure for estimating workers' income (with and without benefit) before layoff (Table 10.7). The effects of total working experience on income are linear (model 3, Table 10.7).

There is no significant difference between the estimations made on income with or without benefits (model 1 vs. 3, 2 vs. 4, Table 10.7), or by using total working experience versus current job tenure after counting benefits into income (model 3 vs. 4, Table 10.7). Therefore, in order to compare the reward mechanism between pre- and post-layoff jobs in the same model specification, the estimations made on income with benefits using current job tenure will be used for analysis (model 4, Table 10.7).

Human capital plays a more important role in earnings before layoff. Both education and job training have positive effects on income. Workers with high school education earned 4% more, and workers with college education earned 14% more, than workers with below high school education. Workers who received on-the-job training also earned 4% more than workers without on-the-job training. But full-time job training did not have a significant effect on income.

Political capital also affected workers' returns significantly before layoff. More political capital ensured better income. In general, party members earned 7% more than non-party members. The income gap between cadres and non-cadres was almost the same for pre-layoff and post-layoff jobs. Cadres earned 17% more than non-cadres.

Therefore the hypothesis that the rewards to education increases in post-layoff jobs is rejected. But the hypothesis that workers' working experience and skills obtained before layoff do not affect their income after layoff holds. Comparing the earnings before and after layoff, on the one hand, the effects of human capital and political capital in general are weakened after layoff. On the other hand, differences based on gender, current job tenure, working load (weekly working hours) and enterprise ownership are strengthened after layoff.

The different reward mechanisms for pre- and post-layoff jobs may partly explain why workers are reluctant to leave their original enterprises until being laid off. First, the benefits from jobs after layoff are worse than those from pre-layoff jobs. Before layoff, workers on average received 76 *yuan* per month as benefits, accounting for 15% of their income, compared to 38 *yuan* per month at post-layoff jobs, accounting for 6% of total income. Before layoff, 72% of laid-off workers in the sample had medical insurance bought by their work place; 84% of workers had pensions financed mainly by their enterprise and 43% of workers had unemployment insurance. After layoff, only 37% of workers have medical insurance, 43% of workers have pensions and 26% of workers have unemployment insurance.

Second, rewards from post-layoff jobs depend more on current job tenures, gender and ownership. Young and male workers have more advantages than older and female workers. Not only does education have no effect on workers' income, the job training and accumulated working experience workers received before layoff also have little effect on their income after layoff. In addition, post-layoff jobs are much harder than pre-layoff jobs. For example, weekly working hours obtained strong significant effects on income at post-layoff jobs. More than 40% of workers were paid at piece rate or hourly rate after layoff (compared to 12% before layoff). This means that laid-off workers have to compete with job market beginners who do not have any prior working experience but are much younger and physically capable.

Therefore, most workers regret being laid off. When workers were asked to pick one out of three choices, only 26% of workers said they did not mind being laid off (not including inner retirement), 37% of workers would like to be laid off in the form of inner-retirement and another 37% of workers would rather work for reduced wages with the same workload instead of being laid off. Fewer young workers regret being laid off: 43% of workers under 35-years-old did not mind being laid off, compared to 21% of workers between 36 to 45-years-old, and 14% of workers who were older than 45-years-old.

The estimation on the returns from the post-layoff jobs reiterate the earlier prediction that workers who are reemployed are more likely to be hired for relatively low-skilled jobs because both education and working experience would not help them much in job attainment and rewards.

Conclusion

Using quantitative research methods, this study examined the effects of human capital and political capital on workers' employment and income, and assessed how these effects differ by types of enterprises. The study found that both human capital and political capital are important determinants for workers' layoff. Workers with more human capital or political capital are less likely to be laid off than workers with less human capital or political capital. In contrast, the jobs available for laid-off workers are in a special segment of the urban labor market in which workers' human capital has only a limited effect on their reemployment status while political capital has no effect.

In addition, the comparison of rewards between laid-off workers' post-layoff jobs and pre-layoff jobs also reveals that post-layoff jobs were mainly jobs requiring only basic skills. Both human capital and political capital have limited effects on workers' rewards from post-layoff jobs. Current working experience is the only human capital variable that significantly affects reemployed workers' income and party membership fails to increase workers' income from reemployment.

The analysis also shows that the old segmentation structure by types of ownership has lost its significance in affecting workers' layoff status or reemployment status. After controlling for all other variables, workers in a privileged position derived from their state-owned or larger sized enterprises did not have more protection from layoff or more advantages in reemployment. The rank and size of enterprises have also lost their significance to a large degree in affecting workers' income. Instead, market performance of enterprises has become the most significant factor affecting workers' layoff status and current earnings. Workers from profitable enterprises are less likely to be laid off than workers from unprofitable enterprises; and earnings from employment in profitable enterprises are much higher than those from unprofitable enterprises.

In summary, consistent with other researchers' findings about the effect of 'institutional persistence' on income (Zhou 2000), this study has found that both human capital and political capital still play an important role in affecting employment in state/collective-owned enterprises. In addition, factors such as ownership, rank and size of enterprises that used to affect workers' well-being do not affect workers' layoff and reemployment. In all, the study suggests that market transition theory may be more accurate in predicting the declining significance of political capital during the market transition, but less accurate in predicting the increasing importance of human capital, since human capital was already an important factor in affecting workers' income and promotion under the planned system (Lin, Cai and Li 1996).

Besides human capital and political capital, age and gender have emerged as important factors in China today, and sometimes they are even more important than human and political capital in affecting workers' layoff status, reemployment and income. Older workers and female workers are more likely to be laid off than younger and male workers. Although we did not find that male workers have advantages over female workers in reemployment, female workers are paid much less than male workers in reemployed jobs. These results are consistent with Appleton and his co-authors' findings (2001) that both education and party membership lost their significance in determining the incomes after layoff, and that the income differentials based on genders and between workers in the SOEs and workers in collective-owned enterprises increase. Other research (Liu *et al.* 2000) also found that the economic reform has increased the gender wage gap in absolute terms. Therefore findings in this research may suggest a new segmentation in the urban labor market, at least in the urban labor market open to laid-off workers, based on 'systematic discrimination' or 'employer taste' at age and gender. Its emergence may be related to the decline of state power and the increasing autonomy of enterprises.

This study can be improved in various ways. First, we need a larger sample from non-state-owned enterprises to better test segmentation by types of ownership. Second, an enterprise-based sampling design and more variations in the types of enterprises (such as ownership, rank, size and economic performance) will help to control for heterogeneity at the enterprises level when examining earnings. Third, the measurement of political capital can be improved. Cadre status in the SOEs and collective-owned enterprises treats both the cadres who are party officials and those who are managers same (Bian 2002). A clearer definition of political capital is needed. Finally, a longitudinal and national representative survey will allow us to evaluate more accurately the transformation of the segmentation structure within regions and the effects of market transition within and between regions.

Continuous research on this important topic is needed because of the rapid development of the urban labor market since the survey was conducted. First, layoff as an intermediate method for unemployment is going to be abolished in China and workers will directly enter unemployment. Each city has made its own schedule for transferring laid-off workers to unemployment. This is another step aimed at placing the SOEs and their workers in the market economy. Although it is still unclear how these new policies will be implemented, it is clear that the urban labor market in China is moving in the direction of a unified labor market integrating the state ownership and non-state ownership.

11 Generational Differences in Mexican-American's Earnings: Comparing the Second, 2.5th and Third Generations[1]

Yukio Kawano, Katharine M. Donato and Charles M. Tolbert II

Introduction

According to the United States Census Bureau (2005), the Hispanic population in the U.S. nearly doubled from 22.4 million to 41.3 million between 1990 and 2004. The Mexicans account for 68% of the increase and comprise 64% of the total Hispanic population in 2004. This growth of the Hispanic population is due not only to the increasing number of immigrants, but also to the growing number of their children who were born in the United States. As a result, one in every five children under 18 is Hispanic and one-third of them are living under the poverty line (Child Trends Databank 2005). Mexican-immigrant parents in particular have very little education and low income (Trejo 1997), which creates a disadvantageous environment for their children.[2]

Although classic assimilation theory predicts that immigrant families overcome their initial disadvantages over three generations through acculturation and adaptation (Gordon 1964), the earnings growth of the Mexican Americans seems stagnant or even declining as they move on to later generations (Waldinger and Perlman 1998). Others worry that continuous Hispanic immigration causes deterioration in the quality of the American labor force and, as a result, demand restrictive or selective immigration policies (for example, Borjas 1999). Restrictionist or not, as Waters and Jimenez (2005) stressed, it is true that the contrast between the discontinued immigration from Europe early last century and the incessant immigration of Hispanics becomes one of the central issues in the current studies of immigration and ethnicity, especially in regards to their adaptation and assimilation. The socioeconomic adaptation of Mexican Americans over generations, in this sense, has much to contribute to the current interest in this research area, as well as in terms of policy implications.

Based on such recognition of the field, we have focused on the earnings of Mexican Americans over several generations. We mainly compare the second and third generations because it is already indisputable that the second and later generations always generate higher incomes than the first generation. A real problem for Mexican Americans is the trajectory *after* the first generation, and whether the path is upward, downward or stagnant. Our analysis suggests, as we discuss in detail in this chapter, that foreign-born parents are a significant determinant for the second and later generation Mexican Americans.

This topic has not been well researched for two practical reasons: data limitation and the relative youth of second-generation Mexican Americans. First, it is difficult to identify generations in the available public data because the information about parents' immigration status is limited. Secondly, researchers were unable to find large enough samples of second-generation Mexican workers because most of them were still too young to work. It is only recently that they became old enough for us to be able to find a number of their adult members in public surveys. This chapter advances the knowledge in this field by introducing a relatively new category, 2.5th generation Mexican Americans, and by its comparison with second and third generation workers.

Studies on assimilation and adaptation

Studies on the socioeconomic mobility of immigrants and their children can be summarized using three perspectives: linear, curvilinear, and segmented assimilation. First, based on the experience of European immigrants, the linear perspective expects immigrants and their descendants to eventually assimilate into the mainstream after about three generations. Smith (2003), for example, using historical census data, found that a Mexican American's income is relatively increasing but the progress from second to third generation had declined in recent years. Gans (1992) also based his studies on the assimilation perspective but with some adjustment. Gans suggested that these ethnic minorities will take a 'bumpy,' rather than a 'linear,' road to assimilation. In the long run, we do not deny the possibility that there will be no difference in socioeconomic status between any race-ethnic groups. Practically, however, the gap between mainstream WASP American and any minorities including Mexican Americans will persist for a long time. We should start from acknowledging the current gap and look into its causes in order to reach reasonable solutions. In this sense, the first perspective seems to have least applicability to the current immigrant adaptation.

Secondly, the curvilinear perspective, also called immigrant optimism, expects greater economic achievement from the second generation than subsequent generations. When plotting the earnings of the first, second and third generations in order, the second generation's overachievement and the third generation's underachievement produce a convex curve. According to this view, the second generation combines the high motivation and high educational attainment to earn more than both first and third generations. The third generation cannot exceed the second because the first generation's motivation transfers to the second generation and diminishes after that. In the earlier empirical studies on this issue, Chiswick (1977) used the 1970 census[3] and reported that the U.S-born 'white' children of at least one foreign-born parent have higher earnings than those having two native parents. Carliner (1980) tested other ethnic groups and he also found higher earnings of second-generation males than the third generation. Livingston and Kahn (2002), using LNPS (Latino National Political Survey) and PSID (Panel Study of Income Dynamics), observed a curvilinear pattern in which second-generation Mexican Americans earn more than the third generation.

This curvilinear theory is extended from earlier research on second-generation children at school. Studies on children's educational achievements and foreign-born parents started much earlier and are continuing (Kao and Tienda 1995; Kao and Thompson 2003; Pong 2003). These studies found that native-born children with at least one foreign-born parent not only achieve better than their foreign-born classmates, but also outperform their third generation classmates. Researchers explain that immigrants' emotional and disciplinary devotion to their children's education and their 'optimism' about their future in the U.S. have a positive effect on the children's aspirations and academic achievement. However, the third and later generations do not achieve as much as the second because their parents are native-born and they do not have as much devotion to education as the first-generation immigrants do. Empirically, however, this hypothesis on school achievements found support only from Asian children, much less from Mexican/Latino and none from black and white children (Kao and Tienda 1995).

To the extent that school achievements affect economic outcomes in the labor market, generational earnings differentials should show a curvilinear pattern. However, these studies had reservations as to how much the second-generation advantage is applied across ethnic groups. Chiswick (1997) pointed out significant disadvantage, not advantage, of having Mexican-born parents. Carliner (1980) also noted that, among the five ethnic groups he tested, only Filipino Americans showed statistically significant decline from the second to third generation. The curvilinear pattern, therefore, may only exist in Asian Americans.

The third view, which we call stagnation or the 'segmented assimilation' perspective, argues that descendants of non-European immigrants will not completely converge with the mainstream population, but assimilate into their own 'segment' in terms of socioeconomic status (Portes and Rumbaut 2001). In this view, ethnic minorities do not reach parity with the American mainstream but lose upward or downward momentum, thus being second or third generation does not make much difference. This perspective, as we will show in this report, explains most appropriately Mexican-American workers' situation. Portes and Hao (2004) found that being Mexican at school implies disadvantage in terms of academic performance as well as aspirations (also see Pong 2003). A little accumulation of human capital leads to low socioeconomic status, and often to the cycle of poverty that immobilizes the Mexican in the American society (Portes and Rumbaut 2001).

Using CPS (Current Population Survey) data, Grogger and Trejo (2002) found no significant differences between second and third-generation Mexican Americans in terms of earnings. This finding contradicts the work of Livingston and Kahn (2002). The disagreement between these two studies is mainly due to the interpretation of statistics in Livingston and Kahn (2002). Based on the sample of 56,000 Mexicans, of which about half are first with the rest being second or third generation, Grogger and Trejo (2002) did not find a statistically significant difference in earnings between second and third generation. Using a rather small sample of only 553 Mexican Americans, Livingston and Kahn (2002) did not find a significant difference between the second and third generations either. However, they concluded that the curvilinear pattern does exist among Mexicans because the regression coefficients for the third generation relative to the second were consistently negative across their models. Consistent or not, however, those coefficients should be considered zero as far as they were statistically insignificant. There is no guarantee that they would find the same coefficients if they used any larger data.

Therefore, Grogger and Trejo (2002) most reliably support the stagnation perspective in the case of Mexican-American workers. Why do they face such disadvantages? It is either because their transition from school to work is obstructed or their opportunity in education is limited. In fact, Fry (2005) reported that Hispanic students are exposed to the worst educational conditions among all race-ethnic groups in terms of school-size, student-to-teacher ratio and students living under the poverty line. There is no doubt that some fractions of Mexican Americans are advancing their socioeconomic status, but other not so small parts of them are left behind at school or in the labor market. In order to study this diversity more closely, we devised an approach using three categories of Mexican Americans: second, 2.5th and third generations.

The 2.5th generation and the assimilation debate

Much research in the past studied three generations from immigrants (first generation) to the children of native-born parents (third generation) via the children of immigrants (second generation), but we think this is unnecessary for two reasons. Firstly, the improvement from first to second generation is incontestable, although the degree of the jump may be of some interest; secondly, the three theoretical perspectives can be examined by comparing the second and third generations. Given the jump from first to second, upward mobility from second to third generation supports linear, flat mobility stagnant and downward mobility curvilinear assumption. We also show statistics of the first generation, native whites and blacks, but this is only for comparative description and not for analysis.

We also pay attention to the fact that second generation persons who have *at least one* foreign-born parent can be split into two groups: those with one foreign-born and another native parent, and those with two foreign-born parents. Most of the past research lumped together these two types of parents, and it was only recently that researchers started to focus on the children of mixed-nativity parents (Jensen 2001; Ramakrishnan 2002). They are called 2.5th generation because they have elements of both second and third generations. These recent studies have revealed that the 2.5th generation constitutes a better part of the native-born Hispanic and particularly Mexican population. Native-born parents provide their linguistic and cultural resources to support their children's advancement at school and labor market, which creates family social capital unique to the 2.5th generation. Another report showed that exogamous Mexican couples (Mexicans married to non-Mexicans) are substantially better educated than endogamous Mexican couples (Duncan and Trejo 2004). In addition, those families with two Mexican-born parents tend to speak only Spanish at home and have low income, which precludes many opportunities for the second generation to accumulate their human capital.

If having one native parent (being a 2.5th generation) is more advantageous than having two foreign-born parents (second generation) or having two native-born parents (third generation), the curvilinear assimilation theory needs an important revision. The theory implies that all second-generation immigrants including the second and 2.5th generations take advantage of the immigrant parents' motivation and their own native characteristics to advance their socioeconomic status further than the third generation does. However, in our observation, the second generation do not advance as much as the third once they excluded the 2.5th generation. It implies that a mixed nativity of parents, rather than a mixed nativity of parents and children, engenders a better adaptation outcome.

Figure 11.1 shows the image of cross-generational adaptation. The solid arrow ADE indicates the observations in previous research in which the second and 2.5th generations are lumped together, which resulted in the stagnant outlook between second and third generations. Arrows AB and AC represent the second and 2.5th generations, respectively, to reflect our latest observations in which the second generation makes less, and the 2.5th generation makes more, than the third generation. How then do these two groups converge in the third and later generations? It is likely that they do not converge. If we can separate the children of the 2.5th generation from those of the second generation, we may have been able to observe this phenomenon. In the data at hand, however, we can only observe the third generation as one group due to the lack of information (grand parents' place of birth). Therefore, the broken lines CF and BE, and the dotted line CE, are only speculative guesses: the upward mobility indicates positive selection and downward negative selection regarding their ethnic identity. For example, the children of the 2.5th generation have a choice of identity between native majority and minority ethnicity because many of them have at least one Mexican-born grandparent. This divergence (CF and CE) is likely if the choice of majority status is associated with their economic success and the choice of minority status economic failure. Meanwhile, the broken arrow BE indicates that most children of the second generation identify themselves with minority because at least two of their grand parents are foreign born.

Our analysis proceeds in two steps. First, we examine the industry and occupation structure of Mexican-American workers after reviewing some descriptive facts, such as wage gaps, demographic and human capital distribution. If segmented assimilation theory is correct, we expect to find that they are structurally trapped in low-status jobs regardless of their generations. The question here is whether the second, 2.5th and third generation Mexicans are different in their composition of industry and occupation. Statistical tests will show if their job structure has changed over generations. Here, we analyze males and females separately and also bring in first

Figure 11.1: Image of cross-generational adaptation

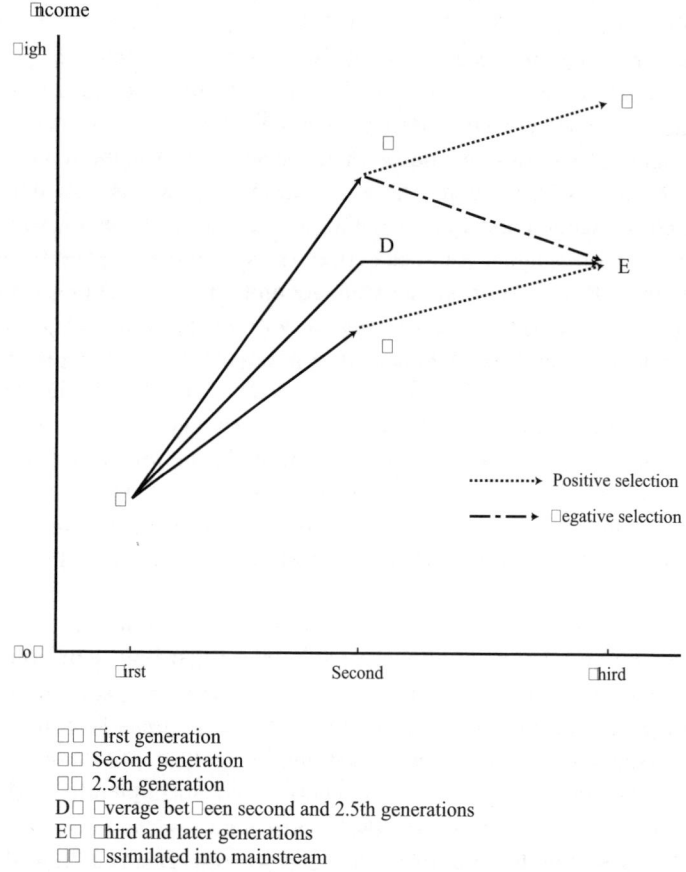

□□ First generation
□□ Second generation
□□ 2.5th generation
D□ Average between second and 2.5th generations
E□ Third and later generations
□□ Assimilated into mainstream

generation Mexicans as well as native non-Hispanic whites and blacks for comparison.

Secondly, we perform multivariate regression analysis to examine the 'third generation decline' or 'second generation overachievement' in second and third generation Mexican-American workers. Using hourly earnings of Mexican workers as a dependent variable, we focus on the effect of being second or 2.5th generation in reference to the third generation, controlling for other demographic, geographic and human capital factors. We expect that the results of the 2.5th generation support curvilinear assimilation theory, but those of the second generation support segmented assimilation theory. Self-selection of ethnic identity is behind these hypotheses, but it is beyond this study's scope to estimate the degree or level of such selectivity – it is only implied by the comparisons between the three generations.

Definition of generations and data issues

We use Outgoing Rotation Group (ORG) sample from Current Population Survey (CPS) Basic Monthly Files collected from 1994 to 2003 (Census Bureau 2002). Monthly samples consist of eight rotation groups. One new rotation group enters the survey every month to replace another which has already had three interviews in the previous months. After the fourth month, one rotation group leaves the sample and comes back to the survey after another eight months to complete four-month interviews again, and then go out of the sample for the last time. The groups at their fourth and eighth interview months are called Outgoing Rotation Group (ORG). We use ORG because information on earnings is available only in this group. Of the fourth and eighth month groups, we keep only persons at the fourth month in order to avoid overlapped persons in the pooled datasets.[4] CPS samples about 50,000 civilian, non-institutionalized, households every month, which enable us to obtain a large number of minority observations. However, it lacks language-related variables such as English proficiency. In addition, there are coding problems in the 'place of birth' item in 1994–96, but it affects mainly those who were born in Asian countries and not Mexican (Census Bureau 1998). Another coding problem that occurred in 1995 led to missing metropolitan status[5].

There are two data issues to consider. First, like any other public surveys, this data does not include those who left the host country (emigrants or out-migration). If there are significant differences between Mexican migrants who stay in the U.S. and those who leave the country, then estimates based on the remaining population may be biased. Thus a longer residence in the U.S. could mean either positive or negative selection depending on the skills of those who left the country, but their data is not available. The many attempts to assess this issue are at best inconclusive, but this is statistically controllable (Grogger and Trejo 2002).

Secondly, unlike longitudinal or panel data, the cross-sectional data such as CPS cannot provide a true picture of intergenerational relationships, which may cause the over- or under-estimation of generational progress (Borjas 1993, 1995). For example, the characteristics of current second generation workers do not necessarily predict the achievement of the future second generation because they grow up in different historical periods and their parents are from different entry cohorts. Entry cohorts can bias such estimations to the extent that different cohort quality is transmitted to next generations. For this research, however, these problems are not very serious because the cohort quality of Mexican immigrants is improving, and thus the earnings of Mexican Americans will be only underestimated (Grogger and Trejo 200; Smith 2003).

Table 11.1 shows how we defined generation categories of Mexican Americans. In order to focus on labor force population, we limit our sample to male and female wage earners (excluding self-employed workers) who are 25 to 59 years old, work more than 10 hours per week, and earn $1–$500 per hour. This definition excludes all students and most non-full time workers from the sample. The final sample is mostly comparable with that in Grogger and Trejo (2002). We categorize generations of Mexicans as follows: all identify themselves as Mexican (Mexican American, Chicano, or Mexicano); first-generation Mexicans are those who were born in Mexico of two Mexican-born parents; the second generation Mexicans are born in the U.S. of two Mexican-born parents; 2.5th generation are also born in the U.S. but have just one Mexican-born parent; and third generation are born in the U.S. of two US-born parents. The sample sizes of the second and 2.5th generations are rather small because of their restrictive definitions. It is also because the age cut-off reduced a number of children from these generations particularly, whereas the first generation does not have many children and the third generation contains all age groups rather evenly. We also excluded cases for which the key variables (ethnicity, birthplaces of oneself and parents) were allocated by the Census Bureau.

Table 11.1: Definition of the three generations

Generation	Mexican origin or descent	Place of birth	Parents' place of birth	Frequency (%ª) Male	Frequency (%ª) Female	Average age Male	Average age Female
First	Yes	Mexico	Both Mexico	11,522 (61.1)	5,443 (44.1)	36.5	37.8
Second	Yes	USA	Both Mexico	1,200 (6.4)	1,122 (9.1)	35.9	36.1
2.5th	Yes	USA	Mexico and USA	1,047 (5.5)	941 (7.6)	39.5	39.5
Third	Yes	USA	Both USA	5,434 (27.0)	5,180 (39.2)	38.4	38.6

Note. a: this percentage is based on sample frequencies.
Source: CPS 1994–2003.

Two issues need clarification. First, the definition of the third generation does not distinguish them from later generations. It may cause a problem if Mexican Americans have many generations like European groups. For Mexicans, however, most third-generation Mexicans are really the third, rather than fourth or fifth, because majority of the immigrants came rather recently (Borjas 1993).

Secondly, since ethnicity in CPS is self-identified by respondents, some American-born Mexicans, particularly the 2.5th generation, would identify themselves as 'other' ethnicity or 'Don't know.' We should include them if they do have a Mexican parent, but then we have to include those whose parents are ethnically non-Mexican but born in Mexico. So we did not mix them into our sample.[6] Just as in the issue of selective out-migration, those who identified themselves as Mexican may be doing so because of the negative connotation inherent to the minority identity (Waters 1990). This negative selection issue is more pronounced in the third generation because self-identified ethnicity is the only way to define Mexican Americans after the second generation.

Characteristics of Mexican Americans

Table 11.2 shows the descriptive statistics of Mexican American workers, displaying male and female results separately. First generation Mexicans, native African American and native White workers are juxtaposed for contrasting purposes. Not surprisingly, foreign-born workers earn much less than any native-born workers do; females earn much less than males do; and native whites earn the most. Among male workers, all native Mexican workers earn more than native black workers, while the two groups of native-Mexican females earn somewhat less than native black females. For both males and females, having one native parent seems to give 2.5th generation workers a slight advantage over the second as well as the third generations.

Mexican-American workers in the 2.5th generation, male or female, are more likely than other Mexican American workers to be older, married, and have high school or higher education; they are less likely to live in central cities; and the female workers are more likely to work part-time. In terms of occupational composition, the 2.5th generation is somewhat more concentrated in high-skill jobs than the other two Mexican-American groups.[7] As Table 11.2 shows, 21% of the 2.5th generation males are in high-skill occupations compare to 17% and 19% of the second and third generation respectively; also 28% vs. 26% in the case of females. The three native-Mexican groups are the largest in the middle-skill level and somewhat less in the low-skill level, indicating that their occupational compositions are somewhere between blacks and whites: blacks have the largest numbers in the lowest level; whites have a large middle layer but the size of the skilled layer is greater than the less skilled.

Industry and occupation composition

Table 11.3 shows the industrial compositions of the three Mexican generations and native blacks and whites in the eight industry classifications, which was reduced from twenty-two categories to secure cell counts. Clearly, the industry compositions of the three groups of native-born Mexicans are different from that of the first generation, and among themselves the compositions look quite alike each other. For example, while nearly a third of the first-generation males are employed in agriculture and construction, only 14 to 18% of native-born Mexicans work in these industries. There are not many females in this category because construction is a particularly male-dominated industry, but the results still show a clear difference between immigrant and native generations due to the shift in the number of agricultural workers. If a worker is native-born Mexican, he or she is more likely than immigrants to find oneself in transportation, communication ④ and service industries ⑦. These industries generally require linguistic and cultural assimilation that first generation immigrants do not possess.

Within native Mexicans, in contrast, there are only small differences: in the case of males, the second generation has a somewhat larger population in retail ⑤ and somewhat less in finance and other

Table 11.2: Mean characteristics of Mexican generation groups, black and white natives, 1994–2003

	Male						Female					
	Mexican 1st Gen	Mexican 2nd Gen	Mexican 2.5th	Mexican 3rd Gen	Native Black	Native White	Mexican 1st Gen	Mexican 2nd Gen	Mexican 2.5th	Mexican 3rd Gen	Native Black	Native White
Hourly Earning ($)[a]	9.77 (.052)	13.39 (.224)	14.90 (.263)	13.89 (.114)	13.02 (.048)	18.02 (.022)	7.98 (.061)	11.45 (.202)	11.87 (.237)	11.30 (.095)	11.69 (.039)	13.84 (.018)
(Median)	8.27	12.73	11.58	12.01	11.15	15.48	6.8	9.6	10.08	9.67	9.78	11.65
Married	0.67 (.004)	0.61 (.014)	0.69 (.014)	0.66 (.007)	0.53 (.003)	0.70 (.001)	0.63 (.007)	0.55 (.015)	0.59 (.016)	0.58 (.007)	0.37 (.003)	0.65 (.001)
High school	0.34 (.004)	0.76 (.012)	0.83 (.012)	0.80 (.006)	0.89 (.002)	0.93 (.001)	0.41 (.007)	0.82 (.012)	0.84 (.012)	0.83 (.005)	0.91 (.002)	0.95 (.000)
Part time	0.04 (.002)	0.05 (.006)	0.04 (.006)	0.04 (.003)	0.05 (.001)	0.03 (.000)	0.18 (.005)	0.14 (.010)	0.15 (.012)	0.15 (.005)	0.11 (.002)	0.18 (.001)
Central city	0.42 (.005)	0.34 (.014)	0.29 (.014)	0.32 (.007)	0.42 (.003)	0.16 (.001)	0.41 (.007)	0.35 (.014)	0.33 (.015)	0.33 (.007)	0.44 (.003)	0.17 (.001)
Occupation[b]												
High skill	0.05 (.002)	0.17 (.011)	0.21 (.013)	0.19 (.005)	0.19 (.003)	0.33 (.001)	0.08 (.004)	0.26 (.013)	0.28 (.015)	0.26 (.006)	0.27 (.003)	0.40 (.001)
Middle skill	0.37 (.004)	0.46 (.014)	0.45 (.015)	0.47 (.007)	0.39 (.003)	0.44 (.001)	0.31 (.006)	0.52 (.015)	0.51 (.016)	0.52 (.007)	0.44 (.003)	0.45 (.001)
Low skill	0.59 (.005)	0.38 (.014)	0.34 (.015)	0.35 (.007)	0.42 (.003)	0.23 (.001)	0.61 (.007)	0.22 (.012)	0.21 (.013)	0.23 (.006)	0.29 (.003)	0.16 (.001)

Notes.
Standard errors are in parentheses.
a: Adjusted to 1998 dollars using Consumer Price Index. Weighted.
b: See footnote 7 for categorization of occupations.
Source: CPS 1994–2003.

Table 11.3: *Industry composition of Mexicans, native blacks and whites, 1994–2003*

	Mexican				NH Black	NH White	Total
	1st gen	2nd gen	2.5th gen	3rd gen			
Male							
①	31.3	17.7	13.8	16.9	8.7	13.0	13.5
②	13.4	11.1	11.9	11.2	12.5	15.2	14.8
③	12.0	9.3	8.9	7.7	9.3	8.0	8.3
④	4.2	11.6	13.0	11.7	15.1	11.4	11.4
⑤	19.4	18.7	17.2	18.5	14.6	16.8	16.7
⑥	9.6	8.0	8.5	7.7	8.6	7.0	7.3
⑦	7.8	14.8	15.5	15.3	18.2	16.8	16.5
⑧	2.4	9.0	11.4	11.0	13.0	11.9	11.5
Total number	11,522	1,200	1,046	5,092	23,220	226,837	268,917
Female							
①	4.4	2.2	1.7	1.9	0.8	2.3	2.2
②	10.3	5.0	5.6	5.4	5.3	5.8	5.8
③	17.9	6.6	4.7	4.6	6.4	5.0	5.5
④	1.7	6.8	4.3	5.5	7.2	4.9	5.2
⑤	19.3	16.0	14.9	18.8	11.6	16.8	16.2
⑥	20.7	8.7	8.5	8.1	8.7	6.7	7.3
⑦	21.4	38.9	45.9	40.9	42.4	43.9	43.1
⑧	4.4	15.9	14.5	14.9	17.7	14.6	14.7
Total number	5,442	1,122	940	4,847	31,230	213,220	256,801

Note. Industry classification:
① = Agriculture, forestry and fisheries; Construction; Mining
② = Manufacturing – durable goods
③ = Manufacturing – non-durable goods
④ = Transportation and communications
⑤ = Wholesale and retail trade
⑥ = Utilities and sanitary services; Private households; Personal services excluding private households
⑦ = Entertainment and recreation services; Hospitals; Medical services excluding hospitals; Educational services; Social services; Other professional services
⑧ = Finance, insurance and real estate business; Auto and repair services; Public administration; Armed forces
Source: CPS 1994–2003.

businesses ⑧ than the 2.5th and third generations. Among the three native Mexicans, the 2.5th generation seems to be most similar to native whites, although it is inconclusive from Table 11.3.

To analyze the degree of cross-generational association in their job composition, we performed Pearson's Chi-square test on selected pairs of these groups; the null hypothesis is the homogeneity of these paired groups. Table 11.4 shows the results of pair-wise chi-square tests of difference and Cramer's Vs to indicate the level of association between jobs and generations.

On the one hand, the differences between first and second generation Mexican Americans are clearly substantial, as are those between the third generation and other native-born blacks and whites. On the other hand, we find fewer differences between second, 2.5th and third generation Mexicans. In industry compositions, for males these three groups are statistically identical; but for females they show some statistically significant differences. In occupation compositions, in turn, native-born Mexican males have mild difference in their composition; native-born Mexican females do not show difference. These twisted results could mean that the males have some occupational mobility within fixed industry, whereas the females have some industrial mobility but not much occupational − earning − mobility.

We also find that, for the males, 2.5th and third generation Mexicans are indistinguishable in terms of both industry and occupation composition, but in terms of occupations the second generation shows some distance from both 2.5th and third after the second generation, but then the 2.5th and third generations find somewhat better-paid occupations than the second generation.

The industrial and occupational compositions of third generation Mexicans are significantly different from those of native blacks and whites. The magnitudes of the Chi-square test scores indicate that they are closer to whites in terms of industries, but they are closer to blacks in terms of occupations. This twist exists both in males and females. These observations imply that third generation Mexican and native whites are working in the same places but the Mexicans earn only as much as blacks do. In order for these interpretations to be substantiated, we should use multivariate analysis to see directions of their differences controlling for other intervening factors.

Determinants of Mexican earnings: generation effects

In the past research on the curvilinear perspective, the key was the second generation who earn more than the first and third generations. In this research, we examine whether this second-generation overachievement is true by distinguishing the second generation from 2.5th generation. We speculate that the apparently stagnant achievement of the second generation resulted from mixing up these two groups into one.

Table 11.4: Tests of cross generational difference in industry and occupation[a]

	Pearson's Chi-square test		Cramer's V
A. Comparison based on 8 industries			
Male			
1st gen. vs. 2.5th gen.	581.3	(<.0001)	.215
1st gen. vs. 2nd gen.	425.8	(<.0001)	.183
2nd gen. vs. 2.5th gen.	10.9	(<.1448)	.070
2.5th gen. vs. 3rd gen.	9.8	(<.1975)	.040
2nd gen. vs. 3rd gen.	7.2	(<.4066)	.034
3rd gen. vs. Blacks	410.3	(<.0001)	.120
3rd gen. vs. Whites	135.0	(<.0001)	.024
Female			
1st gen. vs. 2.5th gen.	549.7	(<.0001)	.294
1st gen. vs. 2nd gen.	595.6	(<.0001)	.301
2nd gen. vs. 2.5th gen.	17.2	(<.0164)	.091
2.5th gen. vs. 3rd gen.	14	(<.0510)	.049
2nd gen. vs. 3rd gen.	17.1	(<.0169)	.054
3rd gen. vs. Blacks	295	(<.0001)	.090
3rd gen. vs. Whites	44.8	(<.0001)	.014
B. Comparison based on 3 occupations			
Male			
1st gen. vs. 2.5th gen.	555.9	(<.0001)	.210
1st gen. vs. 2nd gen.	405.0	(<.0001)	.178
2nd gen. vs. 2.5th gen.	6.3	(<.0438)	.053
2.5th gen. vs. 3rd gen.	3.1	(<.2105)	.023
2nd gen. vs. 3rd gen.	3.7	(<.1548)	.024
3rd gen. vs. Blacks	90.4	(<.0001)	.057
3rd gen. vs. Whites	639.4	(<.0001)	.053
Female			
1st gen. vs. 2.5th gen.	671.1	(<.0001)	.324
1st gen. vs. 2nd gen.	686.1	(<.0001)	.323
2nd gen. vs. 2.5th gen.	2.1	(<.3577)	.032
2.5th gen. vs. 3rd gen.	4.0	(<.1383)	.026
2nd gen. vs. 3rd gen.	0.4	(<.8176)	.008
3rd gen. vs. Blacks	102.2	(<.0001)	.053
3rd gen. vs. Whites	396	(<.0001)	.043

Note. a: These tests were performed on unweighted frequencies.
Source: CPS 1994–2003.

The results of our multivariate analyses on logged hourly earnings of Mexican-American workers are shown in Table 11.5a for males and 11.5b for females respectively. First, we consider three nested models for males. Model I includes basic controls in addition to dummy variables setting to indicate the second and 2.5th generations, leaving out the third generation as a reference group. Controlling for marital status, survey year, and part-time worker status, being a 2.5th-generation Mexican worker gives a positive effect of about 6% on hourly earnings over the third generation. Meanwhile, being a second-generation Mexican worker has a negative and significant effect of about 4%.

Model II incorporates age and education to the basic model to control for the accumulation of human capital. These variables are the sets of dummies assuming their non-linear effects. When human-capital variables are included, the effect of the second generation turned to be positive and insignificant while other coefficients changed only slightly. It indicates that the disadvantage of the second generation is due mainly to their relative youth and low education. The effect of the 2.5th generation remains positive and significant at about 4% after controlling for human capital.

Model III incorporates industry and geographic characteristics. The results indicate that Mexican Americans who work in transportation, communication and professional service receive less than those in durable manufacturing, controlling for human capital and demographic factors. It suggests that they have low-paid jobs in high-paying industries, but in wholesale and retail, they are paid rather well for their human capital. Geographic characteristics are also important determinants of earnings. Central cities and suburbs (balance on MSA) show clearly positive effects over non-Metro (rural) areas. Regions in the U.S. are not significant factors.

In Model III, the coefficients for the second and 2.5th generations are positive 3% and negative 3% with mild significances. It suggests that the effect of the second generation in general is close to zero if we did not distinguish these two groups, because these two effects will cancel each other. This expectation was correct: the coefficient for the combined-second generation dummy is .0003 and p-value .97 which is completely insignificant (full results are not shown – all other specifications remain the same as Model III). As far as Mexican males are concerned, therefore, curvilinear theory had applicability only to the 2.5th generation. As to the second generation, the route from the second to the third generation is upward but rather stagnant.

Table 11.5a: *Multivariate analysis of logged hourly earnings (Male Mexican workers), 1994–2003*

Models	I		II		III	
	Coef.	Pr<|t|	Coef.	Pr<|t|	Coef.	Pr<|t|
Intercept	2.343	(.000)	2.190	(.000)	2.208	(.000)
2.5th generation	.058	(.001)	.044	(.004)	.030	(.044)
Second generation	−.040	(.012)	.015	(.307)	−.028	(.050)
Married	.142	(.000)	.118	(.000)	.120	(.000)
Survey year	.016	(.000)	.012	(.000)	.012	(.000)
Part-time work	−.398	(.000)	−.346	(.000)	−.320	(.000)
Age (drop = 25–29)						
30–34			.076	(.000)	.076	(.000)
35–39			.178	(.000)	.171	(.000)
40–44			.213	(.000)	.201	(.000)
45–49			.206	(.000)	.194	(.000)
50–54			.232	(.000)	.215	(.000)
55–59			.189	(.000)	.184	(.000)
Education (drop = 12 years)						
8years or less			−.342	(.000)	−.303	(.000)
9 to 11 years			−.230	(.000)	−.208	(.000)
13 to 14 years			.127	(.000)	.112	(.000)
15 to 16 years			.425	(.000)	.412	(.000)
17 to 20 years			.567	(.000)	.581	(.000)
Industry (drop = Durable Manufacture)						
Agric. Forest, fish, min, const.					.019	(.323)
Non-durable manufacture					.031	(.179)
Wholesale and retail					.079	(.000)
Transportation and communication					−.118	(.000)
Private hh personal service					−.095	(.000)
Entertainment prof. Service					−.088	(.000)
Finance and pub. admin.					.053	(.015)
Geography (drop = Non-Metro)						
Central city					.101	(.000)
Balance on MSA					.127	(.000)
Not identified					.030	(.096)
Other					.080	(.031)
Region (drop = New England)						
Middle Atlantic					.010	(.930)
East North Central					−.043	(.645)
West North Central					−.087	(.355)
South Atlantic					−.064	(.502)
East South Central					−.161	(.174)
West South Central					−.184	(.069)
Mountain					−.055	(.551)
Pacific					.003	(.973)
California					.033	(.717)
Texas					−.159	(.082)
R^2	.056		.256		.314	

Table 11.5b: Multivariate analysis of logged hourly earnings (Female Mexican workers), 1994–2003

Models	I		II		III	
	Coef.	Pr<|t|	Coef.	Pr<|t|	Coef.	Pr<|t|
Intercept	2.232	(.000)	2.068	(.000)	2.233	(.000)
2.5th generation	.046	(.007)	.021	(.159)	.005	(.723)
Second generation	.012	(.442)	.036	(.011)	−.017	(.221)
Married	.063	(.000)	.037	(.000)	.041	(.000)
Survey year	.013	(.000)	.010	(.000)	.010	(.000)
Part-time work	−.289	(.000)	−.222	(.000)	−.190	(.000)
Age (drop=25–29)						
30–34			.071	(.000)	.073	(.000)
35–39			.120	(.000)	.110	(.000)
40–44			.146	(.000)	.135	(.000)
45–49			.153	(.000)	.142	(.000)
50–54			.178	(.000)	.168	(.000)
55–59			.182	(.000)	.172	(.000)
Education (drop = 12 years)						
8 years or less			−.327	(.000)	−.267	(.000)
9 to 11 years			−.237	(.000)	−.195	(.000)
13 to 14 years			.154	(.000)	.129	(.000)
15 to 16 years			.486	(.000)	.461	(.000)
17 to 20 years			.705	(.000)	.697	(.000)
Industry (drop = Durable Manufacture)						
Agric. Forest, fish, min, const.					−.047	(.238)
Non-durable manufacture					−.056	(.059)
Wholesale and retail					.073	(.012)
Transportation and communication					−.213	(.000)
Private hh personal service					−.220	(.000)
Entertainment prof. service					−.117	(.000)
Finance and pub. Admin.					.007	(.776)
Geography (drop = Non-Metro)						
Central city					.150	(.000)
Balance on MSA					.162	(.000)
Not identified					.057	(.001)
Other					.105	(.005)
Region (drop = New England)						
Middle Atlantic					−.179	(.099)
East North Central					−.139	(.132)
West North Central					−.182	(.053)
South Atlantic					−.170	(.075)
East South Central					−.120	(.294)
West South Central					−.207	(.040)
Mountain					−.179	(.049)
Pacific					−.099	(.303)
California					−.058	(.524)
Texas					−.248	(.006)
R^2	.055		.285		.368	

Table 11.5b displays the same models for female Mexican workers. In Model I, the contrast between the second and 2.5th generations does not appear as it did in the male model: the effect of the second generation is insignificant positive. Nonetheless Model III shows a pattern of coefficients that is similar to the male model, though the coefficients concerning the second and 2.5th generations are insignificant. This is expected because 2.5th and third generation Mexican females do not have as wide gap in average earnings as their male counterparts do: 46 cents vis-a-vis one dollar (see Table 11.2). Probably their concentration in the service industry and the limited occupational mobility of females in the labor market also contributed to their less clear outcomes. It may also be the case that females have less opportunity to utilize the advantage of being a member of the 2.5th generation. As a result, the earnings differences among the three groups of Mexican female workers are mostly explained away by human capital, industry and geographic factors.

Conclusion

In this research on Mexican-American workers, we have clarified and combined the two concepts: intergenerational progress and foreign-born parents. First, we narrowed the issue of intergenerational change to the matter between second and third generations. Three paths were conceptualized: linear progress, decline (curvilinear), or stagnant. Secondly, we pointed out that the traditional definition of the second generation (at least one parent is foreign-born) confounds the effects of having one native-born parent and having two foreign-born parents.

Mexican-American's industry-occupation structure generally stagnates after the dramatic change from the first to second generation. Minor but significant differences divide the second generation males from the 2.5th and third generations in terms of occupational compositions. In the case of females, the second generation is distinguished from 2.5th and third generations in terms of industries. Mexican males seem to move across occupations and females move across industries over generations, but both distinguish the second generation from other two native-born generations. Is this because of the disadvantage of being second generation – having two Mexican-born parents?

Our multivariate analysis revealed that 2.5th-generation Mexican males have an advantage over the third generation, and second generation males have a disadvantage. In the case of females, results were similar to that of males but generational differences are not statistically substantiated. We conclude from these findings that curvilinear theory applies only to 2.5th-generation Mexican males and not to the second generation with two Mexican-born parents. A positive factor behind the immigrant optimism is not the combination of parents' motivation and children's human capital, but the effect of parents' mixed nativity. This finding does not, however, readily support assimilation through intermarriage, because we could not distinguish ethnically mixed parents from mixed generation (but ethnically identical) parents. We also suspect that the decline from 2.5th to third generation is due to the negative selection of Mexican identity.

However, the selection of Mexican identity is not necessarily negative. As to the second generation, they earn less than the third generation even if all other conditions are equal, which implicates mild generational progress by selecting Mexican identity. Some part of the third generation children of the second generation will choose non-Mexican identity and move out of this ethnic group but the rest will remain identifying themselves as Mexican. This and the stagnant industrial mobility observed earlier support segmented assimilation theory. Immigrant optimism does not provide a solution to improve the socioeconomic adaptation of native-born Mexicans.

Remaining issues include non-self-identified Mexicans whom we did not bring into analysis due to their small size and lack of information. Since it is expected that some children of 'mixed' Mexican parents may abandon their Mexican identity, we should find better data and new approach to identify them in future research.

Appendix

See Table 11.A: Mean characteristics of the first and second generations who did not identify themselves Mexican but have certain family connections to Mexico.

Table 11.A: *Mean characteristics of the first and second generations who did not identify themselves Mexican but have certain family connections to Mexico*

	Male			Female		
	1st gen	2nd gen (1)[a]	2nd gen (2)[a]	1st gen	2nd gen (1)[a]	2nd gen (2)[a]
Hourly Earnings						
$[b]	10.12 (.290)	16.52 (.734)	14.66 (1.065)	9.47 (.395)	12.79 (.691)	10.74 (.869)
Median	8.95	13.86	12.03	8.08	10.60	8.91
Age (years)	36.33 (.524)	39.02 (.728)	37.21 (1.326)	37.92 (.821)	38.84 (.727)	38.73 (1.584)
Married	0.75 (.027)	0.64 (.037)	0.64 (.064)	0.64 (.043)	0.46 (.041)	0.52 (.075)
High school	0.42 (.031)	0.92 (.020)	0.85 (.047)	0.60 (.044)	0.87 (.028)	0.79 (.061)
Part time	0.03 (.011)	0.04 (.014)	0.01 (.013)	0.21 (.036)	0.16 (.030)	0.11 (.047)
Central city	0.31 (.029)	0.26 (.034)	0.42 (.065)	0.33 (.042)	0.21 (.034)	0.30 (.069)
Occupation						
High skill	0.06 (.015)	0.31 (.035)	0.20 (.053)	0.17 (.034)	0.32 (.038)	0.20 (.060)
Middle skill	0.39 (.030)	0.46 (.038)	0.61 (.065)	0.35 (.042)	0.45 (.041)	0.54 (.075)
Low skill	0.55 (.031)	0.24 (.033)	0.19 (.052)	0.48 (.045)	0.22 (.034)	0.26 (.066)
N	259	172	58	127	150	45

Notes.
Standard errors are in parentheses.
a: Different parents. See text.
b: Adjusted to 1998 dollars using Consumer Price Index. Weighted.
Source: CPS 1994–2003.

Notes

Chapter 1

1 The percentage varies depending on the arrangement of choices in the questionnaire to a considerable extent. While it was nearly 90% in a survey conducted in 1970s, the figure was about 75% in the 1975 SSM survey. The former survey had three choices (upper-, middle- and lower-middle) and eventually aggregated them to 'middle' in the report, and the latter had two choices (upper- and lower-middle).
2 The goods mean a television set, a refrigerator and a washing machine that everybody wanted to own during the period of high economic growth. Later the desire for ownership shifted to a color television set, an air-conditioner/cooler and a car, and these were known as the 'Three Cs.'
3 Yokohama is a major city with a population of approximately three and a half million people adjoining Tokyo. Sendai is located in northeastern Japan and has a population of approximately one million people. In many aspects Yokohama is much more competitive than Sendai.
4 There are still people in contemporary Japanese society who are the objects of discrimination originating before the modern period. The term *burakumin* refers to people who live in segregated regional communities.
5 The term *furītā*, an abbreviated form of *furī arubaitā* – a combination of the words *furī* (from the English words 'free' and 'freelance'), *arubaito* (from the German 'arbeit') and the English suffix '-er' (represented here by *tā*) –, refers to young people who make a living working at one or more part-time or casual jobs rather than in full-time work. *Nīto* is a borrowing of the word 'NEET,' an acronym term coined in Britain meaning '*N*ot in *E*mployment, *E*ducation or *T*raining.'

Chapter 3

1 This chapter was originally published in *Sociological Theory and Methods*, Vol. 20, No.1, Pp. 45–57. ('Market, Trust, and Inequality: An Agent-based Model of Effect of Market Attractiveness on Trusting Behavior and Inequality.') It is reprinted with permission from the Japanese Association for Mathematical Sociology.
2 Patterson (1999) provides another explanation for this finding. He suggests that people with lower socioeconomic status watch TV programs for a longer duration than those with higher socioeconomic status. Further, increased exposure to TV programs makes people less trustful.
3 The concept of assurance is borrowed from Yamagishi (1998), who presents trust and assurance in contrast with each other.
4 The agent's partner offers the agent one unit of the goods, which gets converted into three units of the goods for the agent. There are two

alternative interpretations of this transformation. First, the agent and his/her partner have different goods; therefore, one unit of the goods from his/her partner is subjectively transformed into three units of the goods for him/her. Second, as implemented in psychological experiments of exchange, an experimenter adds two units to one unit of the goods that is offered by the agent's partner. The same interpretations can be applied to exchanges in the market described below.

5 Note that the 'market' and 'assurance groups' are abstract concepts in this chapter. The market is a place where people transact anonymously under uncertainty, while people follow the norm of mutual cooperation in an assurance group.
6 The model used in this chapter is a modified version of the model proposed by Macy and Sato (2002).
7 The range of the value of propensity lies between 0 and 1 inclusive.
8 Random numbers generated in the fourth and the fifth steps are also uniformly distributed between 0 and 1 exclusive.
9 The agent offers one unit of the goods and receives three units of the good, so his/her payoff becomes 2 (= 3 − 1).
10 The member of group A (B) who has the highest accumulated payoff in group A (B) may be in the market or in group A (B).
11 At this point, we assume that the richer an agent is, the slower he/she learns. This implies that a rich agent does not rapidly decrease his/her propensities even if his/her trust is betrayed. Thus he/she may play the exchange game again at the next iteration.
12 We conducted regression analyses on three models: linear, quadratic, and cubic. The quadratic model fits best among them. (Adjusted R^2s are 0.000, 0.021, and 0.020, respectively.) The average predictor in Figure 3.4 is calculated based on the quadratic model.
13 To check the generality of the finding, we increased the value of X up to 100 to find the average correlation coefficient roughly decreases as X becomes larger. In addition, another simulation with 50 agents was conducted, and we got a pattern similar to that in Figure 3.4, although the decreasing rate is not so high as in Figure 3.4.

Chapter 4

1 The Suzuki family documents used in this study are in the possession of Mr. Suzuki Muneyo of Obanazawa-city, Yamagata. I have analyzed the following: 'Shaku-Myōsyu zen-ni sōrei hikae-chō' (Waki/1821); 'Shaku-Myōsan shinnyo fukō shoshiki hikae' (Kin/1837); 'Shaku-Dōsan inmotsu-narabini-shoshiki hikae' (Sōei/1857); 'Shakuni-Myocho shoshiki hikae' (Sana/1866); and 'Shaku-Dōsho shoshiki hikae' (Sōto/1869).
2 'Obanazawa-mura meisaichō 1857', *Obanazawa-shi shi shiryō* [Historical record of Obanazawa City], vol. 5.
3 'Uzen-no-Kuni Murayama-gun tahata yashiki rippumai sōkei torishirabe chō 1873', *Tendōshi-shi henshū shiryō*, vol. 25.
4 See *Obanazawa-shiritsu Miyazawa chūgakkō sōritsu gojū-shūnen kinenshi*, 2003.
5 'Mura sashidashi meisaichō', *Obanazawa-shi shi shiryō*, vol. 6.
6 *Sōin nikki* [Sōin diary], 2 vols., privately published in 1995.

7 The document is owned by Mr. Suzuki Muneyo, Obanazawa-city, Yamagata prefecture.
8 For the Suzuki family's political activities, see Daisuke Sato (2002).

Chapter 5

1 'Mass employment' indicates the phenomenon in which junior high school and high school graduates from rural areas who found employment in major urban areas migrated en masse to where their employers were located. Special 'mass transport trains' operated by Japan National Railways between 1954 and 1975 provided direct transportation to major urban destinations and are well known among the Japanese.
2 For example, when an individual experiences occupational mobility of some sort, it is impossible to determine whether the move was generated by a temporal change in occupational structure ('forced mobility') or by openness of the society ('pure mobility'). In other words, regardless of whether occupational mobility was generated by a change in the industrial structure or by openness of the society, from the perspective of the person who experienced that move, both represent the same opportunity for occupational mobility and as a result there is no essential difference between the two.
3 Japan's GDP outstripped that of West Germany in 1968 to become second in the world.
4 With regards to this type of migration to cities, Kurasawa (1964), for example, in his survey of 1960 targeting adult males living in Tokyo, identified that more than half of these males originated from areas other than Tokyo and in addition, that 40% of these were second or third sons of farmers. Meanwhile, Maruki (1994), in response to the fact that the total population of the three major metropolitan areas increased by 15.33 million people between 1960 and 1975, 40% of which represented a social increase, stated that 'this was an intense migration never before experienced by Japanese cities.'
5 The data is based on the Basic School Survey. However, data from the Industry and Education Survey is applied to the year 1953.
6 Although the same analysis was carried out for years other than 1966, results were generally similar except for the fact that Hiroshima became more of an oulet prefecture towards the end of the high growth period.
7 Although the practice of the eldest child being the inheritor was the norm in Eastern Japan, in Western Japan it was generally the youngest child that inherited. Refer Takeda (1974) for details.
8 Those migrating from a non-metropolitan area to another non-metropolitan area are excluded from the analysis.
9 Mobility patterns that can be defined other than (1), (2) and (3) are (4) those who moved from a non-metropolitan area to another non-metropolitan area, (5) those who moved from a metropolitan area to a non-metropolitan area and (6) those who moved from a metropolitan area to another metropolitan area. However, as sample numbers in these patterns are extremely limited, they are excluded from the analysis. The sample numbers of each mobility pattern are (1) 210, (2) 52, (3) 72, (4) 12, (5) 2 and (6) 4, respectively.
10 This classification is a simplified version of the SSM general occupational classification in which occupation, employment status and size of company

are combined. Companies with more than a thousand employees and government and public offices are defined as large companies, with companies with less than a thousand employees defined as small and medium companies. Refer to Yasuda and Hara (1982) for details.

11 The size of the company is a continuous variable defined as follows: 1 representing companies with 1 employee, 2 representing 2 to 4 employees, 3 representing 5 to 9 employees, 4 representing 10 to 29 employees, 5 representing 30 to 99 employees, 6 representing 100 to 299 employees, 7 representing 300 to 499 employees, 8 representing 500 to 999 employees and 9 representing companies employing more than 1000 employees or government and public offices.

12 Furthermore, the advantage migrants had is also reflected in economic terms. The average (annual) income is 7.08 million yen amongst migrants, 6.34 million yen amongst metropolitan non-migrants, 5.81 million yen amongst non-metropolitan non-migrants ($df = 2, 304, F = 3.36$ and $p = .036$). If we control for the prestige score of current occupation with ANCOVA, the effect of migration pattern on income becomes insignificant. Therefore we could assume that the difference in first job and that in occupational mobility opportunity between mobility patterns even affect economic status.

Chapter 6

1 We use the estimation method of full maximum likelihood estimation (ML), not restricted maximum likelihood estimation (REML). REML is less biased than with ML in random-effects estimates. However, the values calculated by two methods are almost same if the number of level-2 units is large. ML has the advantage in comparison between two models. For more detail, see Luke (2004).

2 In recent years, there were many papers focusing on social context by HLM, such as the region (Taylor 1998; Sampson et al. 1999; Baumer et al. 2003), country (Curtis et al. 2001; Schofer and Gourinchas 2001) and labor market (McCall 2000, 2001).

3 All the individual level variables are used with grand mean centered, because the intercept variance and intercept-by-slope covariance depend on the origin for the X-variable. It is helpful for the interpretation of parameters. For more detail, see Snijders and Bosker (1999).

4 In this chapter, the best model is found by removing from model 4 the cross level interaction terms and random-effects that do not have significant effects.

5 It is also likely that the tendency disappeared in the 1995 data because the index is the value which is compared with 5 years ago. We need to analyze this possibility further with the data of changes in the long term.

Chapter 7

1 The Japanese old middle class that mainly consists of self-employed workers is more fluid in terms of social mobility than the Japanese new middle class, however.

2 I got permission for using the data from the 2005 SSM Research Committee.
3 Age is not included in the analysis, because it did not have substantial effect on career images.
4 Family workers are included in the category of self-employed workers.
5 Respondents in the agricultural sector are excluded from the analysis because their career and position in the labor market are quite different than those of workers in other sectors.

Chapter 8

1 Permission has been granted by the 2005 SSM Research Committee for use of SSM data in this chapter.
2 The 1985 SSM Survey asked the year of the first marriage while the year of the current marriage was asked in other surveys. However, because remarrying is not very common in Japan and the factor is not considered to vary the analysis result greatly, I have included it in this analysis.
3 Using a larger number of categories reduces the frequency of each cell, making the results less reliable. Also, endogamy is not prevalent among the 'self-employed' (Watanabe and Kondo 1990). For these reasons, I did not use self-employed as a separate category.
4 For explanation of loglinear model, see, for example, Knoke and Burke (1980) and Agresti (2002).
5 Various design matrices are shown at the end of this chapter.
6 In order to obtain the overall pattern, I have weighted each cohort to adjust to the cohort of the smallest frequency (1920–39 marriages).
7 This is partly due to the smaller number of categories in educational background than the status origin.
8 See Figure 8.A for concrete design matrices.
9 BIC (Bayesian Information Criteria) suggests that the smaller the value the better fit the model is. For more details see Raftery (1995). The formula is:

$$BIC = G^2 - df \times \log_e(N)$$

10 The analysis by Shida *et al.* (2000) was based on a shorter period and a smaller sample size, and it employed a different method of analysis, which is the reason why it failed to detect the declining trend.
11 The sample size of marriages in 1920–30s is rather small, which leaves questions as to its accuracy. However, it is important that even including this sample the trend still forms an approximate line.
12 As no changes in the relationship between educational achievement and social status origin have been observed throughout the decades, it is assumed constant here.
13 Although I did not include the table here, testing with BIC has indicated that model 1 was relatively good, while another criteria AIC (Akaike Information Criteria) gives almost same level of fit for all models. As no decisive result could be obtained from information criteria, I gave priority to the result of likelihood ratio difference test.
14 Studies on homogamy incorporating co-habitation include Hamplova (2005).

Chapter 9

1 Ki Hun Kim received support through a special grant from the Center for the Study of Social Stratification and Inequality at Tohoku University under the 21st Century COE Program.
2 Educational reform has several aspects and complexity of the context at national level. The national context is even more difficult to understand, because these are bound up with culturally, historically and politically peculiar features. In this analysis, we only focused on national specific policies related to educational expansion such as the introduction of free and compulsory education.
3 The enrollment rate to secondary school is the ratio of the number of students at secondary schools such as junior high and high schools to the population aged 13–18.
4 The expansion of primary education in the 1930s was not only related to the need for educational opportunities for Korean parents and children, but also a request by the Japanese colonial government as a military strategy. According to Chung (2002), the Japanese Army required the colonial government to change its colonial educational system drastically in order to train the Korean children to become *Kōkokushinmin* (the imperial subjects) as assimilation policies and, for that purpose to enrol and educate all the children in public elementary schools. The aim of this request of the Japanese Army was to draft Korean youths to fight in the war.
5 Previous research in Japan partly insisted that inequalities of educational opportunity decreased over time in secondary education (Ojima 1990). With regard to higher education opportunities for males and secondary and higher education opportunities for females, no such changes have been claimed (Ojima 1990). Aramaki (2000) also came to the same conclusion.
6 The SSM surveys have been conducted every 10 years since 1955. We got the permission for using SSM datasets from the 2005 SSM Research Committee (*http://www.sal.tohoku.ac.jp/coe/ssm/index.html*). We would like to express our gratitude to everyone who contributed to SSM surveys.
7 The JGSS data sets were made available to the authors through the cooperation offered by the Social Science Japan Data Archive (*http://ssjda.iss.u-tokyo.ac.jp/en/index.html*), the Information Center for Social Science Research on Japan, and the Institute of Social Science at the University of Tokyo. The JGSS surveys have been collected by the Institute of Regional Studies, Osaka University of Commerce, and the Institute of Social Science, the University of Tokyo.
8 This study utilized the SIJ data sets collected by the Korean Social Science Research Council in 1990 and 1995. They are provided by the Korean Social Survey Data Archive (*http://kossda.or.kr/*).
9 We study the advancement rate to high school rather than that to junior high school in Japan because junior high school fell in the scope of compulsory education in Japan in 1947.

Chapter 10

1 A Chinese version of this article was published in *Sociological Research* (China), 2006, No.1. Part of this research was funded by the Center for the

Study of Social Stratification and Inequality under the 21st Century COE program, Tohoku University, Japan.
2 Redundant workers accounted for 15% of total labor force in the SOEs in 1994 (World Bank 1995).
3 Layoff is not unemployment in China. Unemployed workers no longer have any relationship with any work organizations and are able to obtain unemployment insurance under some conditions (Unemployment Insurance Regulations, the State Council, 1/1999).
4 'Assuring Livelihood Allowance and Reemployment of Laid-off Workers in SOE', (Communication Ministry of Central Committee of CCP [1999] 2; MOLSS [1999] 13).
5 There were 12.7 million laid-off workers at the end of 1997, 8.77 million at the end of 1998, 9.37 million at the end of 1999 and 9.11 million at the end of 2000. These numbers only included laid-off workers who had not found jobs by the year end (China Labor Statistical Yearbook 1998–2001).
6 Mingpao, 5/17/2000, HK; The Washington Post, 4/4/2000.
7 We will use 'rank' to refer to the levels of governments that administer the enterprises.
8 Dr. Wang Hansheng at Peking University was the Principle Investigator of the project.
9 See Xie (2004) for detail information of the dataset.
10 Enterprises are required to contribute 8% of a worker's wage as medical insurance, 20% as pension fund and 2% as unemployment insurance. Workers who can get reimbursement for their medical expenses are regarded as having medical insurance.
11 According to official definition, an enterprise is defined as small or medium if it has less than 2000 workers, or its sales income /total amount of capital is less than 200 million *yuan*. The enterprise is medium if it has more than 300 workers, its sales income is more than 30 million *yuan,* and its total amount of capital is above 40 million *yuan* (Mingpao, 3/7/2003, HK). Since we do not have enough information on product or capital, we only use the number of workers as the criterion. But there are only few enterprises that have less than 300 workers, so we raise the standard for small enterprises.
12 $(1 - \exp(-0.45)) \times 100\% = 36\%$
13 China Labor Statistical Yearbook, 2002. People's Daily, 9/2/2002.
14 In 1999, there were 83.4 million on-post workers and 6.5 million laid-off workers in the SOEs, and 16.5 million on-post workers and 2.6 million laid-off workers in the collective-owned enterprises. The number of workers decreased by 24% in the SOEs and by 46% in the collective-owned enterprises from 1995 to 1999 (China Labor Statistical Yearbook, 1996, 2000, table 1-1 and 8-1). It means the proportion of workers being removed from the collective-owned enterprises was much higher than that in the SOEs. However, lots of workers in the collective-owned enterprises were removed in the form of unemployment instead of layoff.
15 For example, in Shaanxi Province, the basic living allowance the workers from the collective-owned enterprises obtained was 80% of that of workers from the SOEs. (Shaanxi Provincial Government, [2001] 11).
16 Gan (2000) mentioned 'administrative layoff' in her report. Some local governments assigned quotas to enterprises for layoff. In order to fill in the

quota, some enterprises even laid off the non-surplus workers. A manager interviewed in Tianjin also mentioned the quota problems.

17 China Labor Statistical Yearbook, 2000.
18 China Labor Statistical Yearbook, 2000. Although the definition of the size of enterprises here is different from national statistics, the two definitions are consistent in the way that normally the state-defined medium or large enterprises have more workers than smaller enterprises.
19 China Labor Statistical Yearbook, 2000 (table 1-13, 8-1).
20 It is because the official retirement ages are different for male and female, cadres and non-cadres (including technician). Usually males can retire at 55-years-old, females at 50, male cadres at 60 and female cadres at 55.
21 For example, in a printing firm surveyed in Nanjing, workers laid off at 40-year-old were counted as inner retirement in 1998. However in 1999, 40-years-old workers were not qualified for any more. In another firm, the inner retired workers in 1997 were paid by 720 *yuan*/month –almost the same as what they got before layoff. However those inner retired in 1999 can only get 450 *yuan*/month.
22 In 1998 and 1999, the central and local governments spent 1.3 billion *yuan* encouraging the state-owned textile firms to give up outdated machines and layoff surplus workers. As a result, 1.2 million textile workers were laid off or early retired (People's Daily, 2/20/2000). All female workers above 42-years-old in a surveyed textile firm in Nanjing retired then because of the nice retirement package – nobody dared to miss it. Although the firm managers complained that quality of products got worse dramatically following the retirement of many technicians, they did not stop anybody from leaving because 'this kind of good thing may never happen again.'
23 The direction and significance of the coefficient do not change if age is replaced with total working experience.

Chapter 11

1 Part of this research was supported by the Center for the Study of Social Stratification and Inequality (CSSI), the Center of Excellence (COE) Program at Tohoku University, Japan. An earlier version of this chapter is printed in *Annual Report* 2004, CSSI, Tohoku University pp. 113–134, and presented at the annual meeting of Population Association of America, April, 2005 in Philadelphia. Address all correspondence to Yukio Kawano, Department of Economics, Daito Bunka University, 1-9-1 Takashimadaira, Itabashi, Tokyo 175-8571, or email to: ykawano@ic.daito.ac.jp.
2 According to Van Hook (2004) 32% of second-generation Mexican children under 18 are in poverty.
3 1970 census provided birthplace of respondent's parents. Parents' birthplace question had been replaced by ancestry question after this census.
4 Approximately a quarter of households and individuals overlap from month to month, and a half overlap from year to year.
5 We added dummy variable for missing data.
6 We captured about 800 individual samples whose birthplace and/or that of parents indicates Mexican backgrounds but did not identify themselves as Mexican of any sorts. With the limited information, it is impossible for us to

determine their reasons or true situations in which they chose other ethnic identities. We know, however, that these non-Mexicans earn generally greater hourly wages than those self-identified Mexicans (see Appendix).

7 We made this occupational-skill category based on the average earnings of Mexican workers in both sexes. (1) High-skill occupations include: executive, administrative, and managerial, professional, and specialty occupations. (2) Middle-skill occupations are: technicians and related support, sales, administrative support including clerical jobs, protective and other services, precision production, craft and repair occupations. (3) Low-skill occupations are private household, machine operators, assemblers and inspectors, transportation and material moving occupations, handlers, equipment cleaners, helpers, laborers, farming, forestry and fishing occupations.

References

Agresti, Alan (2002), *Categorical Data Analysis*, (2nd ed.), Indianapolis, IN: Wiley Publishers.
Allen, Mary J. and Wendy M. Yen (1979), *Introduction to Measurement Theory*, Monterey, CA: Brooks/Cole Publishing Company.
Appleton, Simon, John Knight, Lina Song and Qingjie Xia (2001), 'Towards a Competitive Labor Market? Urban Workers, Rural Migrants, Redundancies and Hardships in China', Paper presented at the American Economic Association Conference.
Aramaki, Sōhei (2000), 'Kyōiku kikai no kakusa wa shukushō shitaka (Have disparities of educational opportunity decreased over time?)', in Hiroyuki Kondo (ed.), *Nihon no kaisō shisutemu 3: Sengo Nihon no kyōiku shakai (Stratification system in Japan 3: Educational credentials in the postwar stratification system)*, Tokyo: University of Tokyo Press, pp. 15–35.
Araragi, Shinzō (1994), 'Toshi ijūsha no jinkō kanryū – kison to jinkō U-taan (Population return amongst urban migrants: Existing population and population U-turns)', in Michiharu Matsumoto and Keisuke Maruki (eds), *Toshi ijūsha no shakaigaku (The sociology of urban migration)*, Kyoto: Sekaishisōsha, pp.165–198.
Araragi, Yukiko (1994), 'Chihō jinkō no kōto rison genshō (The phenomenon of rural exodus and move to cities amongst regional populations)', in Michiharu Matsumoto and Keisuke Maruki (eds), *Toshi ijūsha no shakaigaku (The sociology of urban migration)*, Kyoto: Sekaishisōsha, pp.49–82.
Baudrillard, Jean (1970), *La Société de Consommation: ses mythes, ses structures*, Paris: Gallimard.
Bauman, Zygmunt (1982), *Memories of Class: The Pre-History and After-Life of Class*, London: Routledge and Kegan Paul.
Baumer, Eric, Steven Messner and Richard Rosenfeld (2003), 'Explaining Spatial Variation in Support for Capital Punishment: A Multilevel Analysis', *American Journal of Sociology*, 108, pp. 844–75.
Beck, Ulrich (1986), *Risikogesellschaft: Auf dem Weg in eine andere Moderne*, Frankfurt: Suhrkamp.
Becker, Gary S. (1993), *Human Capital: A Theoretical and Empirical Analysis, with Special Reference to Education*, Chicago, IL: The University of Chicago Press.
Bian, Yanjie (1994), *Work and Inequality in Urban China*, Albany, NY: State University of New York Press.
Bian, Yanjie (2002), 'Chinese Social Stratification and Social Mobility', *Annual Review of Sociology*, 28, pp. 91–116.
Bian, Yanjie and John Logan (1996), 'Market Transition and the Persistence of Power: The Changing Stratification System in Urban China', *American Sociological Review*, 61, pp. 739–58.
Bihagen, Erik and Bjorn Hallerod (2000), 'The Crucial Aspects of Class: An Empirical Assessment of the Relevance of Class Analysis with Swedish Data

Covering the Late Twentieth Century', *Work, Employment and Society*, 14, pp. 307–30.

Blau, Peter M. and Otis D. Duncan (1967), *The American Occupational Structure*, Indianapolis, IN: Wiley Publishers.

Blossfeld, Hans-Peter and Yossi Shavit (1993), 'Persisting Barriers: Changes in Educational Opportunities in Thirteen Countries', in Yossi Shavit and Hans-Peter Blossfeld (eds), *Persistent Inequality: Changing Educational Attainment in Thirteen Countries*, San Francisco, CA: Westview Press, pp. 1–23.

Blossfeld, Hans-Peter and Andreas Timm (eds) (2003), *Who Marries Whom: Educational Systems as Marriage Markets in Modern Societies*, Dordrecht: Kluwer Academic Publishers.

Borjas, George J. (1991), 'Immigration and Self-Selection', in John M. Abowd and Richard B. Freeman (eds), *Immigration, Trade, and Labor Market*, Chicago, IL: The University of Chicago Press.

Borjas, George J. (1993), 'The Intergenerational Mobility of Immigrants', *Journal of Labor Economics*, 11(1), pp. 113–5.

Borjas, George J. (1995), 'Assimilation and Changes in Cohort Quality Revisited: What Happened to Immigrant Earnings in the 1980s?', *Journal of Labor Economics*, 13(2), pp. 201–245.

Borjas, George J. (1999), *Heaven's Door: Immigration Policy and the American Economy*, Princeton, NJ: Princeton University Press.

Breen, Richard and John H. Goldthorpe (1997), 'Explaining Educational Differentials', *Rationality and Society*, 9, pp. 275–305.

Breen, Richard (ed.) (2004), *Social Mobility in Europe*, Oxford: Oxford University Press.

Brinton, Mary C. (1998), *Women and the Economic Miracle: Gender and Work in Postwar Japan*, Berkeley, CA: University of California Press.

Buchman, Claudia and Emily Hannum (2001), 'Education and Stratification in Developing Countries: A Review of Theories and Research', *Annual Review of Sociology*, 27, pp. 77–102.

Cai, Yongshun (2002), 'The Resistance of Chinese Laid-off Workers in the Reform Period', *China Quarterly*, 170, pp. 327–344.

Cao, Yang and Victor Nee (2000), 'Comment: Controversies and Evidence in the Market Transition Debate', *American Journal of Sociology*, 105, pp. 1175–89.

Carliner, Geoffrey (1980), 'Wages, Earnings and Hours of First, Second, and Third Generation American Males', *Economic Inquiry*, 18(1), pp. 87–102.

Census Bureau (1998), by A. Dianne Schmidley and J. Gregory Robinson, *How Well Does the Current Population Survey Measure the Foreign-Born Population in the United States*.

Census Bureau (2001), *The Hispanic Population,* Census 2000 Brief.

Census Bureau (2002), *Design and Methodology,* Current Population Survey Technical Paper 63RV.

Census Bureau (2005), 'Facts for Features and Special Editions', CB05–FF.14–3, 8 September 2005, <http://www.census.gov/Press-Release /www/releases/ archives/facts_for_features_special_editions /005338.html> (30 September 2005).

Chang, Sang-su (2003), 'Patterns and Changes of Educational Attainment in

Korea', The Annual Meeting of Research Committee on Social Stratification and Mobility (RC28), International Sociological Association, Tokyo, Japan.

Chang, Sang-su (2004), 'Hangnyeokseongchwiui Gyegeupbyeol-Seongbyeol Gyeokcha (Class and gender differentials in educational attainment in Korea)', *Hanguksahoehak (Korean Journal of Sociology)*, 38(1), pp. 51–75.

Child Trends Databank (2005), 'Children in Poverty', <http://www.childtrends databank.org/indicators/4Poverty.cfm> (30 September 2005).

China Center for Economic Research (CCER), Research Team on Urban Labor Market (1999), 'The Stickiness of Laid-off Workers to Enterprises: Survey on Employment in Jinlin City', *Reform*, 6, pp. 44–52.

Chiswick, Barry (1977), 'Sons of Immigrants: Are They at an Earnings Disadvantage?', *American Economic Review*, 67(1), pp. 376–380, (Errata *AER*, September 1977, p. 775).

Chung, Kyu-young (2002), 'Jeonsidongwonchejewa Singminji Gyoyugui Byeonyong: Ilbon Singminji Jibaehaui Hangukgyoyuk, 1937–1945 (Wartime-mobilization and the transformation of colonial education: The education of Korea, 1937–1945)', *Gyoyukagyeongu (Korean Journal of Educational Research)*, 40(2), pp. 35–64.

Croll, Elisabeth J. (1999), 'Social Welfare Reform: Trends and Tensions', *The China Quarterly*, 159, pp. 685–699.

Cronbach, Lee J. (1951), 'Coefficient Alpha and the Internal Structural of Tests', *Psychometrika*, 16, pp. 297–334.

Curtis, James E., Douglas E. Baer and Edward G. Grabb (2001), 'Nations of Joiners: Explaining Voluntary Association Membership in Democratic Societies', *American Sociological Review*, 66(6), pp. 783–805.

Deng, Zhong and Donald Treiman (1997), 'The Impact of the Cultural Revolution on Trends in Educational Attainment in the People's Republic of China', *American Journal of Sociology*, 103, pp. 391–428.

Dronkers, Jaap (1993), 'Educational Reform in the Netherlands: Did It Change the Impact of Parental Occupation and Education?', *Sociology of Education* 66(4), pp. 262–277.

Duncan, Brian and Stephen J. Trejo (2004), 'Ethnic Choices and the Intergenerational Progress of Mexican Americans', Working Paper Series 2004–2005, No 04–05–02, Population Research Center, University of Texas at Austin.

Erikson, Robert and John H. Goldthorpe (1992), *The Constant Flux*, Oxford: Oxford University Press.

Festinger, Leon (1957), *A Theory of Cognitive Dissonance*, Stanford, CA: Stanford University Press.

Fine, Ben (1998), *Labor Market Theory: A Constructive Reassessment*, London: Routledge.

Forse, Michel and Louis Chauvel (1995), 'Evolution of Homogamy in France: A Method to Compare Diagonal Characteristics of Several Tables', *Revue Francaise de Sociologie*, 36, pp. 123–142.

Fry, Richard (2005), 'The High Schools Hispanics Attend: Size and Other Key Characteristics', *Pew Hispanic Center Research Report*, <http://pewhispanic. org/files/reports/54.pdf> (30 November 2005).

Gamoran, Adam, Yossi Shavit and Richard Arum (2004), 'Inclusion, Not Diversion: Findings from a 15-Nation Study of Expansion and Stratification in Higher Education', The Annual Meeting of Research Committee on Social Stratification and Mobility (RC28), International Sociological Association, Rio de Janeiro, Brazil.

Gan, Yongxin (2000), 'Analysis on the Tendency of Layoff and Reemployment', *Report to Center for the Study of Contemporary China, Tsinghua University, China* <http://www.thcscc.org>.

Gans, Herbert J. (1992), 'Second Generation Decline: Scenarios for the Economic and Ethnic Futures of Post-1965 American Immigrants', *Ethnic and Racial Studies*, 15, pp. 173–192.

Garnier, Maurice, Jerald Hage and Bruce Fuller (1989), 'The Strong State, Social Class, and Controlled School Expansion in France, 1881–1975', *American Journal of Sociology*, 95(2), pp. 279–306.

Genda, Yūji (2001), *Shigoto no naka no aimai na fuan: Yureru jakunen no genzai (A nagging sense of job insecurity: The new reality facing Japanese youth)*, Tokyo: Chūō Kōron Shinsha.

Gerber, Theodore P. (2000), 'Membership Benefits or Selection Effects? Why Former Communist Party Members do Better in Post-Soviet Russia', *Social Science Research*, 29, pp. 25–50.

Gerber, Theodore P. (2001), 'The Selection Theory of Persisting Party Advantages in Russia: More Evidence and Implications', *Social Science Research*, 30, pp. 653–671.

Giddens, Anthony (1991), *Modernity and Self-Identity: Self and Society in the Late Modern Age*, Stanford, CA: Stanford University Press.

Glass, David (1954), *Social Mobility in Britain*, London: Routledge and Kegan Paul.

Gordon, Milton (1964), *Assimilation in American Life*, New York, NY: Oxford University Press.

Grogger, Jeffrey and Stephen J. Trejo (2002), *Falling Behind or Moving Up? The Intergenerational Progress of Mexican Americans*, California: Public Policy Institute of California.

Halpin, Brendan and Tak W. Chan (2003), 'Educational Homogamy in Ireland and Britain: Trends and Patterns', *British Journal of Sociology*, 54 (4), pp. 473–495.

Hamplova, Dana (2005), 'Educational Homogamy in Marriage and Cohabitation in Selected European Countries', Paper presented at the meeting of the ISA Research Committee 28, August 18–21 in Los Angeles, California.

Hankook Gyoyuk 10nyeonsa Pyeonchanwiwonhoe (1960), *Hankook Gyoyuk 10nyeonsa (The 10-year history of Korean education)*, Seoul: Pung Munsa.

Hara, Junsuke (1986), 'Shokugyō idō no nettowaaku (The occupational mobility network)', in Atsushi Naoi, Junsuke Hara and Hajime Kobayashi (eds), *Riidingusu Nihon no shakaigaku 8, shakai kaisō shakai idō (Readings Japanese sociology 8, social stratification and social mobility)*, Tokyo: University of Tokyo Press, pp.214–228.

Hara, Junsuke (ed.) (1990), *Gendai Nihon no kaisō kōzō 2: Kaisō ishiki no dōtai (Strata structure in contemporary Japan 2: Dynamics of social strata consciousness)*, Tokyo: University of Tokyo Press.

Hara, Junsuke (ed.) (2000), *Nihon no kaisō shisutemu 1: Kindaika to shakai kaisō (Stratification system in Japan 1: Modernization and social stratification)*, Tokyo: University of Tokyo Press.

Hara, Junsuke (ed.) (2002), *Kōza shakai hendō 5: Ryūdōka to shakai kakusa (Social change 5: Fluidization and social disparities)*, Kyoto: Mineruva Shobō.

Hara, Junsuke and Kazuo Seiyama (1999), *Shakai kaisō: Yutakasa no naka no fubyōdō*, Tokyo: University of Tokyo Press. (Brad Williams, trans., 2005, *Inequality amid Affluence: Social Stratification in Japan*, Melbourne: Trans Pacific Press.)

Hayashi, Takuya (2002), 'Chiikikan idō to chii tassei (Inter-regional migration and status attainment)', in Junsuke Hara (ed.) (2002), *Kōza shakai hendō 5: Ryūdōka to shakai kakusa (Social change 5: Fluidization and social disparities)*, Kyoto: Mineruva Shobō, pp.118–144.

Higuchi, Yoshio and Zaimushō Zaimu Sōgō Seisaku Kenkyūjo (Policy Research Institute, Ministry of Finance Japan) (eds) (2003), *Nihon no shotoku seisaku to shakai kaisō (Income policy and social stratification in Japan)*, Tokyo: Nihon Hyōronsha.

Hoshi, Atsushi (2000), 'Kaisō kizoku ishiki kenkyū no handan kijun to hikaku kijun: junkyo waku toshiteno nettowaaku no kinō (Criteria and frame of reference in status identification: A function of personal networks in the judgement of one's own status)', *Shakaigaku hyōron (Japanese Sociological Review)*, 51(1), pp. 120–135.

Hout, Michael (1982), 'The Association between Husbands' and Wives' Occupations in Two-earner Families', *American Journal of Sociology*, 88, pp. 397–409.

Hout, Michael, Adrian E. Raftery and Eleanor O. Bell (1993), 'Making the Grade: Educational Stratification in the United States, 1925–1989', in Yossi Shavit and Hans-Peter Blossfeld (eds), *Persistent Inequality: Changing Educational Attainment in Thirteen Countries*, San Francisco, CA: Westview Press, pp. 25–49.

Hur, Su-yeol (2005), *Gaebal Eomneun Gaebal: Iljeha Joseon Gyeongje Gaebarui Hyeonsanggwa Bonjil (Development without development: The situation and essence of economic development during the colonial period)*, Seoul: Eunhaengnamu.

Huntington, Samuel (2004), 'The Hispanic Challenge', *Foreign Policy*, March/April, pp. 30–45.

Imada, Takatoshi (ed.) (2000), *Nihon no kaisō shisutemu 5: Shakai kaisō no posutomodan (Stratification system in Japan 5: Postmodernity and social stratification)*, Tokyo: University of Tokyo Press.

Ishida, Hiroshi (2003), 'Educational Expansion and Inequality of Access to Education in Japan', The Annual Meeting of Research Committee on Social Stratification and Mobility (RC28), International Sociological Association, New York, United States of America.

Ishikawa, Yoshitaka (1994), *Jinkō idō no keiryō chirigaku (Quantitative geography of population migration)*, Tokyo: Kokon Shoin.

Jackman, Mary R. and Robert W. Jackman (1973), 'An Interpretation of the Relation between Objective and Subjective Social Status', *American Sociological Review*, 38(5), pp. 569–82.

Japanese Ministry of Education (1962), *Nihon no seichō to kyōiku (Development and education in Japan)*, Tokyo: Teikoku Chihō Gyōsei Gakkai.

Japanese Ministry of Education, Culture, Sports, Science and Technology (2004), *Japan's Education at a Glance*, Tokyo: National Printing Bureau.

Jensen, Leif (2001), 'The Demographic Diversity of Immigrants and their Children', in Rubén G. Rumbaut and Alejandro Portes (eds), *Ethnicities: Children of Immigrants in America*, Berkeley, CA: University of California Press, pp. 21–56.

Jones, Frank L. (1987), 'Marriage Patterns and the Stratification System: Trends in Educational Homogamy since 1930s', *Australian and New Zealand Journal of Sociology*, 23, pp. 185–198.

Joo, Yikjong (1998), '1930yeondae Jungyeop Ihu Joseonin Jungdeunghakgyōi Hwakchung (The expansion of secondary education in Korea since the mid-1930s)', *Gyeongjesahak (The Journal of Economical History)*, 24, pp. 97–137.

Kalleberg, Arne L. and Aage B. Sørensen (1979), 'The Sociology of Labor Markets', *Annual Review of Sociology*, 5, pp. 351–379.

Kalmijn, Matthijs (1991), 'Status Homogamy in the United States', *American Journal of Sociology*, 97, pp. 496–523.

Kalmijn, Matthijs (1994), 'Assortative Mating by Cultural and Economic Occupational Status', *American Journal of Sociology*, 100, pp. 422–452.

Kalmijn, Matthijs (1998), 'Intermarriage and Homogamy: Cause, Patterns, Trends', *Annual Review of Sociology*, 24, pp. 395–421.

Kao, Grace and Marta Tienda (1995), 'Optimism and Achievement: The Educational Performance of Immigrant Youth', *Social Science Quarterly*, 76(1), pp 1–19.

Kao, Grace and Jennifer Thompson (2003), 'Race and Ethnic Stratification in Educational Achievement and Attainment', *Annual Review of Sociology*, 29, pp. 417–442.

Kariya, Takehiko (2000), 'Gakko, shokuan, chiiki idō (The school, the employment agency and regional migration)', in Takehiko Kariya, Shinji Sugayama and Hiroshi Ishida (eds), *Gakkō, shokuan to rōdō shijō – sengo shinki gakusotsu shijo no seidoka katei (Schools, public employment offices, and the labor market in postwar Japan)*, Tokyo: University of Tokyo Press, pp.31–64.

Kariya, Takehiko (2001), *Kaisōka Nihon to kyōiku kiki: Fubyōdō saiseisan kara iyoku kakusa shakai e (Education in crisis and stratified Japan: From inequality reproduction to a society stratified on the basis of incentives)*, Tokyo: Yūshindō Kōbunsha.

Kase, Kazutoshi (1997), *Shūdan shūshoku no jidai – kōdo seichō no ninaitetachi (The era of collective employment: The instruments of high economic growth)*, Tokyo: Aoki Shoten.

Kennedy, Ruby J. R. (1944), 'Single or Triple Melting Pot? Intermarriage Trends in New Haven, 1870–1940', *American Journal of Sociology*, 49, pp. 331–339.

Kikkawa, Toru (1999), '"Chū" ishiki no shizukana henyō (Quiet changes of middle-social strata identification in Japan)', *Shakaigaku hyōron (Japanese Sociological Review)*, 50(2), pp. 76–90.

Kim, Inhoe, Jae-seon Choe and Myeong-geun Lee (2001), 'Haebang Ihu Bansegiui Hyeonjang Jaryobunseogeul Tonghan Gyoyukhyeonjangui

Jeongchiyeokakjeok Seonggyeok Gyumyeonge Gwanhan Yeongu (A study of political aspects about education using the spot materials since the Korean liberation)', *Hangukgyoyuksahak* (*The Journal of The Korean Society for History of Education*), 23(1), pp. 21–92.

Kim, Ki Hun (2005), 'Educational Expansion and Inequality: Social Class and Gender Differentials in School Transitions in Korea', *Annual Report of the Center for the Study of Social Stratification and Inequality*, The 21st Century Center of Excellence Program, Tohoku University, pp. 135–164.

Kimura, Mitsuhiko (1997), 'Kinndai Chōsen no shotō kyōiku (Primary education in the modern Yi dynasty)', in Shigeru Itaya (ed.), *Azia hatten no kaosu* (*Chaos of development in Asia*), Tokyo: Keisō Shobō, pp. 29–63.

Knoke, David and Peter J. Burke, (1980), *Log-linear Models*, Beverly Hills, CA: Sage Publications.

Kobayashi, Daisuke (2004), 'Kaisō kizoku ishiki ni taisuru chiiki tokusei no kōka (The region as a determinant of social strata identification)', *Shakaigaku hyōron* (*Japanese Sociological Review*), 55(3), pp. 348–366.

Korean Ministry of Education & Human Resources Development and the Korean Educational Development Institute (2003), *Statistical Yearbook of Education*, Seoul: KEDI.

Kosaka, Kenji and Masaru Miyano (1990), 'Kaisō imeije (Images of social stratification)', in Junsuke Hara (ed.), *Gendai Nihon no kaisō kōzō 2: Kaisō ishiki no dōtai* (*Strata structure in contemporary Japan 2: Dynamics of social strata consciousness*), Tokyo: University of Tokyo Press, pp. 47–70.

Kurasawa, Susumu (1968), *Nihon no toshi shakai* (*Japan's urban society*), Tokyo: Fukumura Shuppan.

Lardy, Nicholas R. (1998), *China's Unfinished Economic Revolution*, Washington, DC: Brookings Institute.

Lee, Ching Kwan (1999), 'From Organized Dependence to Disorganized Despotism: Changing Labor Regimes in Chinese Factories', *The China Quarterly*, 157, pp. 44–71.

Lee, Gil-sang (2003), 'Migukjeonggi Chodeunggyoyugui Byeonhwa (Changes in elementary education under the American military government in Korea)', *Hangukgyoyuksahak* (*The Journal of Korean Society for History of Education*), 25(2), pp. 75–100.

Lee, Hye-yeong, Jong-hyeok Yun and Bang-ran Ryu (1997), *Hanguk Geundae Hakgyogyoyuk 100 Nyeonsa Yeongu (2): Iljesidaeui Hakgyogyoyuk* (*A study on history of Korean modern education 100 years (2): The colonial period*), Seoul: Korean Educational Development Institute.

Lee, Kwang-ho (1991), 'Hanguk Gyoyukchije-ui Gujojeok Teukseong – 1945–1955nyeonul Jungsimeuro (A study on the systematic characteristics of Korean educational system in the reorganization era: 1945–1955)', *Godeung gyoyuk yeongu* (*Korean Journal of Higher Education*), 3(1), pp. 131–159.

Lillard, Lee A. and Robert J. Willis (1994), 'Intergenerational Educational Mobility: Effects of Family and State in Malaysia', *The Journal of Human Resources*, 29(4), pp. 1126-1166.

Lin, Justin Yifu, Fang Cai and Zhou Li (1996), *The China Miracle: Development Strategy and Economic Reform*, Hong Kong: The Chinese University Press.

Lin, Nan and Yanjie Bian (1991), 'Getting Ahead in Urban China', *American Journal of Sociology*, 97, pp. 689–720.

Lipset, Seymour M. and Reinhard Bendix (1959), *Social Mobility in Industrial Society*, Berkeley, CA: University of California Press.

Liu, Pak-Wai, Xin Meng and Junsen Zhang (2000), 'Sectoral Gender Wage Differentials and Discrimination in the Transitional Chinese Economy', *Journal of Population Economics*, 13, pp. 331-352.

Livingston, Gretchen and Joan R. Kahn (2002), 'The American Dream Unfulfilled: The Limited Mobility of Mexican Americans', *Social Science Quarterly*, 83(4), pp.1003–1012.

Luke, Douglas A. (2004), *Multilevel Modeling* (Quantitative Applications in the Social Sciences no 143), London: Sage.

Macy, Michael W. and Yoshimichi Sato (2002), 'Trust, Cooperation, and Market Formation in the U. S. and Japan', *Proceedings of the National Academy of Sciences of the United States of America* 99 (Suppl. 3), pp. 7214–20.

Macy, Michael W. and Robert Willer (2002), 'Computational Sociology and Agent-Based Modeling', *Annual Review of Sociology*, 28, pp. 143–166.

Mamada,Takao (1990), 'Kaisō kizoku ishiki: Keizai seichō, byōdōka to "chū" ishiki (Social strata identification: Economic growth, equalization and "middle-stratum" consciousness)', in Junsuke Hara (ed.), *Gendai Nihon no kaisō kōzō 2: Kaisō ishiki no dōtai* (*Strata structure in contemporary Japan 2: Dynamics of social strata consciousness*), Tokyo: University of Tokyo Press, pp. 23–45.

Mare, Robert D. (1980), 'Social Background and School Continuation Decisions', *Journal of American Statistical Association*, 75, pp. 295-305.

Mare, Robert D. (1981), 'Change and Stability in Educational Stratification', *American Sociological Review*, 46, pp. 72-87.

Mare, Robert D. (1991), 'Five Decades of Educational Assortative Mating', *American Sociological Review*, 56, pp. 15–32.

Mare, Robert D. (1993), 'Educational Stratification on Observed and Unobserved Components of Family Background', in Yossi Shavit and Hans-Peter Blossfeld (eds), *Persistent Inequality: Changing Educational Attainment in Thirteen Countries,* San Francisco, CA: Westview Press, pp. 351–376.

Maruki, Keisuke (1994), 'Jo – furusato kō (Introduction: a view on the hometown)', Michiharu Matsumoto and Keisuke Maruki (eds), *Toshi ijūsha no shakaigaku* (*The sociology of urban migration*), Kyoto: Sekaishisōsha, pp.i–v.

McCall, Leslie (2000), 'Gender and the New Inequality: Explaining the College/non-college Wage Gap', *American Sociological Review*, 65(2), pp. 234–255.

McCall, Leslie (2001), 'Sources of Racial Wage Inequality in Metropolitan Labor Markets: Racial, Ethnic, and Gender Differences', *American Sociological Review*, 66(4), pp. 520–542.

Matsumoto, Michiharu and Keisuke Maruki (eds) (1994), *Toshi ijūsha no shakaigaku* (*The sociology of urban migration*), Kyoto: Sekaishisōsha.

Merton, Robert K. and Mathilda White Riley (eds) (1980), *Sociological Tradition from Generation to Generation,* Norwood, NJ: Ablex Publishing Corp.

Minami, Ryōshin (2000), 'Nihon ni okeru shotoku bunpu no chōkiteki henka: Sai-shūkei to kekka (The long-term change in income distribution in Japan: Recalculation and its results)', *Tokyo Keidai Gakkai Shi* (*The Journal of Tokyo Keizai University*), no. 219, pp. 31–51.

Ministry of Labor and Social Security (MOLSS) (1998), *Collection of Official Documents on Assuring the Basic Livelihood and the Reemployment of Laid-off Workers from the State-owned Enterprises*, Beijing: China Labor Press.

Mungyobu (1958), *Mungyo GaeGwan* (*Overview of educational affairs*), Seoul: Mungyobu.

Mungyobu (1959), *Mungyo WolBo* (*Monthly Educational Review*), 47 (August), Seoul: Mungyobu.

Mungyobu (1965), *Handbook of Educational Statistics*, Seoul: Mungyobu.

Nakayasu, Sadako (ed.) (1983), *Showa kōki nōgyō mondai ronshū 5 – nōson jinkōron, rōdōryokuron* (A *treatise on late Showa agricultural issues vol. 5: Rural population theories and work force theories*), Tokyo: Nōbunkyō.

Namiki, Masayoshi (1960), *Nōson wa kawaru* (*The village is changing*), Tokyo: Iwanami Shoten.

Nee, Victor (1989), 'A Theory of Market Transition: From Redistribution to Markets in State Socialism', *American Sociological Review*, 54, pp. 663–81.

Nee, Victor (1991), 'Social Inequalities in Reforming State Socialism: Between Redistribution and Markets in China', *American Sociological Review*, 56, pp. 267–82.

Nee, Victor (1996), 'The Emergence of a Market Society: Changing Mechanisms of Stratification in China', *American Journal of Sociology*, 101, pp. 908–49.

Nomura, Masami (1994), *Shūshin koyō* (*The life-time employment*), Tokyo: Iwanami Shoten.

Nunnally, Jum C. and Ira H. Bernstein (1994), *Psychometric Theory*, New York, NY: McGraw-Hill.

Odaka, Kōnosuke (1984), *Rōdō shijō bunseki: Nijū kōzō no Nihon teki tenkai* (*An analysis of the labor market: The development of the dual structure in Japan*), Tokyo: Iwanami Shoten.

Oh, Seong-Cheo (1999), 'Singminjigi Chodeunggyoyuk Paengchangui Sahoesa- Jeonbukjiyeok Saryeyeongu (A social history of primary education expansion during the colonial period: A case study on Chollabukdo Province)', *Chodeunggyoyugyeongu* (*The Journal of Elementary Education*), 13(1), pp. 5–29.

Ojima, Fumiaki (1990), 'Kyōiku kikai no sūsei bunseki (Trend analysis of educational opportunity)', in Jōji Kikuchi (ed.), *Gendai Nihon no kaisō kōzō 3: Kyōiku to shakai idō* (*Strata structure in contemporary Japan 3: Education and social mobility*), Tokyo: University of Tokyo Press, pp. 25–55.

Parish, William and Ethan Michelson (1996), 'Politics and Markets: Dual Transformation', *American Journal of Sociology*, 101, pp. 1042–1059.

Park, Hyunjoon (2003), 'Educational Expansion and Inequality of Opportunity for Higher Education in South Korea', The Annual Meeting of Research Committee on Social Stratification and Mobility (RC28), International Sociological Association, New York, NY.

Parsons, Talcott (unpublished works in Harvard University Archives)
1938 Letter to Professor Elton Mayo, July 11, 1938.
c.1949 Memorandum: The Problem of Hierarchical Prestige-Ordering of Occupational Roles.
c.1950 Theoretical Problems in the Study of Social Mobility.
c.1951 Memorandum II: Further Theoretical Considerations for a Study of Social Mobility.

1973 Article on Social Stratification, for *Enciclopedia Italiana*, April 1973.
1977 Memorandum: The Problem of the Conference in Cape Town May 1977, July 28, 1977.
1979 *ASC: American Societal Community*.
Parsons, Talcott (1940), 'An Analytical Approach to the Social Stratification', *American Journal of Sociology*, 45, (also in *EST2*, pp. 69–88).
Parsons, Talcott (1949), 'Social Classes and Class Conflict in the Light of Recent Sociological Theory', *American Economic Review*, 35, (also in *EST2*, pp. 323–335).
Parsons, Talcott (1953), 'A Revised Analytical Approach to the Theory of Social Stratification', in Reinhard Bendix and Seymour M. Lipset (eds), *Class, Status, and Political Power: A Reader in Social Stratification*, New York: Free Press, (also in *EST2*, pp. 386–439).
Parsons, Talcott (1954), *EST2: Essays in Sociological Theory*, revised edition, New York, NY: Free Press.
Parsons, Talcott (1955), *Family, Socialization and Interaction Process*, New York, NY: Free Press.
Patterson, Orlando (1999), 'Liberty against the Democratic State: On the Historical and Contemporary Sources of American Distrust', in Mark E. Warren (ed.), *Democracy and Trust*, Cambridge: Cambridge University Press, pp. 151–207.
Phang, Hanam and Ki Hun Kim (2003), 'Hanguksahoeui Gyoyukgyecheunghwa (Trends and differentials in educational stratification in Korea)', *Hanguksahoehak (Korean Journal of Sociology)*, 37(4), pp. 31–65.
Pong, Suet-ling (2003), 'Immigrant Children's School Performance', Working Paper 03–07, Population Research Institute, Pennsylvania State University, PA.
Portes, Alejandro and Lingxin Hao (2004), 'The Schooling of Children of Immigrants: Contextual Effects on the Educational Attainment of the Second Generation', *Proceeding of National Academy of Science*, 101, pp.11920–27.
Portes, Alejandro and Rubén G. Rumbaut (2001), *Legacies: The Story of the Immigrant Second Generation*, Berkeley, CA and New York, NY: University of California Press.
Post, David (1994), 'Educational Stratification, School Expansion, and Public Policy in Hong Kong', *Sociology of Education*, 67, pp. 121–138.
Prandy, Ken and Frank L. Jones (2001), 'An International Comparative Analysis of Marriage Patterns and Social Stratification', *International Journal of Sociology and Social Policy*, 21, pp. 165–183.
Putnam, Robert D. (1993), *Making Democracy Work: Civic Traditions in Modern Italy*, Princeton, NJ: Princeton University Press.
Raftery, Adrian E. and Michael Hout (1993), 'Maximally Maintained Inequality: Expansion, Reform, and Opportunity in Irish Education, 1921–75', *Sociology of Education*, 66(1), pp. 41–62.
Raftery, Adrian E. (1995), 'Bayesian Model Selection in Social Science', *Sociological Methodology*, 25, pp. 111–163.
Ramakrishnan, S. Karthick (2002), 'Second-generation Immigrants? The "2.5 Generation" in the United States', *Social Science Quarterly*, 85(2), pp. 380–399.

Raudenbush, Stephen W. and Anthony S. Bryk (2002), *Hierarchical Linear Models: Applications and Data Analysis Methods*, London: Sage.
Raudenbush, Stephen W. and Anthony S. Bryk and Richard Congdon (2000), *HLM 5: Hierarchical, Linear and Nonlinear Modeling*, Chicago, IL: Scientific Software International.
Raymo, James M. and Yu Xie (2000), 'Temporal and Regional Variation in the Strength of Educational Homogamy', *American Sociological Review*, 65, pp. 773–781.
Research Group on 'Increasing the Employment Chances of Laid-off Workers' (RG1) (2001), 'Research on Increasing the Employment Chances of Laid-off Workers', *Reference for Economic Research*, 11, pp. 25–36.
Research Group of Institute of Labor Science, MOLSS (RG2) (2002), 'Thought about Employment and Solutions under Current Situation', *Reference for Economic Research*, 34, pp. 2–10.
Rona-Tas, Akos (1994), 'The First Shall be Last? Entrepreneurship and Communist Cadres in the Transition from Socialism', *American Journal of Sociology*, 100, pp. 40–69.
Sampson, Robert J., Jeffrey D. Morenoff and Felton Earls (1999), 'Beyond Social Capital: Spatial Dynamics of Collective Efficacy for Children', *American Sociological Review*, 64(5), pp. 633–660.
Sato, Daisuke (2002), 'Bakumatsuki ichi gōnō no seijiteki tachiba to chiiki chitsujo: Ushū Murayama-gun Obanazawa mura Suzuki Gorobee ke no jirei kara (The political standing of a wealthy farmer and regional law and order at the end of the Edo period: The case of Suzuki Gorobee of Obanazawa village, Murayama-gun, Dewa)', *Nihon rekishi*, 654, pp. 38-55.
Sato, Daisuke (2003), 'Gōnō Suzuki Gorobee-ke no jinteki nettowāku: "Nenrei hikae" kara mita kisoteki bunseki (The family network of wealthy farmer Suzuki Gorobee: Some analysis based on the 'New Year Greeting Record')', *Yamagata kindaishi kenkyū (Study of modern history of Yamagata area)*, 17, pp. 1–20.
Sato, Toshiki (2000), *Fubyōdō shakai Nihon: Sayonara sōchūryū (Japan as an unequal society: Farewell to the society where all members felt they belonged to middle strata)*, Tokyo: Chūō Kōron Shinsha.
Sato, Yoshimichi (2002), 'Trust, Assurance, and Inequality: A Rational Choice Model of Mutual Trust', *Journal of Mathematical Sociology*, 26(1–2), pp. 1–16.
Sato, Yoshimichi and Shin Arita (2004), 'Impact of Globalization on Social Mobility in Japan and Korea: Focusing on Middle Classes in Fluid Societies', *International Journal of Japanese Sociology*, 13, pp. 36–52.
Schofer, Evan and Marion Gourinchas (2001), 'The Structural Contexts of Civic Engagement: Voluntary Association Membership in Comparative Perspective', *American Sociological Review*, 66(6), pp. 806–828.
Seiyama, Kazuo (1990), 'Chū ishiki no imi: Kaisō kizoku ishiki no henka no kōzō (The meaning of 'middle' consciousness: The structure of change in strata identification)', *Riron to hōhō (Sociological Theory and Methods)*, 5(2), pp. 51–71.
Seiyama, Kazuo (2001), 'Shotoku kakusa o dō mondai ni suru ka: Nenreisōnai fubyōdō no bunseki kara (How to problematize income disparities? An

analysis of intra-age group inequality)', *Kikan kakei keizai kenkyū* (*Japanese Journal of Research on Household Economics*), 51, pp. 17–23.

Sen, Amartya Kumar (1992), *Inequality Reexamined*, Oxford: Clarendon Press.

Shavit, Yossi and Hans-Peter Blossfeld (eds) (1993), *Persistent Inequality: Changing Educational Attainment in Thirteen Countries*, New York: Westview Press.

Sheng, Shibing (1998), 'The Structural Characteristics of, and Strategic Resolution to Unemployment in China', *Economic Sciences*, 4, pp. 5–10.

Shida, Kiyoshi, Kazuo Seiyama and Hideki Watanabe (2000), '*Kekkon shijō no henyō* (Changes in the marriage market)', Kazuo Seiyama (ed.), *Nihon no kaisō shisutemu 4: Jendaa shijo kazoku* (*Stratification system in Japan 4: Gender, market, and family*), Tokyo: University of Tokyo Press, pp. 159–176.

Smith, Herbert L. and Paul P. L. Cheung (1986), 'Trends in the Effects of Family Background on Educational Attainment in the Philippines', *American Journal of Sociology*, 91(6), pp. 1387–1408.

Smith, James P. (2003), 'Assimilation across the Latino Generations', *American Economic Review*, 93, pp. 315–319

Smits, Jeroen (2003), 'Social Closure among the Higher Educated: Trends in Educational Homogamy in 55 countries', *Social Science Research*, 32, pp. 251–277.

Smits, Jeroen, Wout Ultee and Jan Lammers (1998), 'Educational Homogamy in 65 Countries: An Explanation of Differences in Openness Using Country-level Explanatory Variables', *American Sociological Review*, 63, pp. 264–285.

Smits, Jeroen, Wout Ultee and Jan Lammers (2000), 'More and Less Educational Homogamy? A Test of Different Versions of Modernization Theory Using Cross-Temporal Evidence for 60 Countries', *American Sociological Review*, 65, pp. 781–789.

Snijders, Tom and Roel Bosker (1999), *Multilevel Analysis: An Introduction to Basic and Advanced Multilevel Modeling*, London: Sage.

Solinger, Dorothy J. (2001), 'Why We Cannot Count the "Unemployed"', *The China Quarterly*, 167, pp. 671–688.

Solinger, Dorothy J. (2002), 'Labor Market Reform and the Plight of the Laid-off Proletariat', *The China Quarterly*, 170, pp. 304–326.

Sōmushō Tōkeikyoku (2004), '2-33 Intra-prefectural Migrants, In-migrants from and Out-migrants to Other Prefectures and Net Migration Rate, by Prefectures and Sex (1954–2002)', <http://www.stat.go.jp/data/chouki/zuhyou/02-33.xls> (12 September 2005).

Stark, David (1986), 'Rethinking Internal Labor Markets: New Insights from A Comparative Perspective', *American Sociological Review*, 51, pp. 492–504.

Stark, David (1996), 'Recombinant Property in East European Capitalism', *American Journal of Sociology*, 101, pp. 993–1027.

State Statistical Bureau, P.R. China (1980–2002), *China Statistical Yearbook, 1979–2001*, Beijing: China Statistics Press.

State Statistical Bureau, P.R. China (SSB) and Ministry of Labor and Social Security (MOLSS) (1997–2002), *China Labor Statistical Yearbook, 1996–2001*, Beijing: China Statistics Press.

Sugayama, Shinji and Yukimitsu Nishimura (2000), 'Shokugyō anteigyōsei no tenkai to kōiki shōkai (The development of employment agency administration and its widespread introduction activities)', in Takehiko Kariya, Shinji Sugayama and Hiroshi Ishida (eds), *Gakkō, shokuan to rōdō shijō – Sengo shinki gakusotsu shijō no seidoka katei (Schools, public employment offices, and the labor market in postwar Japan)*, Tokyo: University of Tokyo Press, pp.65–112.

Tachibanaki, Toshiaki (1998), *Nihon no keizai kakusa: Shotoku to shisan kara kangaeru (Economic disparities in Japan: Incomes and assets)*, Tokyo: Iwanami Shoten.

Takeda, Akira (1974), 'Nihon ni okeru sōzoku – Keishō no kankō (Inheritance and succession in Japan)', in Michio Aoki, Akira Takeda, Toru Arichi, Itsuo Emori and Jiro Matsubara (eds), *Kōza kazoku 5: Sōzoku to keishō (Family series vol. 5: Inheritance and succession)*, Tokyo: Kōbundō, pp.303–319.

Takeuchi, Yō (2001), 'Gakureki chūryū ganbō no seisui to gan'i' (The fluctuations and the implications of the desire to attain a middle-stratum position through academic credentials)', *Kikan kakei keizai kenkyū (Japanese Journal of Research on Household Economics)*, no. 51, pp.40–46.

Taubman, Paul and Michael L.Wachter (1986), 'Segmented Labor Market', in O. Ashenfelter and P.R.G. Layard (eds), *Handbook of Labor Economics Vol.2*, Amsterdam: North Holland.

Taylor, Marylee (1998), 'How White Attitudes Vary with the Racial Composition of Local Populations', *American Sociological Review*, 63(4), pp. 512–35.

Toby, Jackson (1980), 'Samuel A. Stouffer: Social Research as a Calling', in Robert K. Merton and Mathilda White Riley (eds), *Sociological Tradition from Generation to Generation*, Norwood, N.J.: Ablex Publishing Corp, pp. 90–110.

Tominaga, Ken'ichi (1990), *Nihon no kindaika to shakai hendō – Chūbingen kōgi (Modernization and social change in Japan: The Tūbingen lectures)*, Tokyo: Kōdansha.

Tomoeda,Toshio (1988), 'Shakaiteki chii to kaisō kizoku ishiki (Social status and social strata identification)', in 1985-nen Shakai Kaisō to Shakai Idō Zenkoku Chōsa Iinkai (ed.),*1985 nen shakai kaisō to shakai idō zenkoku chōsa hōkokusho 2: Kaisō ishiki no dōtai (Report on the 1985 social stratification and social mobility survey 2: Dynamics of social strata consciousness)*, pp. 21–42.

Tomoeda,Toshio and Hideo Kojima (1987), 'Kaisō kizoku ishiki no sūsei bunseki (Trend analysis of social strata identification in post-war Japan)', *Chūō Daigaku Bungaku-bu kenkyū kiyō (Journal of the Faculty of Literature)*, 125, pp. 35–63.

Treiman, Donald J. and KazuoYamaguchi (1993), 'Trends in Educational Attainment in Japan', in Yossi Shavit and Hans-Peter Blossfeld (eds), *Persistent Inequality: Changing Educational Attainment in Thirteen Countries*, San Francisco, CA: Westview Press, pp. 229–249.

Trejo, Stephen J (1997), 'Why Do Mexicans Earn Low Wages?', *The Journal of Political Economy*, 105(6), pp.1235–1268.

Ultee, Wout and Rūd Luijkx (1990), 'Educational Heterogamy and Father to Son Occupational Mobility in 23 Industrial Nations: General Societal Openness or Compensatory Strategies of Reproduction?', *European Sociological Review*, 6, pp. 125–149.

Uunk, Wilfred J. G., Harry B. G. Ganzeboom and Peter Robert (1996), 'Bivariate and Multivariate Scaled Association Models: An Application to Homogamy of Social Origin and Education in Hungary between 1930 and 1979', *Quality and Quantity*, 30, pp. 323–345.

Van Hook, Jennifer (2004), 'Poverty Grows Among Children of Immigrants in US', *Feature Story, Migration Policy Institute* <http://www.migrationinformation.org/Feature/display.cfm?ID=188> (30 September 2005).

Veblen, Thorstein (1899), *The Theory of Leisure Class: An Economic Study in the Evolution of Institutions*, New York, NY: Macmillan.

Walder, Andrew (1986), *Communist Neo-Traditionalism: Work and Authority in Chinese Industry*, Berkeley, CA: University of California Press.

Walder, Andrew (1992), 'Property Rights and Stratification in Socialist Redistributive Economies', *American Sociological Review*, 57, pp. 524–39.

Walder, Andrew (1996), 'Markets and Inequality in Transitional Economies: Toward Testable Theories', *American Journal of Sociology*, 101, pp. 1060–1073.

Walder, Andrew (2002), 'Market and Income Inequality in Rural China: Political Advantage in an Expanding Economy', *American Sociological Review*, 67, pp. 231–253.

Walder, Andrew, Bobai Li and Donald J. Treiman (2000), 'Politics and Life Chances in a State Socialist Regime: Dual Career Paths into the Urban Chinese Elite, 1949 to 1996', *American Sociological Review*, 65, pp. 191–209.

Waldinger, Roger and Joel Perlmann (1998), 'Are the Children of Today's Immigrants Making It?', *The Public Interest*, 132, pp. 73–96.

Wang, Hansheng and Zhixia Chen (1998), 'The Re-employment Policy of Government and Individual Behavior Strategy of *xia-gang* Workers', *Sociological Research*, 4, pp. 13–31.

Wang, Zhaoming (2000), 'The New Urban Poverty in China', *Economist*, 2, pp. 74–79.

Warde, Alan (1994), 'Consumption, Identity-formation and Uncertainty', *Sociology*, 28(4), pp. 877–898.

Warner, William L. and Paul S. Lunt (1941), *The Social Life of a Modern Community*, Yankee City Series, 1, New Haven, CT: Yale University Press.

Warren, Brian L. (1966), 'A Multiple Variable Approach to the Assortative Mating Phenomenon', *Eugenics Quartery*, 13, pp. 285–290.

Watanabe, Hideki (1998), 'Kekkon to kaisō no sūsei bunseki (Trend analysis of marriage and social stratification in Japan)', in Hideki Watanabe and Kiyoshi Shida (eds), *Kaisō to kekkon, kazoku* (*Marriage, family and stratification*), 1995 SSM Research Series vol. 15, 1995 SSM Survey Research Committee, pp.113–130.

Watanabe, Hideki and Hiroyuki Kondo (1990), 'Kekkon to kaisō ketsugō (Marriage and class coupling)', in Hideo Okamoto and Michiko Naoi (eds), *Gendai Nihon no kaisō kōzō 4: Jyosei to shakai kaisō* (*Strata structure in contemporary Japan 4: Women and social stratification*), Tokyo: University of Tokyo Press, pp.119–145.

Waters, Mary (1990), *Ethnic Options: Choosing Identities in America*, Berkeley, CA: University of California Press.
Waters, Mary C. and Tomás R. Jimenez (2005), 'Assessing Immigrant Assimilation: New Empirical and Theoretical Challenges', *Annual Review of Sociology*, 31, pp.105–25.
Whyte, Martin and William Parish (1984), *Urban Life in Contemporary China*, Chicago, IL: The University of Chicago Press.
Whyte, William H. (1956), *The Organization Man*, New York: Simon and Schuster.
World Bank (1995), 'Staff Appraisal Report: China Labor Market Development Project', Report No. 14602–CHA.
Wright, Erik O. (1997), *Class Counts*, Cambridge: Cambridge University Press.
Wu, Xiaogang (2002), 'The Effect of Market Transition in Urban China', *Social Forces*, 80, pp. 1069–1099.
Wu, Xiaogang and Yu Xie (2003), 'Does the Market Pay off? Earnings Returns to Education in Urban China', *American Sociological Review*, 68, pp. 425–442.
Xiao, Lichun (1998), 'The Status Quo and Development of Laid-off Workers in Shanghai', *Chinese Demography*, 3, pp. 26–37.
Xie, Guihua (2004), 'Market Transition of Laid-off Workers in Urban China', Dissertation Submitted to Department of Sociology, Johns Hopkins University.
Xie, Yu (1992), 'The Log-multiplicative Layer Effect Model for Comparing Mobility Tables', *American Sociological Review*, 57, pp. 380–395.
Xie, Yu and Emily Hannum (1996), 'Regional Variation in Earnings Inequality in Reform-Era Urban China', *American Journal of Sociology*, 101, pp. 950–92.
Yamagishi, Toshio (1998), *Shinrai no kōzō (The Structure of Trust: The Evolutionary Games of Mind and Society)*, Tokyo: University of Tokyo Press.
Yagamishi, Toshio and Midori Yamagishi (1994), 'Trust and Commitment in the United States and Japan', *Motivation and Emotion*, 18(2), pp. 129–66.
Yasuda, Saburo (1964), *Shakai idō no kenkyū (A study of social mobility)*, Tokyo: University of Tokyo Press.
Yasuda, Saburo and Junsuke Hara (1982), *Shakai chōsa handobukku, daisanpan (Social survey handbook, 3rd edition)*, Tokyo: Yūhikaku.
Yokoyama, Akio (1980), *Kinsei kasen shū-un shi no kenkyū (Study of river transportation in the pre-modern period)*, Tokyo: Yoshikawa Kōbunkan.
Yu, Wei-hsin (2001), 'Taking Informality into Account: Women's Work in the Formal and Informal Sectors in Taiwan', in Mary C. Brinton (ed.), *Women's Working Lives in East Asia*, Stanford, CA: Stanford University Press.
Zang, Xiaowei (2002), 'Labor Market Segmentation and Income Inequality in Urban China', *The Sociological Quarterly*, 43, pp. 27–44.
Zhang, Huiming (1998), *The Logic of Reform on Chinese State-Owned Economy*, Taiyuan (China): Shanxi Economy Press.
Zhao, Wei and Xueguang Zhou (2002), 'Institutional Transformation and Returns to Education in Urban China: An Empirical Assessment', *Research in Social Stratification and Mobility*, 19, pp. 339–375.

Zhou, Xueguang (2000), 'Economic Transformation and Income Inequality in Urban China: Evidence from Panel Data', *American Journal of Sociology*, 105, pp. 1135–74.

Zhou, Xueguang, Phyllis Moen and Nancy B. Tuma (1998), 'Educational Stratification in Urban China, 1949–1994', *Sociology of Education*, 71, pp. 199–222.

Zhou, Xueguang, Nancy B. Tuma and Phyllis Moen (1997), 'Institutional Change and Job-shift Patterns in Urban China, 1949 to 1994', *American Sociological Review*, 62, pp. 339–365.

Index

2003 National Survey on Work and Daily Life 132

adaptation 216, 218, 221, 235
admission quota system 169
advancement rate 5–6, 166, 242
  to higher education 6
agent-based model xii, 32–3
allocation of possessions 22
apartheid in South Africa 26–7, 29
Appleton, S. 198, 201, 205, 214
Araragi, S. 109
Araragi, Y. 89
Arita, S. 127
Arum, R. 165
assimilation 23, 216–17, 226, 235, 242
  curvilinear 221, 223
  segmented 217, 219, 222–3, 235
assurance group 32, 34–6, 38–9, 41–3, 238

backward-looking rationality 130
basic equality 6–13, 16
  achievement of 6
Baudrillard, J. 125
Beck, U. 125
Becker, G. S. 131
Bendix, R. 88
Bian, Y. 184–7, 200, 214

binary logistic regression 173
Blau, P. M. 140
bloc 142
  blue-collar 142
  white-collar 142, 151, 157
Blossfeld, H-P. 142–3, 158, 163
Borjas, G. J. 216, 224–5
Breen, R. 147, 158, 164
Brinton, M. C. 127
Bryk, A. S. 117
Buchman, C. 163
Bush-Mosteller algorithm 37
by-product hypothesis 142, 144, 146, 152–3, 157

Cai, Y. 184, 214
capital xiv, 26, 33, 90, 130–1, 136, 138–9, 184–8, 191–2, 194–200, 203, 205, 208, 211–14, 231
  financial 33, 137
  human xiii, 130–1, 137, 139, 184–8, 191, 194–200, 203, 208, 211–14, 219, 221–3, 231, 234–5
  political xiii, 184–8, 192, 194–9, 205, 211–14
  social xii, 33, 130, 136–7, 185, 221
career xiii, 19, 104, 107, 127–37, 175
  image xiii, 129–37
categories of gifts 54

Chang, S-s. 170
Chiswick, B. 218–19
class xiii, 20–4, 27–8, 112–17,
    120–1, 124–7, 140, 163–5,
    171–3, 175, 178, 180–1, 240
    identification xiii, 112–17,
        120–1, 124–5
    middle 23–4, 127, 164, 240
    status 21, 23–4, 28
cognitive dissonance 130
college graduate 10, 16, 110,
    127, 131, 136–7
compulsory education 145, 166,
    171, 175–6, 180, 242
Congdon, R. 117
consociational Democracy 28
covariation 142, 144
cross-generational association
    228

de-strata group 11
Deng, Z. 163, 166
Densely Inhabited Districts
    population 116
double-track system 175
Dronkers, J. 163, 165
Duncan, B. 221
Duncan, O. D. 140

education xiii, 6–7, 10–12, 21,
    23–4, 28, 93, 97, 99, 110,
    117, 126, 131–2, 136–40,
    143, 145, 149, 152, 163–8,
    171–81, 187–8, 191, 195,
    199–200, 203, 205, 209,
    211–12, 214, 216, 218, 220,
    231, 237, 239, 242
    higher 5, 28, 88, 92, 110, 142,
        146, 149, 152, 165, 167–71,
        178, 180–1, 199, 226, 242
    new 171, 173–5, 181

old 166, 167, 180
utilitarian value of 12
educational continuation 163,
    171, 180
educational reform xiii, 163–6,
    169, 180–1, 242
educational revolution 23–4
EGP schema 172
employer taste 214
employment agency 96–7, 99,
    102, 105, 110
employment status 130–2, 137,
    184, 186–7, 203, 207, 213,
    239
endogamy 141, 149, 241
enrollment rate 166–7, 242
Erikson, R. 172
ethnicity xiv, 12, 27–8, 216, 221,
    224–5

fairness 17
Fine, B. 187
firm size 130–1, 136
Foci of Integrative Balances in
    the Societal Community 29
Fry, R. 220
funeral record 47, 49
furītā 14–15, 237

Gamoran, A. 165
Gans, H. J. 217
Garnier, M. 163
Genda, Y. 15
gender xiv, 5, 12, 19, 127, 130,
    132, 137, 169, 172, 180, 185,
    193, 195, 197, 202, 212, 214
general openness hypothesis
    143, 157
Giddens, A. 125
globalization 127
Goldthorpe, J. H. 164, 172

goods xii, 4–7, 10, 32, 35–6, 42, 51–7, 61, 64, 68, 72, 76, 80, 90
  basic 7, 10
  upper 10
Gordon, M. 216
graduation quota system 168, 178
greater competitiveness 8
Grogger, J. 219–20, 224

Hannum, E. 163, 185
Hao, L. 219
Hara, J. 3, 6–8, 12, 104, 174, 240
Heckman probit model 208
high growth period in Japan xiii
Higuchi, Y. 8
homogamy xiii, 140–59, 241
  relative 148, 151, 153, 157–8
  status xiii, 140–2, 144, 157–8
Hoshi, A. 113
Hout, M. 141–2, 164

in-marriage 141, 148–9, 152, 157
in-marriage rate 141, 148–9
  origin-specific 148
industrialization xi, 27, 143–4, 148, 157–8
inequality xi–xiv, 3–19, 29, 31, 112, 126, 163–5, 171, 175–6, 178, 180, 200
  educational 164, 170–1, 175, 181
  expanding 8
  new xii
  of opportunity 4–5, 8
  of possession 4
institutional persistence 184, 213
intellectual community 8, 11

intergenerational disparity 14
intra-class correlation 115
Ishikawa, Y. 88
issue of the second and third sons of farmers 96

Japanese employment practice 127–8, 131, 133, 136, 139
Japanese General Social Survey 171
Jensen, L. 220
justice 25, 112, 171
  distributive 17
  procedural 17

Kahn, J. R. 218–19
Kalleberg, A. L. 185–6
Kalmijn, M. 140–3
Kao, G. 218
Kariya, T. 16, 96
Kennedy, R. J. R. 142
Kikkawa, T. 113
Kim, K-H. 163, 170, 242
kinship solidarity 20–1
Kluckhohn, F. 19
Kobayashi, D. 112–14, 120
Kojima, H. 113
Kondo, H. 140–5, 241
Korean Labor and Income Panel Study 171
Kosaka, K. 113

labor market xiii, xiv, 91–3, 99, 127–39, 184–8, 192, 213–15, 218, 220, 234
  Japanese xiii, 127, 130
laid-off workers 183–4, 188–97, 200–8, 212–15, 243
latent structure 158
layoff xiii, 183–4, 186–208, 210–15

Index

Lillard, L. A. 165–6
Lin, N. 185
Livingston, G. 218–19
Logan, J. 184–6, 200
logit model with random effect 194
loglinear model 147–8, 151, 241
long-term employment practice xiii, 127–33
Loubser, J. 27

Macy, M. W. 32, 42–3, 130, 238
Mamada, T. 113
Mare, R. D. 142–3, 164, 172–3
Mare model 173
market xii, xiii, 8, 31–42, 68, 92, 130, 133, 136–9, 142, 158, 183–8, 192, 201, 205, 207, 212–15
 attractiveness xii, 33, 41–2
 transition 184–7, 214–15
marketization 187
market transition theory 184–7, 214
Marx, K. 20
Maximally Maintained Inequality hypothesis 164
Mexican American 216–20, 224–6, 231
 2.5th generation 216–17, 220–31, 234–5
 first generation 217–26, 229, 234
 second generation 217–26, 229, 231, 234–5, 244
 third generation 216–31, 234–5
migration xiii, 88–93, 96–110, 114, 124, 223, 225, 239–4
Minami, R. 4
minorities xii, 12–13, 30, 217, 219

Miyano, M. 113
mobility xiii, 4, 19, 24, 32, 42, 88–9, 97, 104, 106–9, 113, 125, 127, 145, 158, 164, 171, 217, 220–1, 229, 234–5
 forced 89, 239
 geographical 42, 92, 99
 horizontal 24
 intragenerational 106–7
 pure 89
 social 19, 24, 88–9, 127, 140, 142, 157, 184
 vertical 24
Moen, P. 163, 166, 185–6
moral 20
 authority 20
 evaluation 20
multinomial logit model 173, 176, 178
multinomial logit regression 133, 137

Nee, V. 184, 187
nīto 14–15, 237
Nomura, M. 133
non-migrant 101–8, 240

Obanazawa village 48–50, 52, 54–5, 57
objective class situation 112, 126
occupation 6, 9, 13, 21–4, 97, 104, 110, 117, 125, 140–1, 145–6, 149, 151, 172, 222, 229, 234
old labor allocation system 184

Park, H. 169–70
Parsons, T. xii, 18–29
Patterson, O. 31, 237
political capital *See* capital, political

Pong, S-l. 218–19
population change 114–16, 124
Portes, A. 219
Post, D. 163, 165, 243
power xi, 20, 22, 25–6, 185, 199, 214
power persistence 199
prestige 4, 18–20, 22, 102, 116, 240
probit model 205, 207–8
Putnam, R. D. 32

Raftery, A. E. 164, 241
Ramakrishnan, S. K. 220
random-intercept model 116–17, 120
random-slope model 116–17, 120
Raudenbush, S. W. 117
regional disparity in opportunity 88
Relative Risk Aversion hypothesis 164
Rhoodie, N. 27
Rumbaut, R. 219

Sato, D. 47, 64, 76, 239
Sato, T. 8, 16
Sato, Y. 31–4, 42–3, 127, 238
saturation hypothesis 144, 157–8
segmented labor market theory 184–6
Seiyama, K. 6, 8–10, 174
Sen, A. 17
seniority-based wage system 10, 127
Shavit, Y. 142, 163, 165
Shida, K. 141–4, 154, 241
Social Inequality and Justice Survey 171

social mobility 19, 24, 88–9, 127, 140, 142, 157, 184
survey in Newton 19
social network xii, 113, 130, 188
social stratification xi–xiv, 3–4, 11–12, 14, 18, 20–1, 25, 140–1, 145, 158
Solinger, D. J. 183
Sørensen, A. B. 185–6
spatial characteristics xiii, 112–14, 120, 124, 126
specialized training college 133, 136–7
SSM xiii, 4, 6, 13, 97, 99, 108, 111, 113–15, 126, 145, 171–2, 237, 239
state-owned enterprise 183, 192, 214
status attainment hypothesis 143
Stouffer, S. 19
stratification xi–xii, xiv, 3–4, 17–25, 52, 97, 113, 140, 171, 184, 187, 242–4
subjective perception 112–13
Suzuki 47–52, 54–5, 57, 61, 64, 68, 72, 76, 80, 84, 238–9
family 47, 49–52, 55, 57, 61, 64, 68, 72, 76, 80, 84, 238–9
Gorobee 47–9, 51, 54, 57, 61, 64, 68, 72, 76, 80
systematic discrimination 185, 214

Tachibanaki, T. 8
Thompson, J. 218
Tienda, M. 218
Timm, A. 143, 158
Tominaga, K. 96

Tomoeda, T. 113
transition between schools 164, 165, 173
Treiman, D. 163, 166, 170, 200
Trejo, S. J. 216, 219–21, 224
trust xii, 31–6, 41–2
Tuma, N. 163, 166, 185–6

Yasuda, S. 89, 240
Yokoyama, A. 61
Yu, W-h. 130

Zhou, X. 163, 166, 184–6, 200, 213

U-turner 108
Unidiff parameter 147–8, 154–5
universalistic performance value 21
Urban Labor Market Integration Project 188
Uunk, W. J. G. 141–3

value-pattern 21
variegation and individualization of goals 10, 13
Veblen, T. 125

Waldinger, R. 216
Wang, Z. 183
Warde, A. 125
Warner, W. L. 18
Warren, B. L. 142
Watanabe, H. 140–5, 241
Waters, M. C. 216, 225
Whyte, W. H. 125, 186
Willis, R. J. 165–6
work-sharing between age groups 15
Wright, E. O. 140

Xie, Y. 143, 147, 185–6, 243

Yamagishi, M. 42
Yamagishi, T. 32, 42, 237
Yamaguchi, K. 170
Yankee City Study 18